Fighting for
Social Justice

Fighting for Social Justice

The Life Story of David Burgess

David S. Burgess

Foreword by Bill Moyers

Wayne State University Press   Detroit

Library of Congress Cataloging-in-Publication Data

Burgess, David S., 1917 –

    Fighting for social justice : the life story of David Burgess / David
S. Burgess ; foreword by Bill Moyers.

      p. cm.

Includes bibliographical references and index.

    ISBN 0-8143-2899-7 (alk. paper)

    1. Burgess, David S., 1917 – . 2. United Church of Christ — United
States — Clergy — Biography. 3. Church work with the poor — United States.
4. Fellowship of Southern Churchmen. 5. Trade-unions — Officials and
employees — Biography. 6. United States. Foreign Service — Officials and
employees — Biography. 7. Peace Corps (U.S.) — Indonesia — Biography. 8.
UNICEF — Officials and employees — Biography. I. Title.

    CT275.B78522 A3 2000

    285.8'092 — dc21

                              00-008716

My autobiography is dedicated to my

beloved wife, Alice, and our five wonderful children

Laurel, Lyman, John, Genie, and Steve

Contents

Contents

Foreword

I HAVE RARELY met anyone who fulfilled more completely than David Burgess my idea of the Christian pilgrim. Like Thomas à Kempis, Dave would imitate Christ, but he is too honest about his imperfections to claim distinction in attaining the aspiration. (He is, by his own admission, an ordinary man; but as G. K. Chesterton observed, "All men are ordinary men; the extraordinary men are those who know it.") In many respects a traditionalist, he has kept himself open to currents running from other depths, so that the Creation story of Genesis remains vital to his heritage while the creation spirituality of Matthew Fox intrigues his present quest. He has battled the "principalities and powers" of this earth—encountered their corruption, hypocrisy, and treachery— yet finds it impossible to hold grudges even against those who most thwarted him. At heart he is a radical, but practices negotiation instead of confrontation. He admits freely to anguish over the conflict of serving the poor and supporting his family. Open to the "still, small voice" that is heard with greatest certainty in solitude, he has nonetheless thrust himself out into the raucous, clamoring world to serve the sacred in secular surroundings.

His life has spanned this brutal century. Born as war raged across the trenches of a continent, he graduated from Oberlin College on the eve of the great conflagration. Yet wherever he could find the moral equivalent of war, Dave placed himself squarely on the front lines. In his youth he helped desperate coal miners build homes for their families and worked alongside migrant farmers and sharecroppers. As a labor organizer he took on cotton barons and textile magnates. Humbled but not defeated by the "Georgia realities" of the Deep South, he turned to equally daunting realities elsewhere: in India with the Foreign Service; in Indonesia with the Peace Corps; in twelve nations of East Asia with UNICEF, including war-torn Vietnam and Cambodia and the war-created new nation of Bangladesh; and finally, back home again in Newark,

New Jersey, the innermost inner city, riddled by crime, wrecked by crack, and gripped by despair. But in Newark, where others saw only the grimy streets and the squalor of projects, Dave saw, in the people struggling to make life there, the image of God. So for eleven years he fought the good fight—for affirmative action and public housing, against poverty and pollution. He was the very incarnation of the ecumenical spirit in a city wounded and fragmented by division and faction.

Gritty battles there were. He tackled city hall, corporate greed and perfidy, and at times, his own shaken self. For as Dave Burgess confesses, the heartiest pilgrim can experience spiritual torpor, the deadliest disease of all, for it contains the incubus of boredom and disenchantment and of cynicism itself. Like Jacob, he wrestled with the uninvited and unnamed Stranger—and prevailed. But as Jacob was scarred by the struggle, so Dave Burgess, too, limped from the field. What true pilgrim escapes unscathed?

His life has been a testimony to idealism in action. But the arc of his passage over these eighty-three years reveals a great deal of America's own passage. The issues of social justice that compelled him—poverty, the needs of working people, discrimination, inequality—are still with us. But whereas a young man committed to justice years ago could join the trade union movement or any number of progressive organizations marching to the left of Franklin Roosevelt, today both the Republican and Democratic Parties have become vassals of corporations and other wealthy interests, and the advocate of social reform has few places to sign up. If you are to breathe new life into the meaning of citizenship, recapturing the notion of citizens as moral agents, we will need models and mentors, of whom there are no finer exemplars than David and his wife, Alice. Little heralded for lives of steadfast witness, they pressed on. Ever faithful to each other and their calling—even in the midst of doubt and disappointment—they embody the best of their activist generation. In the words of Robert Kennedy, whom Dave much admired in the 1960s, "Few have the greatness to bend history itself, but each of us can work to change a portion of events, and in the total of all these acts will be written the history of a generation."

His own generation's history would be incomplete without this story told by Dave Burgess. He and Alice continue to draw from deep aquifers of faith "to do justly, and love mercy, and to walk humbly with their God." No pilgrim has left surer footprints of faith and service.

Bill Moyers

Preface

IN THE SOUTHERN California town of Claremont in the early 1930s, they were a common sight: men in dark, sometimes ragged clothing, sitting listlessly atop boxcars that rolled down the shiny steel tracks leading toward Los Angeles. The blight of the Great Depression had settled over America; these penniless travelers were hoping to find work in the city, though most would not. I was a teenager growing up in Claremont at the time, and I remember watching the men many times, silently, wondering how they endured their plight, what they thought as they looked out over our affluent middle-class college community. I was intensely aware that while they were probably headed toward panhandling and a night on the pavement, I was well fed and clothed and, as the son of a college professor, had claims to a soft bed.

In my early years, for reasons I cannot entirely explain, I began to identify with the poor, the hungry, and the homeless. It crept up on me in stages, but by the time I was halfway through high school, I had begun to think I had a mission in life, to serve God by serving these people. It has at times created friction with my peers—some of my classmates in Claremont, I'm sure, saw me as distant and over-serious—but it has carried me along ever since with great recharging energy. Through it all, I have tried to take to heart the words of Jesus, that "Everyone to whom much is given, of him much will be required" (Luke 12:48, RSV).

Along the great road of life, I have been privileged to play a role in two of the great social movements of the twentieth century, though generally on the minority, unpopular side of the fight. The first was the peace movement. The Second World War was the seminal event for my generation, but I was never in uniform. Instead, I was part of the small group of pacifist activists who resisted our country's entry into the conflict. As a new seminary student, I set out to try to live by Christ's Sermon on the Mount, with its admonition that we should not resist evil, that if one cheek is struck, the other should be turned. I was also much influenced by student politics of the 1930s, and the writings of thinkers such as Reinhold Niebuhr, my theology professor at seminary. Over time, the horrors of what Hitler wrought in Europe brought me to believe that there are times when armed force must be applied, but I have remained through my life a pacifist by instinct, putting my word and vote in for peace, always skeptical that bombs and guns can ever solve any problem, no matter how good the intentions. That seems to me as true as ever as I put the finishing touches on this book in mid-1999, when U.S. forces do battle with foes in Iraq and Yugoslavia with no end in sight.

The second movement that drew me was the global battle for economic justice. In the twentieth century, new technology has helped bring on an explosion of wealth, but we have learned almost nothing about spreading it around in an equitable way. In the 1940s, inspired by the ideals of the New Deal, I worked with migrant workers in the South who helped put the best food in the world on American tables but often were themselves underfed and living in unspeakable hovels. In the 1950s, I helped unionize textile workers who clothed our country during the great economic boom decade but could hardly afford to buy what they made. In the 1960s and 1970s, my attention was largely turned overseas, to poor countries such as Bangladesh and Indonesia, where multinational corporations often walked off with much of what their hard-working people produced. In the 1980s, I worked to try to correct the forces impoverishing America's inner cities—Newark, New Jersey, in particular, where I was pastor at two churches and headed the Metropolitan Ecumenical Ministry.

I suppose I am still a New Dealer at heart. I believe that government can play a crucial role in correcting the ills of society; I saw it happen during the Depression and many times in my life later on. I have voted Democratic in most every election (though by no means do all Democrats of today hold to the old values of their party). I have always been distrustful of corporate power, yet at the same time, I have never believed in state ownership of the economy, mindful of how badly that approach has worked when Communist countries have tried it.

As a young man I decided to become a minister, but I rejected the notion that Christianity is only a spiritual quest. I signed on fully to the ideal of the "social gospel." The Bible offers many words that point to a duty to attack the social ills that we encounter on earth. I often drew inspiration from St. Paul's admonition to the professing Christians who so easily blended in with the corrupt ways of society in first-century Rome. In his letter to members of the church, he counseled: "Do not conform yourself to the standards of this world, but let God transform you inwardly by the complete change of your mind. Then you will be able to know the will of God—what is good and pleasing to Him and is perfect" (Romans 12:2). This passage is quoted in many churches today, including many run by conservative pastors with no interest in social justice. These conservative pastors and church members often overlook the fact that anyone who submits to St. Paul's admonition is forever changed totally in mind and heart by God. This often motivates the person to work for earthly justice and the transformation of society itself. I believe that in some small way, I was touched in the way that St. Paul mentions, and that it became the central motivation of my life.

I hope that my story can be useful to today's younger Americans. Today's world is different from the one I was born into. Microsoft, a company whose product is not steel or automobiles, but electronic impulses inscribed on disks, has emerged as the corporate titan of the day; labor union membership has declined; the notion of government as an engine of positive change is out of fashion; and few young men and women of today will hold a job for life, or live in the same place for more than a few years. Yet today's younger people, I believe, have concerns common to my generation's, in the form of apprehension about the future and desire for a more equitable division of our country's wealth. The fight for social justice goes on, though the names and dates and places change. To my mind, it is as fundamental to human existence as eating and breathing.

In looking back over my life, I note that it had its share of defeats. But when I lived through them, I often recalled the words of Norman Thomas, former presidential candidate of the Socialist Party and one of my heroes in my younger years: "There are no lost causes, only causes that have not yet been won." Happily, I've been privileged to be part of the winning phase more than a few times as well, such as the purchase of the Delmo Homes projects in Missouri by their farmworker tenants in 1945, the reduction of childhood diseases in Thailand in the 1960s, and the saving of nine thousand public housing apartments in Newark that were scheduled to be dynamited in the 1980s. Win some, lose some, but never give up. With that approach, I've been able to keep going.

This book had its genesis in a yellowing manuscript that sat on my bookshelf for many years and which at times I would take down and read. It was the memoirs of my own father, John Stewart Burgess, a deeply compassionate and motivated man who was in many ways a role model for me. He had started writing it after suffering a heart attack in 1940. He never finished it; another attack killed him in 1949.

The manuscript acquired new meaning for me in 1989, when I followed in Dad's footsteps and suffered a heart attack. Like his, it was the result of too many hours on the job and the attendant anxieties. As I recovered, things passed through my mind that I now knew had gone through Dad's. It was time to assess and record, to claim accomplishments and acknowledge compromises and failures. I made up my mind to gather up a lifetime's worth of diaries, letters, reports, and memories and distill them into a book. It was what Dad had done, but unlike him, I told myself (ever the overachiever), I would finish the job. But as had happened a half-century before, things got delayed. Once I recovered my strength, I did what Dad had done: I went back to work full-time, running an ecumenical ministry in Newark. The writing didn't really get under way until I retired from the ministry and my wife, Alice, and I moved from New Jersey to the small town of Benicia, California, in September 1990. Here, for the first time in my adult life, I was not holding down a full-time job or looking for one. I had time on my hands, and as has always been my way, I filled it. Most every morning I rose early to sift through the past and bang away at my computer.

In my efforts to recall distant events, I soon discovered that my memory was fragmentary and my ability to describe vividly the daily sights and sounds of the past faulty. That led me to a not entirely welcome conclusion: over the course of my life, I frequently allowed my tendency to think serious thoughts to overshadow my power to feel and imagine. I found I could often recall the cause and objective of the hour quite clearly, but too often the people who had stood beside me, the homes I had lived in, the food I had tasted, were a blur.

For me there's a poignant scene in Thornton Wilder's play *Our Town,* when God brings back from the dead a young woman named Emilie to relive her twelfth birthday on earth. Sadly, she finds that her beloved mother and father are so preoccupied with daily worries and plans for tomorrow that they have no time for their daughter even on her twelfth birthday. She cries out to her mother: "Oh Mama, just look at me one minute as though you really saw me. Let's look at one another. I can't go on. It goes too fast. Take me back—up the hill to my grave. But first: wait. One more look. Good-by, good-by world. Good-by to clocks ticking and Mama's sunflowers. And food and coffee. And new ironed dresses and hot baths, and sleeping and waking up. O earth, you're too wonderful for anybody to realize. Do any human beings ever realize life while they live it, every, every minute?"[1]

I wish today that I had lived my life more in that spirit.

So, accepting my limitations, but thankful that God has blessed me with caring parents, good health, my beloved wife, and our five children, I am completing my autobiography as I pass my eighty-third milestone. I do it to gain a greater understanding of myself, and I hope that through it I will convey the essence of my life to family and friends but also to strangers who will know me only in these written words. If this book should cause anyone to want to go deeper, my personal papers can be found in the archives of the Walter Reuther Library at Wayne State University in Detroit.

My deep-felt thanks go to many people who helped and encouraged me in this writing. Our son-in-law Ron Castro spent long hours correcting the original and much too lengthy manuscript and making it look good on a computer screen. Stewart Burns, an author and historian, applied his considerable editing skills to my words. Our son John helped me make the story more readable and relevant to younger generations.

Lending encouragement and advice along the way was my friend of half a century, Victor Reuther, and new friends such as Leslie Hough, former director of the Walter Reuther Library, and Arthur B. Evans, director of the Wayne State University Press. And of course I owe more than I can ever repay to Alice, who shared with me so many of the events recounted here, and who in recent months has put up with losing me day after day to the computer keyboard and the pull of the past.

David S. Burgess

1

A Boyhood in China, 1917–1926

MOST EVERY LIFE owes its start to what seems a chance encounter. In my case, it occurred on a tennis court in Kyoto, Japan, in the year 1908. There my parents, two young Americans who had traveled abroad with the Christian missionary movement of a century ago, first cast eyes on each other.

They were, if a son can be allowed such a judgment, unusual, gifted people. John Stewart Burgess was a cheerful, though somewhat self-doubting man who had come to Japan after college on a one-year English-teaching job with the YMCA to "see what this missionary business was all about." He made the trip much to the dismay of his own father, who had arranged for him a plush banking job in New Jersey, only to see it turned down for something in a strange, far-off country and paying no great salary. What really interested my father (he was a Princeton graduate) was scholarship, the new discipline of sociology in particular. Later he became engrossed in the building of a "New China." Throughout what lengthened into many years in Japan and then China, he never considered himself a missionary, having, I think, too much respect for the cultures in which he lived. If he spread his strong Christian faith, it was through empathy and power of example, not preaching. He was endlessly curious about Asian society and loved spending social time away with the locals. His memoirs contain an amusing account of attending a Japanese gathering. Showing your stuff in song-making was (and still is) a common pastime when the Japanese get together, so he let loose with "My Gal's a Corker, She's a New Yorker."

In fact, his gal wasn't a New Yorker—she was born in Chicago in 1881 and grew up in Japan. Bearing the name Stella Cornelia Fisher, she was the daughter of some of the first American missionaries (Baptists, they were) to arrive in the country after it opened to the West in the mid-nineteenth century. It was rather unusual in those days to educate a girl beyond high school, but she was sent home to the States for college, at the University of Chicago and later Kalamazoo College, then returned to Japan and worked for the YWCA. Mother was a strong-willed woman, a poet, one of the original feminists. She made no secret that she didn't care much for the missionary crowd, often seeing its people as dry and self-important. She might have stayed in the United States after college had her mother not fallen seriously ill back in Japan. I believe that through much of her life, my mother had to accept that her mind spun round at a faster rate than those of most of the missionaries around her.

The family annals don't record whether the newly introduced Americans played each other that day on the tennis court in Kyoto. If they did, I would guess that my mother won.

They were married in 1909 and soon moved to China, where my father had been offered a job with the YMCA. As they tried to start a family, there followed two sad losses, a common experience given the times and sanitary conditions of the country where they were living: their first child, John, died before age three of blood poisoning; their second son, Donald, was born prematurely and lived only a few days. But I arrived safely in the world on June 15, 1917, shortly after our country's entry into the First World War. I had the good medical fortune to be born in the United States, at the Presbyterian hospital in New York City, during a rare visit my parents made in that period to their home country. A month later we were all in Beijing, or Peking as it was known then.

Peking

The first home I remember was a large brick house within a compound in back of the Peking YMCA where my father worked. The walls enclosed a pocket of American affluence and order. We ate well, dressed in clean clothes, and took hot baths. Servants kept things running smoothly. My brother Vinton (born in 1919) and I were watched over by my mother and a Chinese woman whom we called "Amah." By the age of two, Vinton and I were fluent in both English and Mandarin Chinese.

Beyond the walls were the full chaos and cultural richness of China of the early twentieth century, a society that was just casting off its imperial tradition. Not far from our home, the famous "last emperor," Pu Yi, was living as a virtual prisoner inside the Forbidden City palace. The country had taken only a few faltering steps beyond feudalism. I remember well the shouts of street peddlers hawking spicy sweet potatoes, soups, persimmons, and steamy rice. I can still picture the haggard faces of old and wistful women hobbled by bound feet, some carrying babies on their backs. Most old men wore pigtails. In the streets were wagons drawn by laborers and rickshaws drawn by small, lean men. There were herds of sheep, goats, and water buffalo, and funeral possessions with weeping mourners dressed in white—to the Chinese the symbol of death.

Perhaps it was the contrast between the two sides of the compound walls that first instilled in me a sense of how unjust the world can be in distributing wealth and other bounty. I was aware at a very early age that my daily entitlements of food, shelter, and care simply did not hold for the people outside the compound walls. Probably it was my parents who first got me thinking in this direction. They were raising Vinton and me to be "good and moral" sons who desired to help less privileged people. I remember that when I was about six, I walked with my father one day down a nearby street and we came upon a British man in a white suit and pith helmet beating a rickshaw man with a metal cane. My father explained to me that this white man regarded the yellow-skinned rickshaw man and all Chinese as inferior and therefore did not hesitate to swing his cane that way. At times the suffering struck even closer to home: one day our cook informed my parents that the frozen corpse of a beggar lay on our front steps.

Certainly my father was one of the few Americans in Peking who knew firsthand the life of the city's poor. His work with the YMCA and the years of sociology research that he began in Peking brought him into contact with prisoners in shockingly squalid jails, the neglected mentally ill and deranged, street prostitutes, the victims of leprosy and tuberculosis, the ill-housed and homeless, and the hosts of beggars crowding the streets every day. In 1919 he and Sydney Gamble, a Proctor and Gamble heir working in China, published a book entitled *Peking: A Social Survey.* I still have a copy. It remains the premier social survey of the city in that period.

Dad was by no means all seriousness, though. When he traveled, he always seemed to return home loaded with little gifts for my mother, my brother, and me. He was a great storyteller, regaling Vinton and me at bedtime with a serial tale of a baseball team of animals, each one playing a different position. He drew funny pictures of the animal team members. I can only remember getting one spanking from him. My mother was generally the more somber of the two, quick to express her displeasure with judgmental eyes when Vinton and I did something wrong. I would say that ours was not an expressive family, something which in later years would be the case with my own.

Mother kept herself busy during my father's frequent absences by translating into English many ancient Chinese poems and essays. She wrote her own poetry as well, much of it about life in the Chinese capital, and published a book of verses entitled *A Peking Caravan.* Her unease about being part of the well-fed missionary community and her deep sensitivity to the poor outside the gates of the compound are clearly expressed in a poem she wrote during the cold winter of 1924:

Three square meals,
And then comes tea—
Thin slabs of toast suggesting jam,
Or scones to be butter crowned.
Sandwiches with savory tang,
Honeyed walnuts, pastry, tarts and macaroons.
Dulset cakes of tireless artistry.
Gay voices floating through
Ambrosial whiffs of pungent tea,
Mellifluous coffee.
Well nourished men, overnourished wives.

I wonder if he's at it yet,
The old man I saw as I rode here
Propelled by human brawn.
His toil-wrapped hands caressed the willows
Growing by the city's moat,
While, furtively, his fumbling fingers
Clutched the tenderest twigs and tucked
Them into gunny sacks beneath his arm.
Willow leaves, you know,
Boiled with the bark of elm—
In a discarded tin—
Makes easier that gnawing, grinding pain,
and adds a little fuel
To the flickering embers of an old's man's life.

Another cup? Yes, two lumps, please
Another slice of cake—you've just begun.[1]

Just after the end of the First World War, Dad left the YMCA to become head of the sociology department at the newly established Yenching University on the edge of Peking (today it is known as Beijing University). He told me years later that he enjoyed the most productive period of his academic career during his time at the university in the 1920s. He saw his teaching as furthering the emergence of a modern China that would take its place among the community of nations. Along the way, he was quite literally witnessing history, the division of China into the two political forces that would dominate its history up to the present time. Roughly half of his leading students, he told me, became officials in the Nationalist government of Chiang Kai-shek. The other half later joined the Communist Party and worked under Mao Tse-tung before and after the party took power over all of the Chinese mainland in 1949.

Tungchow

All parents keep secrets from their children. One that mine held was why our family moved in 1924 from Peking to an American compound near the small town of Tungchow thirty miles from Peking. Perhaps they felt the air and sanitation were better. My father worked at the university on weekdays but returned to Tungchow for Saturday and Sunday. Vinton and I were not put into the local American school. Instead, our mother instructed us using Calvert home-teaching materials sent from Baltimore. Although my brother and I missed our classmates at the American school in Peking, we learned to cope.

Frequently Vinton and I accompanied the family cook into Tungchow to purchase vegetables, fruits, sides of beef and pork, and live chickens. Even after all these years in China, my American sensibilities could get a shock from everyday life in this country. I recall feeling horrified when the cook chopped off the chickens' heads with a sharp knife and left the headless chickens thrashing about on the ground. There were disturbing sights in the town as well. China was by this time descending into civil war between countless rival warlords and political factions, and at times the violence came frighteningly close. On the streets of Tungchow we saw many soldiers of a warlord who had recently captured the town. Our cook told us one day that during the previous week a general serving a defeated warlord had been beheaded in the town square before a large crowd. But the escalating violence resulted in what for me was the highlight of our two years near Tungchow: the arrival of a company of American Marines, sent by the embassy in Peking to protect us and other American families in Tungchow from attacks by warlord armies. My brother and I liked the Marines because they soon became our coaches in baseball and football, sports that much fascinated us and made us feel closer to our own faraway country.

We were to move to that country sooner than I had expected, in June of 1926. For this move, I did get an understanding of the reasons. One was that my parents wanted us all to be close to good doctors. They had lost those first two children to disease, and continued to grieve about this. Vinton had had a mastoid operation and Dad a near-fatal bout with typhoid fever. In addition, my father had hatched a new ambition: he wanted to earn a Ph.D. in sociology at Columbia University. My parents thought long and hard, and finally made the decision to leave. Looking back, it seems it should have been an easy call for an American family with small children. The day we left Peking the army of Chiang Kai-shek and rival forces were lobbing artillery shells over the city in a battle for control of it.

Soon we were steaming east aboard an ocean liner. Asia slipped over the horizon and from my thoughts as well, though the place was in my blood now and would draw me back. I had just turned nine, and was feeling very excited. A long journey and a new country lay before me.

2

A Privileged Adolescence in the Great Depression, 1926–1935

WE DISEMBARKED FROM our ocean liner in San Francisco in late June of 1926 and took a train across the continent. My brother Vinton and I passed much of the trip with noses pressed to the windows, fascinated by the mountains, the farmland, the riches of this new country we were passing through. Eventually we reached Morrisville, Pennsylvania, where we were welcomed to the home of my grandparents William and Clara Burgess. Here I was exposed to a whole new way of thinking to go with this new country.

William Burgess was a wealthy man (the family had made a fortune in the pottery business), a lifelong Republican, and a member of the U.S. Tariff Commission under the presidencies of Warren Harding and Calvin Coolidge. Vinton and I were told to call him "Grandfather Bobbin," but the name did little to make him approachable. With a booming voice and thick beard, he seemed to me a bit like an Old Testament prophet, best dealt with from a distance. He had lots of views that had never been heard in our home. I remember well that during our visit, he complained to my father that newly arrived Irish and Italian immigrants were defeating worthy Anglo-Saxon politicians at the polls and were on the verge of taking over both the Republican and Democratic Parties. He was shocked to learn that Socialist Party leader Norman Thomas had been my father's classmate at Princeton.

Three years after our visit, my grandfather met a tragic end. On the floor of the U.S. Senate, he was denounced by Democrat Thaddeus Carraway of Arkansas, who headed a committee investigating lobbyists in Washington. In a speech, Carraway charged that the chief representative for U.S. pottery makers, my grandfather, was corrupting members of Congress with money and all manner of special favors. Grandfather later appeared before Carraway's Senate committee, and with tears in his eyes denied the charges in detail.

He acknowledged giving corporate campaign contributions to members of Congress, but said he had stayed well within the law. After the hearing, he returned to Morrisville and quickly contracted pneumonia. Within a week he died, and we in the family, believing firmly that he was innocent, always said that he had died from a broken heart. He had been a pious lifelong Presbyterian, and his funeral was large and well attended. I was there with many other family members, and for the first time in my life, I saw my father cry. The day after the funeral my father went to Washington, where he pleaded with Senator Carraway to make a speech in the Senate to clear my grandfather's name of the false charges. The senator refused.

Life in White Plains

For our first two years in America, my family lived in a white-shingled house in White Plains, New York, forty miles north of Manhattan. Five days a week, my father commuted by train to Columbia University. He burned the midnight oil at home and earned the Ph.D. in two years. My mother went on a series of lecture tours to many cities, reading her own poetry and lecturing about the culture and future of China.

For me and Vinton, entrance into this new society was not without pain. On my first day as a fourth grader in a White Plains grammar school, my classmates scornfully laughed at my Lord Fauntleroy pantaloons and long white stockings. Hearing that I had come from China, some kids called me a "yellow chink" and "slant-eyes." The next day I came to school dressed in conventional American boys' attire of the time—white shirt, white pants, and black sneakers. I soon made friends among the neighborhood boys, however. To prove to myself and others that I was really an "All-American boy," I refused to speak Mandarin at home, much to my parents' displeasure. My memory of that language soon disappeared.

That year I joined a Boy Scout troop and the local YMCA, where I played basketball, lifted weights, ran on the track, and swam in the pool. With friends I went to the local movie theater on Saturday afternoons and saw Douglas Fairbanks, Mary Pickford, shoot-'em-up Westerns, and thrillers such as *West of Zanzibar*. On a fall afternoon I shared a cigar with a friend and became violently ill. I never smoked again.

In 1927, the New York Giants became my lifelong baseball heroes when I went to the Polo Grounds and saw them soundly defeat the Pittsburgh Pirates. My enthusiasm for the sport sometimes took strange forms: when no other family member was home, I would pose before a full-length mirror as a pitcher throwing a blazing fastball or as a batter knocking out a towering home run.

I dreamed more than once that someday I would become like Bill Terry, the Giants' first baseman.

In summers, we spent time in the New England outdoors. We stayed at Mountain Rest in the Berkshires, a vacation spot for overseas missionaries on leave in America. On Sundays we attended the Congregational church in the nearby village of Cummington. That, I learned years later, was a foreshadowing of the chance encounter that would lead to my own marriage. A pretty and vivacious girl named Alice Stevens lived next door to that church and attended services on Sundays. We did not meet that summer, though we must certainly have sat just a few feet from each other on a number of occasions. On Thanksgiving Day thirteen years later Alice and I were married in the sanctuary of this same church.

My somewhat precocious interest in politics and the rights and wrongs of the world continued. I felt admiration for a White Plains neighbor who had invented a pie-making machine but never tried to patent or sell it commercially, out of fear, he said, that it would put hundreds of bakers out of work. I heard the news on the radio in 1927 that Governor Alvan Fuller of Massachusetts had refused to commute the death sentences of the Italian anarchists Sacco and Vanzetti. I felt he was a hard-hearted man for that. Mom and Dad kept me up on events in China. One day we had a visit from Jimmy Yen, one of my father's former students, who would go on to head programs for mass literacy in China and later in other Asian countries.

After receiving his doctorate in sociology at Columbia in June of 1928, Father decided—against Mother's wishes—to return to China. We were all lonely in his absence (he was again heading the sociology department at Yenching University), but we learned to get along without him. I earned good grades at the grammar school and made new friends. I was pleased when my mother told me in the spring of 1930 that Dad was returning to America and that we were all going to move to southern California, where he had been named an associate professor of sociology at Pomona College in the town of Claremont.

But my elation was short-lived: I was about to get an introduction to a serious illness, the first of a number that would complicate my adolescent years and, I think, build in me endurance that I was able to draw on many times later in my life. A week after hearing the good news about Dad, I became suddenly ill with encephalitis, commonly known as sleeping sickness, which inflames the brain and spinal cord. The mosquito-borne disease caused me to sleep twenty hours a day. Alarmed by my deteriorating condition, our family doctor had me rushed by ambulance to the Presbyterian hospital in New York City, the place where I had been born. Fluids were drawn from my backbone, and nurses rubbed cocoa butter all over my skin to increase my blood circulation. It was a thoroughly frightening, debilitating experience. My recovery was slow, but recover I did and with the family moved west.

Three Golden Years in California

In 1930, Claremont was a small college town then surrounded by orange groves and free of today's smog. We settled in, and everything I've learned since indicates that my father was soon one of the more popular professors at Pomona College. The living room of our new home a block from the campus became an informal meeting place for students and faculty alike. Claremont agreed with me too: I was feeling better now, and ninth and tenth grades at the local public high school were among my most happy years. There were about forty kids in my class. On Friday or Saturday nights about half of us would show up at dance parties at the homes of various class members. In an awkward and stumbling manner, I learned to dance and to carry on conversation with girls. On Sunday evenings most of my friends and I went to the youth fellowship at the Community Congregational Church. You could get a driver's license at age thirteen back then, so some of us drove our family cars to shuttle loads of kids to the beach or up Mount Baldy. Now and then a boy and a girl fell in love and "went steady," but most of us remained unattached as loyal members of our friendship group.

At our high school, the elderly Miss Willow struggled to teach me the fundamentals of Latin. English teacher Miss Hull surprised me when she remarked that I had "some real writing talent." Coach Martin kept me as a second stringer on the baseball field and the basketball court. Once I scored two baskets, and in a baseball game I hit a winning two-bagger. How could life be better than this? I wondered.

In fact, it was a bit like China. The Burgess family was well housed and well fed. My father had the good fortune to be at work in the middle of the Great Depression. But during these years, Claremont was often full of hungry men and women going from door to door and begging for food and other handouts. On many days I saw them riding the roofs of passing freight cars headed to Los Angeles. Claremont also had a large Mexican-American community, most of whose members were poor and lived south of the tracks. Their sons and daughters attended our high school, but they were always on the fringes of student society and were never invited to become members of our social group.

Father had been a friend of the poor in China, and he played the same role in Claremont—though here it would get him into trouble. He negotiated a pact between dairy farmers and orange-grove managers in which they agreed to exchange milk and oranges that they otherwise would have destroyed. (Trying to raise prices by reducing supply—destroying produce—was a common tactic among farmers, even though so many people were going hungry at the time.) Father met with Francis Townsend, author of the Townsend Plan to give all elderly citizens a monthly pension of $200, and the novelist Upton Sinclair, who unsuccessfully ran for governor of California in 1934. They were both considered radicals by the general public. Father invited Townsend and Sinclair to outline their reform programs before his classes at Pomona College. He became friends with progressive Democrat Jerry Voorhis, a part-time teacher at Pomona who was elected to Congress in 1936 but defeated ten years later by the young Richard Nixon. We were all Democrats in my family—we rejoiced when Franklin Roosevelt was elected president in 1932.

In the spring of 1933, my golden years came to an abrupt end. The president of Pomona College, Charles K. Edmonds, who had recruited my father back in 1930, informed him that he would be terminated in June, saying that the depressed economy and resulting cash crisis at the college gave him no choice. My father believed that the real reasons for his termination were his association with Townsend and Sinclair, his role in the barter agreement, and his friendship with Voorhis, whom Edmonds terminated at the same time.

High School near Philadelphia

In 1933 my father got some unexpected and very welcome news: he was asked to head the ten-professor sociology department at Temple University in Philadelphia. The family drove cross-country to Pennsylvania, Dad trusting me enough at the wheel to give me long driving lessons as we went. We began a new life in Philadelphia. Father worked his magic again in the classroom. His imaginative new course on the family drew hundreds of students. He was elected honorary chairman of the black YMCA on the Temple campus. In 1935, always a man ahead of his time, he led a civil rights march down Broad Street in Philadelphia. I admired his brave and crusading spirit.

Life was proving difficult for me, however. I had been used to a class of just forty kids in Claremont; now I had to adjust to being one of more than four hundred boys and girls in the eleventh grade at Cheltenham High School. And sickness struck again: while my mother was at Kalamazoo College to receive an honorary degree, I suffered my first epileptic seizure, right there in the classroom, in full view of my fellow students. To avoid a recurrence, I began taking phenobarbital pills every night. Then, in early 1934, I came down with a sore throat and high fever, interspersed with cold chills all over my body. I was taken to Temple University Hospital, where a Dr. Kolmer, a cardiac specialist, examined me. That night he informed my parents privately that I had a most severe form of rheumatic fever—so severe, in his opinion, that I would probably die before I reached the age of twenty. I wasn't told about that assessment until years later, but I was aware, lying in bed by myself, that I was in very deep danger. One day I recall weeping at the despair of it all.

But, as had happened with my other illness, I began to recover. As I regained my strength, I became aware that Dr. Kolmer, and my mother as well, viewed me as an invalid. They wanted me to rest all the time, to avoid exercise and contact sports, and to cut back my hours at school. I did reduce my school hours, but when it came to physical activity I went entirely in the other direction. Determined never to be sickly, I began running two to three miles each morning, an activity that often drew stares in this pre-jogging era, and did push-ups and sit-ups every day. Of my own volition, I avoided what we today call junk food, ate three good meals a day, never smoked, and avoided all forms of alcohol. This was the basic regimen I would continue for the rest of my life.

During the summer of 1934 I persuaded my father to hike with me for five days down the Appalachian Trail in the Green Mountains of Vermont. Surrounded by natural beauty, I rejoiced that somehow I had regained my health. At the end of the hike, Dad had a surprise suggestion—that I finish high school not at Cheltenham High School but at Blair Academy, a boarding prep school in the hills of northwest New Jersey. In the 1990s we would look on such a separation from my parents as strange, but in those days going off to boarding school was common enough among people of our station. Father knew the problems I'd had at Cheltenham and was looking for a way to ease the stress on me, I think. I agreed to go, though I harbored skepticism about how well I'd like an elite and high-priced prep school.

Blair Academy

I entered Blair in the fall of 1934. As I had expected, the place was a way station to Ivy League universities for the sons of wealthy businessmen and stockbrokers. Most had money enough to return home on weekends and to cruise local bars and nightclubs. After returning to the dorms on Sunday night, they delighted classmates with stories about their heavy weekend drinking and their real or imaginary sexual exploits. I was the son of a man who had never earned more than $10,000 a year, and that was not a formula for social success at Blair. During my first weeks, I was the victim of hazing in several forms. Water was thrown over my transom. I was accused of being both a "queer" and a virgin. I was challenged to wrestle or box by classmates bigger and stronger than I. Yet despite these distractions I received high grades in my classes, wrote stories for the school newspaper, and joined the academy choir. I sang on Sundays at the local Presbyterian church, though I found the pastor there to be boring and hopelessly otherworldly. I played soccer for the first time, but failed to make any varsity team. I kept running those two to three miles each morning before breakfast. I was in excellent physical shape now.

In early 1935 I was shocked when the Blair headmaster told me that I could not graduate from Blair that June because I had not earned sufficient credits during my junior year at Cheltenham High School. Having no desire to spend another year at Blair, I came up with my own plan: without telling my parents or the headmaster, I wrote letters to Swarthmore, Carlton, and Oberlin Colleges asking to be admitted as a freshman in September. I got no reply from Swarthmore or Carlton, but much to my surprise a letter arrived in late April from Dean Bosworth at Oberlin informing me that, despite my lack of a high school degree the coming June, I could enter Oberlin as a freshman in the fall. It's hard to imagine such a thing happening today, but times were different then. I joyously accepted the offer.

The summer of 1935 passed quickly. Again putting aside advice to avoid exercise, I got a job as a landscaper at the YMCA Silver Bay Conference Center on Lake George. I learned to type, swam out to the float on the lake each day without fear, and won a lead role in a local production of the Gilbert and Sullivan operetta *HMS Pinafore*. I also attended weekly chapel services and developed a more serious commitment to the Christian faith. For the first time in my life, I began reading the Bible. The reason, I think, was that I was becoming aware of tragic events in America and abroad and believed that I would find guidance in the pages of Scripture. My teenage mind was pondering questions like these: What was the Christian response to Hitler's persecution of the Jews? Should the European powers and America stop Hitler from expanding Germany's borders? Italy had invaded Ethiopia, and I was very moved by the address its leader, Haile Salassie, gave to the League of Nations. A continent away in India, Gandhi was confronting British rule with pacifist tactics. Jesus had followed the pacifist route against Rome, the imperial power of his time, so did that mean that a true believer in Jesus must be a pacifist? With the Great Depression showing no sign of ending, I was also becoming very interested in the still-widening chasm between the rich and the poor at home and began to wonder what a Christian should do about it. The United Auto Workers seemed to me to have the right approach—they were staging a series of militant but nonviolent sit-down strikes in the auto plants of Detroit and elsewhere. The speeches of a UAW organizer named Walter Reuther impressed me; he would later have a deep influence on my life.

Soon the end of summer arrived. Feeling excited in the same way that I had when my family left China, I packed up and set off for Oberlin.

3

Student Activist, 1930s-Style, at Oberlin College, 1935–1939

FOR THIS SOLEMN and intense young man of eighteen, Oberlin College proved to be a perfect fit. Before the Civil War, Oberlin had become the first college in our country to admit women and African Americans. Its abiding idealism was symbolized by the words appearing over a campus memorial arch for the victims of the Boxer Rebellion in China: "The blood of martyrs is the seed of the church." The legacy of evangelist Charles Finney and theologians Henry Churchill King and Edward Increase Bosworth made Oberlin a continuing bulwark of liberalism and a center for open intellectual inquiry. It was a place of moral inspiration to thousands of graduates who left it to devote their lives to the service of humanity in America and overseas. Oberlin shaped me in many important ways. As I stated in the class handbook at my fiftieth reunion in 1989, "Oberlin helped me to realize that my life will have no lasting meaning until I devote it to helping folks less privileged than myself. I have tried to make this a constant theme and goal in my life journey."

In the four years following my arrival, Oberlin professors opened my mind and heart to the world of the past and present. To name but a few, Professor Jessie Mack helped me to appreciate the poems of the nineteenth-century romantics. Professor James Hall from the Music Conservatory helped me to develop a lifelong taste and preference for classical music. The behavioral psychologists Luke Steiner and Lawrence Cole forced me to question the validity of my faith. American historians Carl Wittke and Robert Fletcher persuaded me to major in history rather than economics. They advised me when I wrote a lengthy study of how Samuel Gompers, president of the American Federation of Labor, was a firm opponent in 1914 to our nation's entrance into the First World War but became a jingoistic enthusiast for that war three years later. Oberlin was much more than the classroom for me, however. I kept up my exercise, listened to the music of Glenn Miller, had some romantic interests, and got very much involved in student politics.

Today we sometimes talk as if American student activism was invented in the 1960s. In fact, the late 1930s were a time of strong campus involvement in social and moral issues fed by the continuing crisis of the Depression, the rise of fascism in Europe, the Spanish civil war, and the ever-greater certainty of a new world war. At Oberlin you could find a broad mix of liberals, Communists, Christian activists, anarchists, and idealists, as well as ordinary Democrats and Republicans. Among the idealists I would count Paul MacEachron, a friend who after his sophomore year sailed for Spain and joined the international volunteer unit known as the Abraham Lincoln Brigade. He died in Spain fighting the fascist forces of General Francisco Franco. Paul's commitment and moral purity much impressed me. I had no taste for the two mainstream parties' complacency, or the student Communists' hardheaded tactics and dogmatism. Though many people today would say that the old-line Communist Party USA was never anything more than a fringe movement, I can say from experience that there were quite a few party members in student politics in those days. They were generally young, righteous, manipulative, willing to roll over everyone to achieve their goals, all the while voicing unending praise for the paradise called the Soviet Union.

I was by now thoroughly set as a liberal and a Christian, and found quite a few organizations in which I could pursue those convictions. I joined a group called the Peace Society and attended its monthly meetings on peace and war. I was also a member of the Oberlin chapter of the American Student Union, where I more than once spoke out against its "fellow travelers"—the term used in those days for people who were secretly in league with the Communists. But it was the YMCA that got most of my attention. During my freshman year I taught in a Y-sponsored Sunday school at an orphanage on the edge of town. The next year I joined a small student group that met at the home of the famed theologian Walter Horton to discuss the Christian faith, the direction of our lives, and (as students always do) the meaning of life and death. In my junior year I served on the Oberlin YMCA cabinet, and as a senior I was thrilled to be elected by the whole Oberlin student body as new president of the college YMCA.

My view of the world and my choice of future callings were shaped by my summer experiences in those years. I spent the summer of 1937 at the first university "work camp," a cooperative venture in western Pennsylvania sponsored by the American Friends Service Committee. We volunteers built homes for and with coal miners and their families. We walked the picket line with striking miners and became well acquainted with organizers of the newly formed United Steel Workers Union–CIO. At the end of that summer I envisaged myself as a future CIO organizer.

I spent the summer of 1938 at the YMCA-YWCA presidents' school at Union Theological Seminary in New York City. Several times we visited the slums of nearby Harlem. We studied the Bible together, and most of us found it was filled with contradictory road signs.

In the summer of 1939, soon after my graduation from Oberlin, I boarded an ocean liner and sailed to Europe to visit six countries and attend the World Conference of Christian Youth in Amsterdam as a YMCA delegate. Everywhere we turned during that visit, we saw evidence that war was coming soon. In Trafalgar Square in England, signs declared that "We must be prepared." Hamburg residents were allowed only two eggs per person each month, the rest presumably being salted away for the army. Our young Nazi guides in Germany were confident that the Polish city of Danzig would be soon be occupied by the German army as a matter of "historical necessity" and that neither Britain nor France would intervene. I was very impressed with egalitarian Denmark, where, according to the Danes, "few have too much and still fewer too little." But I was brought back to the reality of the coming war when I saw from the front porch of the Danish Folk School in Elsinore two huge German battleships powerful enough to sink the whole Danish navy in an hour. To me the Palace of Nations in beautiful Geneva, Switzerland, had a hollow, ghostlike charm most fitting to the predictable failure of the League of Nations to prevent the oncoming war.

But the highlight of my trip was the ten days at the first World Conference of Christian Youth in Amsterdam, where I was one of fifteen hundred student delegates from seventy-five nations. During debates on the conference floor, the "social-action gospel" that delegates from the United States, England, and India pressed often clashed openly with European fundamentalism, the doctrine of original sin, the primacy of faith in Jesus Christ as the Son of God, and the literal interpretation of the Bible. At times, divisions between the delegates were based not on theological doctrine but on war and national hatred. Japanese and Chinese delegates would not converse—the Japanese army had already invaded China. Despite such divisions, the growing war clouds, and the anticipated deaths in the coming war, the conference was an inspiring experience for me and most other delegates. I learned at the end of the Second World War that some of the most conservative and fundamentalist delegates, with whom I had strongly differed, fell into the hands of Nazi torturers, but were not broken by them because of the strength of their Christian faith. I will always remember the final worship service, which ended with delegates reciting the Lord's Prayer en masse, each in his or her own tongue.

After four years, my time at Oberlin neared an end, and I wrestled with what to do after graduation. I was blessed with a variety of options involving college YMCAs, seminaries, law schools, and unions. In the end, I chose none of these. Instead, I accepted a one-year government internship in Washington administered by an agency called the National Institute of Public Affairs. I had always been interested in government. I wanted to hook up with some agency or New Deal lawmaker working to address the country's social problems. And I admit that I wanted to rub shoulders with powerful decision-makers. As it turned out, I arrived in Washington just as most people there were starting to turn their attention away from problems at home and toward what was happening overseas. On September 1, 1939, Hitler's army launched its blitzkrieg attack on Poland, detonating the Second World War.

4

Learning the Ways of Washington, 1939–1940

WAR IN EUROPE or not, the internship went on. Thirty-five of us recent college graduates arrived in Washington that fall, in many cases looking to turn our temporary government jobs into permanent careers. In the first days we traded gossip freely on the question foremost in our minds: where would we be assigned? I ended up in the Wage and Hour Division of the Department of Labor, which had the difficult task of enforcing a 1938 federal law stipulating forty cents an hour as the minimum wage for workers engaged in interstate commerce. My first supervisor assigned me the rather tedious task of drafting a series of administrative rules. In ensuing weeks I did manage to get out and around, though, and sat in on congressional hearings in which members of the House and Senate were examining the effects of the wage and hour law on small businesses and large industrial plants. Critics of the law of course claimed that it would bankrupt many small firms. Supporters argued that workers needed a much higher minimum wage than forty cents an hour. I knew easily which side I was on. But alas, the debate is much the same sixty years later.

During the Christmas vacation, the job brought some real excitement: I joined a division inspector on an unannounced visit to a textile plant in Philadelphia. This company was rumored to be paying its workers less than the mandated minimum wage and denying them overtime pay. Without warning, we walked into the plant and for the next three hours examined the company's books and interviewed, behind closed doors, more than two dozen employees. Then the inspector told the company manager that his firm was in violation of minimum wage requirements and faced stiff fines. What made an impression on me was the inspector's frankness and bold approach, the arrogance of the manager, and the timidity of many employees.

Then it was back to the dreary task of drafting those regulations for the Wage and Hour Division. In the end I was saved by an old family friend—

Jerry Voorhis, my father's colleague from Pomona College days. Jerry was then a Democratic congressman representing a district that included the town of Claremont I had loved so much. I paid a visit to his office, and he greeted me warmly. I told him I would be most pleased to become an unpaid research assistant on his Capitol Hill staff. To my delight, he agreed and in a few days my transfer to his office was official. I felt now that I had the kind of job I'd come to Washington for. My first assignment was to draft letters to constituents answering questions or explaining Voorhis's position on various issues. Voorhis was a member of the House Un-American Activities Committee (HUAC), and when he could not attend its sessions I was sometimes sent to listen and report back to him. The committee was headed by a wily and bigoted congressman from Texas named Martin Dies. Voorhis told me that House Speaker Sam Rayburn had appointed him as the sole liberal on the committee mainly to keep an eye on fellow Texan Dies's unpredictable and at times outlandish behavior. These days we often think that the committee's outrages began a decade later in the times of Senator Joseph McCarthy, but having attended those meetings, I can say that in 1940 the committee and some well-coached accusatory witnesses were already busy ruining lives by bringing false charges of Communist sympathy or activity against often innocent souls who were hauled before the committee. I sometimes disagreed with the views of the accused, but felt they had a right to express them. Voorhis was the only HUAC member who sometimes sided with the accused and publicly condemned the tactics of Dies and his staff.

Two or three nights a week my fellow interns and I gathered at the office of the internship program to swap stories about our work and hear lectures by leading civil servants and lawmakers. I made some lasting friends in the intern group, notably James MacGregor Burns, who went on to be a renowned historian and presidential biographer.

One night our group had the good fortune to visit the White House as guests of First Lady Eleanor Roosevelt. We had been ushered to seats in the East Room when she came through the door and greeted us very warmly. She talked freely of events in Washington, and her statements about HUAC were far from complimentary. She spoke of the war in Europe and other issues facing Congress and the president. I found her entirely charming. In reply to somewhat hostile questions from some of my colleagues about her husband's policies, she showed the ability to answer evenhandedly and at the same time to laugh pleasantly and relieve the moment of tension. I found myself wishing I had this rare ability.

I liked Mrs. Roosevelt and had come to Washington as a firm believer in the New Deal, but during my time in the capital, I discovered that the president's major concern now was not the ill-housed and ill-fed of America, but how to aid the allies in Europe and put America on a war footing in preparation for joining them. This was troubling to me. By 1940 I had come to consider myself a pacifist. Step by step, I had resolved to follow the nonviolent ways of Jesus Christ as outlined by his words in the Sermon on the Mount: "But I say to you, Do not resist one who is evil. But if any one strikes you on the right cheek, turn to him the other also; and if any one would sue you and take your coat, let him have your cloak as well. . . . Love your enemies and pray for those who persecute you" (Matthew 5:39–40 and 44). I believed firmly that a true Christian must be a pacifist, as Jesus had been, that violence invariably begets violence and corrupts the people who engage in it. I had got inklings of this as a schoolboy—bullies were always best dealt with by turning away from them. As I grew older, I began to feel that history was full of examples of the evil of war and that this verity was playing itself out again in the expanding conflicts in Europe and Asia. I read extensively about pacifism and found lots of reasoned arguments for it, particularly in the writings of A. J. Muste and Douglas Steere. I was also impressed by the works of the American Friends Service Committee, which then, like today, put into quiet action the pacifist tradition of the Quaker faith.

At the same time, I can say there was some confusion in my views: while my head was purely pacifist, my heart was not entirely so. I couldn't imagine standing by, for instance, if my father and mother were attacked, or if I was walking on a union picket line with fellow strikers and we were set upon by scabs and company police. There were times, I suspected, when preservation of self and loved ones demanded that some level of violence be employed.

My divided mind reflected the sentiments of the American public at that time. There were two firm camps concerning the war. Supporting Roosevelt's goal to make American the "arsenal of Democracy" were people like Congressman Voorhis, European Jews who had come to America to escape Hitler, a majority of my own generation, and most church leaders whom I admired. Opposed to FDR's war policies were Socialist Party leader Norman Thomas, United Mine Workers President John L. Lewis, the conservative America First organization, the American Communist Party (at least until the Nazi invasion of the Soviet Union in June 1941), and most Quakers. This last group now included my parents, who had recently converted to that faith and become members of a Quaker meeting in Philadelphia.

When the internship ended in June 1940, many of my colleagues enlisted as officers in the fast-growing U.S. armed forces. Amidst my uncertainties, I applied for admission to two law schools (I thought that as a lawyer I might make a contribution to labor struggles) and Union Theological Seminary. Again I had a health crisis: an almost bursting appendix was removed at Temple University Hospital. But I recovered and worked that summer at a conference center on the shores of Lake Winnipesaukee in New Hampshire. Here I taught English to Jewish refugees and got news that my dear father had suffered his first heart attack. I have a powerful memory of being filled that summer with doubt and uncertainty about my future. But finally in late August, the pacifist, spiritual side prevailed. There was no dramatic epiphany with thunder booming. Rather, I concluded that I needed to keep searching. Seminary seemed the best place to do that. I entered Union Theological Seminary in September 1940.

5

Tumult at Union Theological Seminary, 1940–1942

AT UNION I quickly got involved in militant pacifist politics—too quickly, it turned out. I had been at this Manhattan seminary only a few days when I became aware of a group of fellow students planning to make a dramatic statement against U.S. entry into the war in Europe. They announced they would jointly refuse to register for the first peacetime draft in U.S. history, which the federal government had scheduled to take place in October of 1940. Soon I was attending meetings of the group and was very much in awe of its leaders. One of them was David Dellinger, who struck me as one of the most forceful and self-confident personalities I had ever met. Dellinger paid a visit to me, as he did to virtually every student at Union, to urge me to join with them.

Soon I did. On October 12, I signed a statement declaring myself against war in all forms and announcing my refusal to submit to the draft. It felt good to have allied myself with this group of militants—I was making a bold statement about the key issue of our times, and in a nonviolent way. As the October 16 deadline approached, we all joined together one evening in the seminary's small James Chapel and sang the hymn "Rise Up, O Men of God." We wanted to be noticed by the press, and we were. Ours was one of the few cases of organized resistance to the draft in a country where public opinion, shocked by the daily bombing of London by Nazi warplanes, was moving in favor of entering the war in Europe. Quite a few newspaper articles about us appeared. The *New York Times* dubbed us the "Union Twenty."

Pressure was being brought against us from many sources. Our critics claimed that we didn't understand the theology of pacifism. Others said we were embarrassing Union and harming our future careers as ministers. Union President Henry Sloan Coffin, whom almost every student referred to as "Uncle Henry" (with varying degrees of affection), met with us individually and as a group to argue the case for registering. It seemed to us that this man, fundamentally cautious and conservative, was in part acting to counter the unwanted attention we were bringing to his beloved seminary. In his large and imposing office, he made the very practical observation to us that we all could register as conscientious objectors and under the law be free from the draft. My father joined the chorus, telephoning me to plea that I register.

As our campaign progressed, we all kept up a unified front publicly, but in private I and eleven others among the twenty were having doubts. It may sound self-serving, but I think I can honestly say today that though the prospect of prison was truly frightening, I believed at the age of twenty-three that I had the courage to endure it. The problem was that I was still wondering if I really was a consistent pacifist. Though I remained firmly against war as an institution, I continued to harbor that hypothetical willingness to use violence in response to attacks on striking pickets or my family. I could imagine people in Europe feeling that way as the Nazis came after them. I began to sway. In the end, just eight of the twenty went through with the planned defiance of the law, but I was not one of them. On the morning of the deadline day, in the silence of my own dorm room, I reached the decision that I would register. I went quietly to the seminary office and filled out the papers, claiming status as a conscientious objector. On November 14, police arrived at the Union campus, arrested the eight (now called the "Union Eight" by newspapers), who were led by Dellinger, and took them handcuffed to jail in a police wagon. It was a very sad day for me. I felt full of guilt and in many ways unqualified to become a Christian minister.

In ensuing weeks, I cast around for a new moral direction. One morning I stumbled across these words of Dr. Martin Dibelius in his book *The Sermon on the Mount* about the meaning of Jesus Christ as the messenger of God:

> The deeds and works of Jesus Christ were signs of the Kingdom of God. Nothing more and nothing less. Nothing more, for they introduced the Kingdom of Heaven on earth; nothing less, for they are far more than advice and prescriptions for life during our age. . . . His miracles are a revelation of heavenly forces and a proclamation of what God is going to do. His entire personage is like a signal from heaven announcing that there is another world and that the other world is moving toward this earthly world.[1]

Suddenly I was full of hope. I realized for the first time in my twenty-three years that the morally impossible demands of Jesus Christ on me and other believers were far less important than the faith that through him "the other world is moving toward this earthly world." The welcome exposure to this new reality calmed my heart. Suddenly I found myself on my knees at the foot of my bed giving thanks to God.

After a trial, the Union Eight were given two-year sentences, to be served at the federal prison in Danbury, Connecticut. I and others did what we could to support them from the outside, including helping their wives and girlfriends, several of whom were working among low-income families in Newark, New Jersey. All eight were released after a year. But Union's President Coffin would not allow any of them to return to Union unless they swore not to agitate for peace. None were prepared to make this promise. Six went to the Chicago Theological Seminary, but the other two—David Dellinger and Merideth Dallas—served one more year in jail because they did not enter a seminary and refused to sign up for the draft. Dellinger in particular never gave up the fight for pacifism. He became the primary radical pacifist in America during the entire second half of the twentieth century. He was one of the famed Chicago Seven arrested in connection with the street disturbances at the 1968 Democratic Party convention in Chicago.[2] Another one of the Union Eight was George Houser, who for many years headed the American Committee for Africa and was active in the African liberation struggles. In 1994 he was received as an honored state guest of the republic of South Africa by the then newly elected president, Nelson Mandela.[3]

Despite all the turmoil, I did settle down to my studies after the eight were jailed. I found the classrooms of Union a very stimulating place. Professor Julius Bewer helped me to understand the relevance of the Old Testament prophets to the twentieth century. Professor Ernest Scott broadened my knowledge of the New Testament, particularly the absolute pacifist demands of Jesus Christ to those of us who claim to be believers.

But by far the professor who had the most effect on me at Union was the impassioned theologian Reinhold Niebuhr, or Reiny, as we all called him. He was at the height of his powers as a lecturer, the writer of many books and articles, and a kind of national moral compass who influenced officials in Washington and around the country. I remember him too as the reported author of the prayer that has inspired countless members of Alcoholics Anonymous: "God, grant me the serenity to accept the things I cannot change, the courage to change the things I can, and the wisdom to know the difference."

Long before Pearl Harbor, Reiny was campaigning openly for America's entrance into the war in Europe, believing strongly that there are times when it is God's imperative to fight. He poured scorn on the Socialist Party and its leader, Norman Thomas, and on the American Communist Party for its frequent changes in party line as dictated by Moscow. Though Reiny was an imposing figure in class, I sometimes got up the courage to make the case for my own pacifist outlook. When I did so, he listened with respect, but responded that I had something basically wrong: Jesus was a pacifist and a moral absolutist, yes, but he did not expect flawed and sinful men and women like you and me to be able to follow in his footsteps.

In his lectures, Reiny scarcely mentioned the Holy Spirit, prayer, or the hope for life after death. There was an anti-mystical quality to his beliefs— God was not to be seen as a daily companion. In the words of David Dellinger in his book *From Yale to Jail,* Reiny made God "the wholly other—a distant, unapproachable, basically unknown and unexperienced monarch."[4]

As intimidating as Reiny could be in class, I saw another side of him on Sunday evenings, when I would leave my dormitory room and go to his apartment, where he and his British wife, Ursula, would receive groups of students. The sessions often lasted two or three hours. He was relaxed and witty, eager to enter into the give-and-take of arguments about theology, domestic politics, and the wars around the world.

In time, I came to believe that Reiny's brand of Christian "neo-orthodoxy" was too pessimistic. It underestimated the capacity of human beings to be born again spiritually, to rise above the tragedies of their lives and to improve society and human institutions around them. But I was greatly indebted to him for setting me straight for life on two counts: he made me more aware of my own pride and selfishness and my tendency to make excuses for my failures, and he helped me to understand the pervasive evil of the "principalities and powers" of this world and the sinful structure of what he called "immoral society" in America and other nations.

Knowing Reiny was a high point of my time at Union, but by far the most important event of those years—perhaps of my whole life—had nothing to do with him. It occurred in February 1941. The place was the national YWCA headquarters in New York City, at a meeting of the Peace Commission of the National Intercollegiate Christian Council (NICC). I was also on a committee to plan a national NICC meeting of college and university students scheduled for December, and so was a young woman named Alice Stevens, who was the co-chair of the NICC and a senior at Berea College in Kentucky. Watching her across the table during the committee meeting, I was smitten by her radiant beauty and confident manner. Later I invited her to be my guest at the Rainbow Room atop Rockefeller Center. To my surprise, she accepted my invitation. We sipped Cokes and for more than two hours talked about our lives and hopes. We discovered our near meeting as children, when I attended the church next to her house in her Massachusetts village of Cummington. We both fell in love that night.

We were busy people and managed to see each other only one more time in New York City before my first seminary year ended. That summer Alice came to visit me in Gibraltar, a small town south of Detroit, where I was serving as summer pastor in a blue-collar church. Early in September we were again together at a planning meeting of the NICC on the campus of Eden Seminary near St. Louis. The first night there, we walked into a small park, sat on a bench, and kissed and hugged. We agreed there to be engaged and to marry before the end of the year, though we knew that our parents would feel that we were moving too fast.

Alice had won a scholarship to Union starting in the fall of 1941. That term, I roomed at the men's dormitory while Alice was across the street in McGiffert Hall. After completing our homework each night, we would go to the lounge at McGiffert and court. Often the talk was personal, sometimes it was work—such as the NICC assembly to be held soon after Christmas at Miami University in Ohio, with Alice as the co-chair.

I was anxious to get my parents on our side for the impending wedding, so we invited them to meet us at an undergraduate house in Princeton where my father had boarded in 1904 and 1905 during his senior year. They greeted Alice kindly, but soon were doing what I expected they would—advising us to postpone the wedding. They were concerned, among other things, that we had known each other for such a short time. Under these circumstances, how could we be so sure marriage was right? Put it off until June of 1942, they strongly advised. After we talked for more than two hours, my parents hadn't budged an inch. At the close, we invited them to attend our wedding in Cummington on Thanksgiving Day. They reluctantly accepted our invitation.

The following week Alice and I visited Union President Coffin to tell him about our plans. He wasn't happy either. "In the entire history of this seminary," he said, "couples have been married before an academic year or after an academic year but never in the middle." He threatened to cancel our scholarships if we went through with our plans. We told him, as politely as we could, that our minds were made up. Fortunately for us, Coffin never carried out his threat.

Alice's parents finally gave their blessing to our plans. On Thanksgiving Day of 1941 we were married in the old white-shingled church next to Alice's house in Cummington. I was late to the ceremony because I had cut my face while shaving, but that was really the day's only snafu. I will always remember the "Wedding March," with beautiful and vibrant Alice coming down the aisle on the arm of her father, Ashley; the words of the church pastor, Carl Sangree; our exchange of vows; the prayer of blessing as we knelt before Dr. Eugene Lyman, my father's former professor and Alice's distant relative;

our memorable kiss; and going down the aisle with Alice on my arm and the greetings of dozens of well-wishers, many of them Alice's relatives. We walked next door to a reception at the Stevens home. Near the end of the evening, Alice's father drew me aside and said, "I want you to take care of my little girl." I promised him I would.

We spent our wedding night at the Parker House Hotel in Boston. Next morning we took a train from Boston to a quaint fishing village on the coast of Maine. Here in a small seaside lodge, we fully enjoyed our brief honeymoon making love and hoping for a long life together. We got that wish. A half century later, on November 20, 1991, at our new hilltop home in Benicia, California, overlooking the waters of the Carquinez Strait, we celebrated our golden wedding anniversary with some of our children and grandchildren.

The joy of our wedding in 1941 was soon followed by the tragedy of war. Like everyone of that period, I will forever recall when I got the news of Pearl Harbor. I was eating a brown-bag sandwich that Sunday afternoon at the East Side's John Hall Settlement, a Presbyterian mission to the urban poor where I was assigned as a student assistant. The radio was on, and suddenly the announcer broke in with news that Japanese planes had attacked Pearl Harbor. I felt physically ill, knowing that the war would result in suffering and death for millions of human beings. Soon I was on a subway back to Union. I got off at the subway station at the corner of Broadway and 116th Street and felt so distraught that I ran down Broadway to find Alice at our apartment and share the news with her. That kind of behavior was very common in that day. Some Americans, like Alice and I, were sad. Others were glad that the long wait was finally over.

Later that month we traveled by train from New York to Miami, Ohio, for the quadrennial NICC assembly. The war dominated the proceedings. I still opposed entering it, but I was in the minority. Even the American Communist Party and the American Student Union, long against it, now enthusiastically backed America's entry. It was the Nazi invasion of the Soviet Union that had really changed the party line. Factional politics were in full swing st the assembly. I recall seeing an American Student Union staff member in the balcony giving hand signals to some delegates on the floor, indicating that they should vote against an antiwar resolution of the Peace Commission which I had helped to write. My resolution was soundly defeated. On the last night of the assembly, with Alice in the chair, I spoke about a resolution under debate. A few minutes later, I asked for permission to speak again. Alice informed me in no uncertain terms that I was out of order and should sit down. Knowing we had just been married, the delegates broke out in noisy applause. I left Miami proud of Alice for leading the gathering with such grace and confidence.

Just after Christmas of 1941, Alice and I moved to a small apartment for married couples in Union's McGiffert Hall. We studied hard and made good grades. But amidst our books, examinations, and first year of marriage, we were restless. We wanted to get out and get started with our real life, not talk about it from an ivory tower. We consulted with many people and in the early spring of 1942 made a serious decision: we would leave Union for a year and work with migrant farmworkers, whom we saw as perhaps the most needy and exploited group in our country. So, in the late spring of 1942 we were hired by Edith Lowery, head of the Home Missions Council of the Federal Council of Churches, to work with migrants in southern New Jersey and southern Florida. She hired us both with a joint salary of $1,500 a year, plus ten cents for every mile we drove on church business in our 1932 Ford coupe. We loaded it up and set out, feeling excited and singularly devoid of regrets.

6

Missionaries to Migrants, 1942–1943

WHEN WE LEFT New York that summer, I was twenty-five, Alice twenty-three. We had lived rather sheltered lives, though just how sheltered we were yet to discover. During the next fourteen months, we lived and worked alongside Italian and Slavic families from the slums of Philadelphia who came to southern New Jersey during the summer months to pick blueberries and scoop cranberries. We befriended black migrants up from the South, and Bible-thumping preachers with flocks of saved sinners. We met poor white families from Georgia whom the crop-destroying boll weevil had forced onto the road to work other people's fields. At times we managed to touch the lives of migrant adults and children alike in New Jersey and southern Florida. They touched our lives as well, making us more mature, more understanding, and more aware of the injustices that they and millions like them had suffered.

We began with simple things, in a small town just a few hours' drive south from New York City called Whitesbog, New Jersey. Here poor families from the slums of Philadelphia came in the summer to work in the fields and packing sheds owned by the White Company. We had an invitation to come to this place, a gesture of compassion from the reigning figure at the family-owned company, the matronly Miss White. Concerned for the welfare of the children, she had asked the representatives of the Home Missions Council to help establish a day-care center and other facilities for them. That June, Alice and I arrived in the little town and, working with three other outsider staff members like us, opened a center for infants and children and a recreation program for teenagers. We also conducted Sunday school and worship services on Sunday mornings for children and adults alike.

Wanting to be fully knowledgeable about conditions of the workers' lives, we visited all the workers and their children in the deteriorating dormitories that the company provided for them. We soon noticed that while outwardly friendly to us, the workers regarded us as part of the company structure. To change that view, we decided that we would take turns working in the fields and packing sheds three days a week. I was in good shape, but wasn't prepared for the physical demands of the work these people did every day. The sun shone hot, the air was muggy, and my fingers got cut and scraped as I groped for the elusive blueberries or leaned down to gather cranberries in a heavy pronged scooper. After a few days, all of us had aching backs and weary arms but a few earned dollars in our pockets, which were quite welcome, given our rather low Home Missions salaries. The white migrants from Philadelphia, the black migrants from the South, and the resident blacks began to view us differently. They regarded us, as one of them told me, as "one of us" and not mere paid functionaries of Miss White and her ever-present foremen. He was exaggerating, I'm sure, but it showed we'd made some progress in changing the workers' view of us.

Working in Southern Florida

As it turned out, we didn't stay long in Whitesbog. Like the people we met there, we soon became migrants ourselves. In mid-September 1942, responding to instructions from the Home Missions Council, Alice and I arrived by car at the Pahokee Farm Labor Camp near the Everglades in southern Florida. Run by the federal Farm Security Administration, it was one of a chain of such camps established by New Deal programs to aid farm-labor families who lived for long periods on the road. Our camp was for whites only, segregation being the order of the day in Florida in the 1940s. The camp manager took us to a single-room house furnished only with a bed, tables, chairs, an inside water pump, and an adjoining outhouse. Paying $2.10 a month in rent, we lived there for the next eight months.

The camp was surrounded by fertile fields of fruits and vegetables. Most of the field workers were black, earning twenty to thirty cents an hour. Most workers in the packing sheds, where produce was sorted and boxed for shipment, were white and earning thirty-five to forty-five cents an hour. Life was hard for both groups. The field workers were trucked to the fields at 8 A.M. but often could not start work until two hours later when the dew had evaporated. Often they were paid their daily wages well after sundown. The white packing-shed workers were paid nothing when the conveyer belts broke down or when vegetables were slow in being delivered from the fields.

Alice and I worked two or three days a week in the fields or sheds, as we had done in New Jersey. We soon discovered that the black workers enjoyed greater unity as a group than the whites did. Perhaps that was because of the abject physical danger they faced. In this area of Florida, blacks were denied the most basic police protection. If local whites believed that a black man had insulted a white man or woman, it was not uncommon for his corpse to be found in the fields or floating in a drainage canal the next day. I remember several instances of such violence. On December 2, 1942, the body of a murdered black man was found in a nearby bean field. He still had several dollar bills in his wallet, indicating that his assailants were not common thieves but self-appointed defenders of the white race. A few days later a white packing-shed owner boasted to me that he had killed nine blacks during his lifetime.

It was not only African Americans who faced violence, however. The following week this same packing-shed owner threatened Simon Jones, a white resident of our migrant camp who sometimes freelanced as a trucking contractor signing up workers to pick beans in nearby fields. Jones had driven his truck to the nearby black district of nearby Belle Glade and offered black workers the rather high rate of sixty-five cents per hamper of picked beans. The shed owner threatened Jones with a beating if he did not reduce the offer. For two days Alice and I worked for Jones, picking those beans. But then the son of the shed owner accosted Jones and shouted, "There will be a killing if you don't change your ways." Fearing for his life, Jones left the camp by truck the next day and returned to his hometown in southern Georgia.

Though we tried to fit in, Alice and I were often regarded as different by the camp's people. When they heard our Yankee accents, they concluded quite correctly that we were college graduates. When I was heard typing far into the night (I wrote an occasional magazine article during our time there), the rumor spread that I was actually an FBI agent gathering evidence about our neighbors' past scrapes with the law. But slowly, trust of us increased among our farm-labor neighbors. Our work in the fields helped, as did Sunday school classes and a worship service we conducted. In the services, Alice played the piano while I preached and, with the assistance of a guitar player, led gospel songs.

At the camp community center on Friday nights, we started a recreation program of games and folk dances. I formed a Boy Scout troop and Alice a small Brownie troop. Using bats, balls, and gloves donated by nearby churches, we organized baseball games for boys and girls alike. We were disappointed, though, that attendance at Sunday school and church and at our recreation programs was often low. We attributed that to our Yankee accents, our tendency to appeal to the mind rather than the heart, and our ignorance of the ways of the South.

After a while we changed tack. We sponsored a series of revival services with the help of local clergy, and people started coming in larger numbers. Later we founded the nondenominational Camp Pahokee Community Church.

Alice and I were happily surprised when on New Year's Eve 1943 about two hundred of our neighbors attended our service. At a minute before midnight I blew out the lone candle on the wooden altar, spoke of events of the past year, and lit a fresh candle of hope to honor the coming of the new year. I knew that among our migrant friends there were many common concerns—the possible death of their sons on the battlefields of Europe and Asia, the threat of a crop freeze, homesickness for the towns where they grew up, spiritual loneliness—but at that midnight hour, as we all sat together giving thanks to God, most appeared happy, united, and at peace within themselves and with their neighbors in the camp.

That Old-Time Religion

We got a taste of a very different kind of religion from Preacher Daniels, or Brother Daniels as he liked to be called, the pastor of an unpainted and dilapidated Church of God surrounded by a bean field on the edge of Pahokee. One day he came to our door to invite me to attend a revival at his church the next night. As he stood at our doorway, he asked me to answer some serious questions: "Have you ever been saved, Brother Burgess, so that the temptations of this world are like water running off a duck's back? Have you ever been sanctified so that you know that Jesus is coming? Ever been blessed by the Holy Ghost so you're ready to jump to the ceiling and shout 'Glory, glory'? Do you want to beat the devil at his own game before you slip forever into a dusty grave, before you burn in Hell with ten black devils poking at your sinful heart?" As politely as I could, I avoided answering his questions but assured him that I'd come to the revival the following evening.

The next night I arrived at the church just as a nearby packing shed was shutting down and people were starting to enter the church. First came Sister Cox, a shapely woman of about thirty with three children (her drunkard husband was not present). Rumor had it that some years earlier she had been saved through faith from the profession of prostitution. Her dingy dress was in contrast to her beautiful long hair, her joyous face, and her hope that many of the people there would be "brought to the Lord" that night. Then Old Man Herring stalked in. He was a hard-drinking carpenter from Turpentine County in Georgia. He greeted me in fatherly fashion: "So you're coming around to attending a church where the folks believe the Bible from cover to cover." In past conversations he had told me that belief in the literal interpretation of the Bible transformed pedestrian preachers into pulpit-pounding rousers. Then came tired mothers hugging their babies, and old men in coveralls with hands hard from spreading beans on conveyor belts. Next came boys and girls herded in by parents and other kinfolk and made "to sit up and act right" during the long revival service. In a few minutes all the pews were filled and the latecomers were left standing at the back and sides of the church sanctuary.

Then the singing began as a piano player pounded out gospel tunes. It was like nothing I had ever heard before. Some people sang through their noses like cowboy singers. Others sang the way most church folk do—soft and clear at first, but then louder and louder. Most men did not sing or even hum. They stood silently, swaying a little and keeping the rhythm with their feet. Some women sat, cried a little, and rocked their little ones to sleep. Song followed song. The tempo grew faster and the singing louder as the man at the piano hit the keys with greater force. The words of the songs told stories of sadness and bliss, hellfire and Elysian fields, curses of the damned and the harp-playing "saved" praising God in the highest.

When Pastor Daniels believed the congregation was "sung out," he began to preach: "You and me, who are we? We're just common folk living in this black muck, workin' ourselves to the bone so our young ones can eat. We're just workin', hoein', wonderin', worryin', schemin' to keep body and soul together. We don't have no home. We can't go back to Georgia." Heads nodded in approval, and shouts of "Amen!" arising from the people showed that he was touching their hearts. Daniels continued, "But folks, there's a place where you don't have to work, don't have to slave, don't have to scheme. But no pig, no matter how fancy he's dressed, can go through them pearly gates to Heaven. A dog can't either, but you can go." His voice rose to a shout, "But you can't go to Heaven unless you're saved, sanctified, and filled with the Holy Spirit from head to foot, unless you're washed in the blood of the lamb, unless you're free of this sinnin' business—whorin', dancin', smokin', cards, and all that."

Daniels finished his lengthy sermon with the question: "Is there any man or woman who wants to be saved, saved from backslidin'?" For a moment no one uttered a word. Then a small girl spoke her lines, obviously having been coached by her parents in advance: "I've been saved, sanctified, and filled with the Holy Spirit." Preacher Daniels thanked her with the words, "There's a brave little girl not frightened to speak up for the Lord." Then a woman with a baby in her arms stood up and spoke out, "I need the help of the Lord. You all pray for me." I discovered later that she was a woman of thirty-five burdened with raising three children alone.

Now was the time for Sister Cox to testify. "Brothers and sisters"—her voice was growing more and more confident—"I was one time taking up wicked things of this world—gamblin', dancin', smokin', and all like. But one night in a country church in south Georgia I got saved. I looked up when I was kneelin' at the sinners' rail and saw Jesus a-hangin' up on the cross, bleeding for you and for me—yes, for me and for you. I knew then I was headin' straight to Hell. I felt myself backslidin' and slippin'. Then Jesus, that glorious savior, reached out his hands and pulled me up away from Hell. I was washed in blood and was done forgiven for my many past sins. I no longer lust for movies, dancin', smokin', and all like. Then a few weeks ago I came right here to this Church of God—but not to one of them stuck-up and cold and big churches in downtown Pahokee. This is a happy church tonight, Brother Daniels, and it's full of happy and saved folks." Sister Cox stopped to catch her breath as cries of "Amen!" and "Glory be!" filled the church. Other testimonies quickly followed from the old and young alike. Some of the people knelt and uttered loud prayers. Finally, preacher Daniels gave the closing prayer. Then the people rose as one, left the church, and walked along the bean fields and down dark paths toward the labor camp or Pahokee.

I went home too, feeling exhausted and intrigued. It was of course like no service I'd ever led. Daniels struck me as an essentially sincere man, and his flock as people reaching out from sheer desperation. I was troubled by his depiction of the proper life as a series of self-denials, but over the course of our time in Pahokee, we saw often how life could get out of hand.

Life on the Edge, Life without Hope

Gradually Alice and I gained some understanding of our migrant neighbors and how we could minister to them. We discovered that they distrusted government officials, police officers, employers, and anyone in a position of authority. Being on the road so much left them feeling permanently out of sorts. One woman in the camp spoke of her alienation in these words: "I felt the presence of God in my home church back in Georgia. But to me God is not present in the Everglades and its miles of muddy marshlands and endless fields of unpicked fruits and vegetables and dirty, hot, and crowded packing houses." Her voice seemed to me to be the same one we hear in the fourth verse of Psalm 137, written by a Hebrew in exile in Babylon: "How shall we sing the Lord's song in a foreign land?"

Such estrangement, Alice and I felt, weakened their desire to plan and made them unresisting victims of circumstances. The average father of a migrant family had no permanent job or the prospect of finding one and was thus not a good role model for his sons and daughters. The average mother was similarly insecure. Young men of draft age laboring in the fields or packing sheds had little to look forward to other than joining the military to kill or be killed by Germans or Japanese. Most migrant couples married at a young age and, lacking birth control devices, conceived many children. Because of their transient lives, most families felt little concern for the welfare of their neighbors in the camps. They tended to live from day to day without hope for a better future.

We left Pahokee in May 1943, on instructions from our church superiors. In a report to our supervisor, Edith Lowery, we made some recommendations for our successors. Bring books to read. Pray frequently and cultivate a spiritual life. At least one day every week, get away from the camp and its residents. Start your work slowly at the camp. Remember that although you are well educated, you never graduated from "the school of hard knocks" as your neighbors have. Before you launch any programs, visit, talk casually, listen, and get acquainted with your neighbors at their homes and workplaces. Watch for small and sometimes unexpected ways to assist them. Above all, befriend and inspire the young. Remember that despairing people often cover their pain by being outwardly bossy, by gossiping and seemingly trusting no one outside their family circle. Don't be discouraged by the seeming irresponsibility of some of the adults. But remember that in contrast to adults, most young people are responsive to an outsider who shows genuine sympathy and understanding.

Bridgeton—Seat of the Confederacy in South Jersey

In May 1943 we drove our Ford coupe up the East Coast, and finally stopped in Bridgeton, New Jersey, the state's major center for picking and packing fruits and vegetables. In those days, it was a town of twenty thousand dominated by Seabrook Farms Company, the Deerfield Packing Company, Owens Illinois Glass Factory, and the Ritter Cannery. It was also gripped by terrible racial and class tensions, as wartime labor shortages resulted in large numbers of poor blacks and whites moving to Bridgeton from the South. It was very unusual in this town for companies not to get their way. When the Farm Security Administration announced plans to build and operate a huge migrant camp at nearby Big Oaks, many local officials spoke out against it, not wanting the influx of outsiders. But executives of Seabrook Farms, needing the labor, persuaded key local leaders to approve the plans, and construction got under way. The Big Oaks camp opened in January 1943. At the urging of Seabrook Farms, a federal agency called the War Manpower Commission brought in hundreds of black migrant workers from the Caribbean islands and black and white migrants from the South to work for Seabrook Farms and other cannery companies in the area. As the Big Oaks camp filled to capacity, the local school board refused to admit the camp's migrant children to public schools, claiming that most of them had communicable diseases. In desperation, the Big Oaks camp manager recruited two Works Progress Administration teachers to instruct the camp's sixty grammar school children at the camp's mess hall.

In Bridgeton in those days there was not a single black-owned business. Blacks were denied jobs in the police force, fire department, and post office. In 1942 a white policeman shot and killed an unarmed local black man who was allegedly driving off in a stolen car. The victim bled to death because an ambulance did not arrive until a half hour later. Alice and I observed during our stay in Bridgeton that white policemen delighted in arresting blacks downtown on Saturday and Sunday nights, beating them with billy clubs, and handcuffing them around light posts before taking them to police headquarters and charging them with disorderly and drunken behavior. The head of the Bridgeton draft board assured worried whites that within a year he would get "every God-damned nigger off the streets" by drafting each of them.

At the end of our first week in Bridgeton, I had an insight into race relations: the typical white man in Bridgeton assumed his own superiority and therefore looked for signs of inferiority in his black counterparts. When he met an uneducated and uncouth black who drank, cursed, and was unfaithful to his wife, the white man's worldview regarding blacks was confirmed. But when he met educated and cultured blacks, maybe ones who asserted their constitutional rights as equal citizens, the white man looked upon them as disturbers of the peace who secretly encouraged their poorer fellow blacks to engage in acts of violence against whites.

Alarmed by the racial tensions, I went to a meeting of Bridgeton's white ministerial association. Here I recommended that a selected group of white clergy meet informally with black clergy to discuss ways to improve racial relations. My recommendation was promptly ignored. By the time I left, I could see where most of these clergymen stood. One delighted his colleagues with what he believed to be a very humorous story. It seemed that a certain black man named Sambo returns from the North to visit his former hometown in South Carolina. Having forgotten southern ways, he knocks on the front door of a white man's home and asks for food. Opening the door, the white man says, "No, Sambo, just go around to the back door where you belong and I will give you all you can eat."

Many times I ran directly into hostility against migrants and against me in Bridgeton. Once, for instance, I spoke at a monthly meeting of the Kiwanis Club about the conditions of agricultural migrants, hoping I might elicit some sympathy for them. But during the question period, one club member asked: "Why does Seabrook and the federal government bring hundreds of migrants to Bridgeton and dump them on us?" The following day a club member met me on the street and pointing his finger at me said, "You are that damned minister who wants to free them God-damned niggers rather than keeping them in their place."

About the only sympathetic reception I got from local whites was at a local radio station owned by New Jersey Congressman Elmer Wene, a liberal Democrat. He asked me to talk on the radio three times about the conditions of local migrants. The first time I arrived at the station, the receptionist was hesitant to let me into the studio because, as she explained the following day, "You looked more like a high school student than a minister of the gospel." I did in fact look like a high school student in those days, something that probably didn't help when I tried to approach the members of the white establishment.

Soon after we arrived in Bridgeton, Alice and I discovered that six white families who had been our neighbors at the Pahokee labor camp were now living in primitive quarters known as Farm Center Camp next to the Seabrook Farms plant. They had naively believed the promises of Seabrook recruiters in Florida that upon coming to Bridgeton they would get a brick company house to live in, steady employment during the four summer months, and free medical care. But after arriving, they found that the housing was squalid, that only a few of their family members were employed by Seabrook Farms, and that there was no free medical care. At the Farm Center Camp, the families were housed in sixteen-by-sixteen-foot cabins with screened doors and windows but no glass windows. The cabins stood less than twenty-five feet from drains full of toilet refuse and industrial waste from the Seabrook plant. For several weeks the families cooked on open fires outside their cabins until the company got around to providing kerosene stoves for each cabin plus cold-water community showers, one for men, the other for women. Wanting to live near our old neighbors, Alice and I moved to a similar small cabin at the Farm Center Camp. Alice went to work on the plant's twelve-hour night shift, six nights a week.

Meanwhile, I became, in effect, a labor union representative, taking up the grievances of migrant workers with officials at Seabrook and the Deerfield Packing Companies as well as with state and federal agencies. There was certainly no shortage of points to argue—the housing was awful, some of the workers had pneumonia, there were no child care facilities, and women were paid only forty-five cents an hour—but my efforts seldom met with success. Often state officials rejected my recommendations, attributing the camps' deplorable conditions to "bad planning" by the Seabrook and Deerfield companies. In the meantime, Alice and I conducted church services on Sunday afternoons at the Farm Center Camp. We purchased an old piano with money from local churches where we found rare sympathy for us and our work. The local Seventh Day Adventist church gave us old hymnals. We borrowed benches from the Seabrook cafeteria and obtained the free services of a blind guitarist and a skilled pianist. My sermons—in contrast with those in my Pahokee days—were brief, informal, and Bible-based, full of stories and emotion.

We had a gospel sing on Wednesday nights and an adult Bible class on Thursdays nights.

Our special and most supportive friend during those hectic days in Bridgeton was Norman Graves. The town's sole black high school graduate in 1921, he was unable over the years to get a job he wanted as a policeman or fireman. So he became a barber. Though he later won an election to the Bridgeton City Council, he was denied a seat by the local board of elections. To improve race relations, Graves and his wife founded a local chapter of the Fellowship of Reconciliation (FOR), an activist pacifist-related national agency. But eventually Graves and his wife dissolved the FOR chapter because of lack of white support. Despite all of these difficulties, he never lost his idealism and hope for a better future. In June of 1943 Graves helped me start a recreation center for blacks in downtown Bridgeton. A local company purchased some furniture for the center, and members of a black Boy Scout troop painted the building inside and out. At the center a black minister showed movies on weekends, and a group of Jamaicans sponsored Saturday night dances.

Alice and I left Bridgeton in mid-August of 1943, satisfied with our modest accomplishments there. We were soon succeeded by a black minister and his wife. One of our parting recommendations to them was this: preach a revolutionary gospel in which Jesus Christ is not a distant abstraction but a living, everyday companion in the struggle to liberate the exploited poor. To Alice and me, a key lesson of the previous fourteen months was that spiritual redemption was not enough. Now more than ever, we wanted to do our part in overcoming racial and class injustices that hold so many people in degrading poverty.

7

Chaplain to the Southern Tenant Farmers Union, 1944–1947

FEELING THAT I NEEDED to finish my Master of Divinity degree, I returned to Union Theological Seminary in the fall of 1943. Alice selflessly left her own seminary studies and took a job to support us. In May of 1944 came a milestone event in any ministerial career: at a ceremony at Broadway Tabernacle Church in New York City, I was ordained into the Congregational and Christian Churches denomination, later to be called the United Church of Christ.

The ceremony was something of an anticlimax. Alice and I were eager to get back to work with migrants, but we felt that our previous employer, Edith Lowery, had tended to avoid controversial issues. What we'd done in the camps the previous year, really, was to try to relieve some of the pains of the migrants through such things as church services and day care. But we weren't attacking the things that caused those pains in the first place. So after ordination, we looked elsewhere. We were able to persuade Truman Douglas, who then headed my denomination's Home Mission Board, to assign me as a chaplain to a labor organization we felt was facing the issues head-on—the Southern Tenant Farmers Union (STFU). The board agreed to pay me and Alice, who was my most important fellow worker, a total salary of $1,750 a year. We were also given a modest travel allowance and a small house trailer, which we hitched to our faithful 1932 Ford coupe. The trailer would be the roof over our heads for the next eighteen months.

The STFU had been founded back in 1934 by fifteen tenant farmers and sharecroppers—seven black and eight white—and a very unusual man named H. L. Mitchell, a dry cleaner by trade and a longtime follower of Socialist Party leader Norman Thomas. The union's first goal was limited—to organize popular support for a congressional bill mandating that plantation owners share their New Deal federal subsidy payments with the tenant farmers and sharecroppers who worked their land. This goal was achieved early on. Federal dollars flowed to these rural poor, giving them much-needed cash at a time when the economy was in a downspin.

But leaders of the STFU sought a broader objective as well: to bring to the farm economy a form of collective bargaining already existing in urban factories and industries. The union wanted to force plantation owners across the South to recognize it as the sole bargaining agent for tenant farmers (who paid their rent in cash), sharecroppers (who paid owners with a portion of their crops), and day laborers (who were hired for simple wages). In a few places, this goal was realized. When Alice and I first signed on, for instance, about two thousand STFU members were working at a Campbell Soup Company plant in Camden, New Jersey, with the union acting as their bargaining agent. In my first STFU assignment, for four summer months in 1944, I was not only the STFU members' chaplain but also their union representative in Camden with the Campbell Soup Company.

For the most part, though, the STFU never established itself in a conventional bargaining position. That was partly because in 1934 plantation owners in many states launched a long campaign of violence and intimidation against the STFU. Several STFU leaders died in that struggle. Union factional politics also took a toll. In the late 1930s, the STFU was affiliated with the United Cannery, Agricultural, Packing and Allied Workers Union–CIO but broke away to protest alleged Communist influence in that organization. That move cost the STFU dearly in union dues, and a major decline in union membership began. The number of active STFU locals in the South dropped from two hundred in 1939 to fewer than forty in 1942.

In September 1944, after my summer work representing STFU members at the Campbell Soup Company in Camden, Alice and I drove with our house trailer to Memphis, Tennessee, where the STFU had its national headquarters. There I met again STFU President Harry ("H. L." or "Mitch") Mitchell. He was a tall, somewhat gaunt man with a full head of hair, a doctrinaire socialist who sometimes wore old rumpled suits. He gave me a surprise assignment: to go out into the cotton counties of Arkansas, find former STFU members, and try to revive their interest in the union.

Thus one morning I found myself driving in a heavy rain along a dirt road in Arkansas. As I turned onto a bridge, the car began to skid. It came to rest with one wheel over the edge of the bridge above a deep river. My heart racing, I got out, calmed myself, and took stock of the situation. Years later, I realized that the car, close to falling into the swollen river, but refusing to drop, was an apt metaphor for the condition of the STFU in rural Arkansas at that time.

On that trip I called at a small black church near the Arkansas town of Cotton Plant to attend what I hoped would be a large gathering of former union members. When I opened the church's door in the blackness of night, I saw a few candles and only six people, all former STFU members, in the front pews. As we talked, it soon became clear that they were not enthusiastic about their young visitor's suggestion that they get involved with the STFU again. They expressed fear of violence by plantation owners and the owners' allies among the local police and sheriffs. That night I slept at the home of a black pastor, who with typical hospitality welcomed me with coffee at midnight and insisted that I take the bed normally used by him and his wife, which was by far the house's most comfortable. The next day I headed down more dirt roads to another church and rendezvous, where I found only four former members of the STFU. They too displayed little desire to rejoin the union. With work scarce in the area, they were more interested in asking me about opportunities—like those at the Campbell plant in New Jersey—to harvest and pack fruit and vegetables on the East and West Coasts.

Among these workers, whites and blacks remained divided as ever. I remember a white woman, the wife of a poor tenant farmer, asking me apprehensively during one of these trips to Arkansas if there was any "mixing of the races" in schools which migrant children attended in south Jersey or in the states of Oregon and Washington. I told her the truth—that the schools in these states were not segregated—and she didn't seem to like it.

A number of times I came face-to-face with the oppressive powers of the region, notably the Farm Bureau Federation and the National Cotton Council, two organizations representing the wealthy cotton-farming moguls. One day in November 1944, I drove to the small town of Osceola in eastern Arkansas for a hearing sponsored by the Extension Service of the U.S. Department of Agriculture. Present were cotton planters and also dozens of local police and sheriffs, whose presence seemed intended to intimidate. The purpose of the hearing, held in the town's courthouse, was to discuss establishing not a minimum wage but rather a *maximum* wage for all cotton pickers. The plantation owners wanted an agreement that no worker would be paid above a certain wage—this was the level of their collusion. In his testimony, the rotund president of the Cotton Council, Oscar Johnson, declared that refusal to set a maximum wage "would put many local cotton farmers out of business." That outlandish claim was heard over and over again that day from plantation owners, police officers, and lawyers in the pay of cotton companies. As the sole dissenting voice, I was apprehensive about the hostility in the hearing room. Nevertheless, I took the witness chair toward the end of the hearing and made a case against the maximum wage. I noted that many of the planters could afford to pay more than they did, especially in view of the fact that German and Italian war prisoners being interned in the area were working their fields. I criticized planters for forcing tenant farmers and sharecroppers off the land, and then hiring them back as low-paid day laborers, so as to take advantage of a loophole in a federal law that allowed planters to share none of their federal aid payments if they had no long-term tenants or sharecroppers farming their lands.

As I left the courthouse, a burly pistol-packing deputy sheriff stopped me and asked why I wasn't in Europe fighting the Nazis. He warned: "You'd better get your ass out of this county for your own health and welfare." I lost no time getting into our Ford coupe and heading for the bridge over the Mississippi River and our home in the trailer park in Memphis.

Happily, in my Arkansas travels in 1944 and 1945, I never faced anything like what had happened to veteran STFU organizer C. E. Creasy ten years earlier. I heard his tale one day after stepping past a hunting dog and knocking on the door of his run-down home.

"Is this the house of C. E. Creasy?" I asked when the door opened a crack.

"What's left of him," came the answer.

Old Man Creasy was a grizzled but lively guy. His wife held a two-day-old baby, their own, which rather surprised me given the advanced age of both parents. Creasy sat me down in a rocker, poured some coffee, and began talking. Over the course of a long conversation, he told me about the time in 1935 when he and a colleague named Griffith were trying to recruit black sharecroppers for the STFU. When the two STFU organizers went to a café in the town of Crawfordsville, they were seized by two deputy sheriffs, handcuffed, forced into a police car, and driven to the sheriff's office. There they were dragged to a bench inside the adjoining jail. The local sheriff appeared. "The mean son-of-a-bitch sheriff," as Creasy describe the man to me, asked the two prisoners: "Why did you God-damned Communists talk with them useless and trouble-making niggers yesterday afternoon?" Meanwhile, a deputy sheriff was on the phone inviting some of the leading plantation owners to come to the jail right away. When they arrived, the sheriff abruptly hit Creasy and Griffith, who were still handcuffed, knocking them to the floor. Recalled Creasy: "Those bastard planters were soon circling me and Griffith and kicking our heads and bodies. I almost blanked out. But after a minute or so the beatings stopped. Out of fear of injuring us, one young planter was shouting to his colleagues, 'Stop! Not a God-damned one of you is going to kick these two men again.' Griffith and I got up and sat on the bench again. The sheriff then said to us, 'You've got five minutes to walk back to your car. Drive out of Crawfordsville forever. If you ever come back, you'll both be strung up.' "

I spent several months traveling in cotton counties of Arkansas, but I elicited little enthusiasm from former STFU members about reviving the organization. One thing dampening their enthusiasm, I learned, was that they felt abandoned by the union's president, Harry Mitchell. They all knew that since 1934 the planters had put a price on his head and warned him never again to visit cotton towns, including Tyronza, the founding place of the STFU. Mitchell seemed to take that warning to heart, and stayed away. I was always a bit surprised by that. After a few months on the job, I came to share some of the same frustrations with Mitchell that I heard from people in the countryside.

I urged him to make some serious changes. In May of 1945, I wrote him recommending that he meet in Memphis once a month with his Arkansas and southeast Missouri organizers now on the unions payroll, order some new educational material, solicit money from national unions of both the AFL and the CIO, recruit new leaders to move things along in the postwar years that were coming, and, most importantly, hire a new organizing director from the ranks of the labor movement. Mitchell carried out a few of those suggestions. Two years later he hired Barney Taylor, a United Auto Workers staff member, as the new STFU organizing director. Taylor conducted successful organizing campaigns in California and Louisiana, but he never made progress in Arkansas. Over time, the union evolved into more of a rural protest movement than a dues-collecting union.

Mitchell remained active with the union through the rest of his life. He helped César Chavez form the United Farm Workers Union in California, and dispatched other organizers to create unions among the cane workers and fishermen in Louisiana. During the last years of his life, he and his wife, Dorothy, lived in Montgomery, Alabama. From there he traveled to colleges and universities and conventions of academic historians to tell the STFU story. Ten years before his death in 1989, he wrote his autobiography, *Mean Things Happening in the Land*.[1]

In our age of greed and public indifference to social justice, I was impressed by the dedication of this keeper of the flame. During his fifty-five years as a labor leader, Mitchell consistently acted upon the moral axioms of his mentor, Norman Thomas. Mitchell's death in 1989 marked the end of the STFU he helped to create, but not the end of the continuing battle for social justice in rural America.

During my work with the STFU, I began to realize that my seminary training had not equipped me to deal with many of the people I was meeting now— plantation owners, the victimized poor, Pentecostal preachers, members of a complacent middle class, and conservative mainline congregations. Certainly Niebuhr's emphasis on original sin, the sin of pride, and the fallen nature of man and man-made institutions made me keenly aware of the evil of the ruling principalities and powers. But his theological doctrines did not strengthen my ability to combat these powers. Out of my own sense of despair and the growing doctrinal chasm between me and neo-orthodox theologians such as Niebuhr, I wrote an article for the *Christian Century* of December 6, 1946, entitled "Wake Up Theologians." In it I stated:

> Instead of receiving the full loaf of the Christian Gospel in words and deeds, the dispossessed migrants, tenant farmers and sharecroppers . . . have too often received the stone of paternalistic Christian charity. The true and dedicated minister to the rural poor must choose his place with the poor in their ongoing struggle against the powerful—not looking down from a high balcony but marching on the highway with God's needy people.[2]

That was how I saw myself—marching on that highway, though in Arkansas it was often in fact only a narrow muddy road. The people I met along it were poor and deserving of a better break in life. Still, I couldn't escape the feeling that I, Mitchell, and the STFU were failing them.

8

The Battle to Save the Delmo Homes, 1945–1947

LIFE CAN TURN around in a hurry. Early in 1945, I was still moping over my failure to revive the Southern Tenant Farmers Union in the cotton counties of Arkansas. Then one morning I was in the union office in Memphis when Harry Mitchell showed me an article in the *Memphis Commercial Appeal*. It said that Congress was considering a bill to sell to the highest bidder 579 homes that the federal government had built in southeast Missouri for farm-labor families back in 1940. These were the so-called Delmo Homes, built and managed by the Farm Security Administration (FSA). Making up ten separate projects, they stood in the some of the best cotton-growing land in the country, the southeast area of Missouri known variously as the "bootheel" or "swampeast Missouri."

I soon learned that Mitchell had played an important role in a fight that had led to the homes' construction. After the First World War, owners of large cotton plantations had dominated the region's economic and political life. At the bottom of the social scale were sharecroppers and tenant farmers, often living in dismal shacks owned by planters. The Depression had come, and planters had done well with New Deal federal subsidy payments. But they were unhappy with the 1937 law that the STFU had helped to enact requiring them to share their federal subsidy payments with the people who worked their lands. So the cotton plantation owners moved to take advantage of a big loophole in the law which allowed plantation owners who had no tenants or sharecroppers on their land to keep all the federal subsidy payments. In late 1938, many plantation owners in Southeast Missouri notified their tenant farmers and sharecroppers that their services were no longer needed, and that no later than January 1, 1939, they and all their family members must vacate the planter-owned shacks where they lived. Often the owners intended to hire them back as day laborers who by law could not collect a portion of the owners' subsidy payments.

But a few days before this January 1 deadline, the unexpected happened. Tenant and sharecropper families, both black and white, gathered at a black church near Sikeston, Missouri. A man named Owen Whitfield, a black farmer in the bootheel and a former STFU staff member, stepped to the pulpit and spoke. "Would you rather go on living the way you have been living or would you rather die?" he asked the people. They answered in unison, "We'd rather die!" Then Whitfield shouted, "I agree. But let's not die unseen and unheard-of. Let's find some way to let the people of this nation know what's going on here."

So on eviction day of January 1, 1939, the people did move out of their shacks. But they didn't go off in search of new ones. Instead, they moved their earthly belongings—battered tables, woodstoves, clothes, and everything else you found in their poor rural homes of the day—to sites on the sides of Highway 61, which runs north and south through the heart of the Missouri bootheel. As snow began to fall, they hoisted signs to dramatize their plight. Soon a roadside demonstration was in progress, day and night, and in ensuing days it was reported by newspapers and radio stations all over America. Quickly the protest became a national symbol of the fight for rural justice.

Alarmed, the planters wired the governor of Missouri and demanded that he send state troopers to evict the demonstrators. Local sheriffs and police were already trying to do that: in some cases they loaded some of the demonstrators, together with their family members, into trucks and discharged them in distant cotton and corn fields without food, water, or shelter, sometimes in the middle of the night. Many of the remaining demonstrators foresaw defeat as growing numbers of state troopers drove up and down Highway 61, stopping here and there to pressure them to leave.

Seeking moral and financial support, Mitchell and fifteen of the demonstrators traveled by train to Washington to lobby members of Congress. Mitchell himself managed to get in to see three influential members of the Roosevelt administration—Harry Hopkins at the White House; Aubrey Williams, who led the National Youth Administration; and Will Alexander, head of the FSA. At Mitchell's request, Alexander phoned Mrs. Roosevelt's appointments secretary and arranged a meeting with her the next day. Thirty years later, in a book about the Delmo fight, Mitchell recounted how at the meeting he had asked for help in getting the Missouri National Guard to provide tents and field kitchens to the demonstrators: "Mrs. Roosevelt replied, 'I have heard about it. I have read about it. I will ask Franklin tonight to get this done. And I will do more. Where can I send some money to the STFU?' "[1]

As a result of White House intervention, things began to happen. The National Guard delivered a few tents and field kitchens to the demonstrators, and FSA head Alexander called a press conference in Washington. With Missouri

Senator Harry Truman and some White House staff members at his side, Alexander announced that the FSA would make loans to plantation owners so they could build new houses for tenant farmers and sharecroppers. The FSA would also pay for the construction of 579 homes at $1,200 apiece for farmworkers at ten locations in southeast Missouri. Three of the projects would be for whites and seven for blacks—this was still very much the era of official segregation. Each project would have an FSA manager, a community center, and an elected council of home residents.

The Delmo Homes (the name was a contraction of a nearby Mississippi delta and the postal abbreviation for Missouri) were completed in 1940, and were soon fully occupied at rent of $3.50 per month per family. Many of the tenants and sharecroppers moving in were veterans of the roadside demonstration. Most local planters, of course, strongly opposed building the homes, fearing the communities would become recruiting grounds for the STFU, which would then fight to force up farmworkers' wages.

Although the planters had been defeated for the time being, in 1945 they began to get their way in Washington. The usual suspects—leaders of the American Farm Bureau Federation, the National Cotton Council, and allies they had developed in the Extension Service of the Department of Agriculture— persuaded Congressman Wayne Hayes of Ohio to submit a bill to Congress authorizing the immediate sale of all the Delmo Homes to the highest bidder. Congress passed the bill, and it became law just after President Roosevelt died and Harry Truman was sworn in in April 1945.

Meanwhile, former congressman Frank Hancock of North Carolina had become the FSA's new administrator. He promised Congress he would liquidate the agency before he left office. Fortunately for the Delmo residents, Hancock had a problem—he was an alcoholic. His addiction meant that he was frequently absent from his office in Washington. Standing in for Hancock during his many absences was a very decent and caring man and New Dealer from Alabama named Pete Hudgens, the FSA's deputy administrator. Pete proved to be our secret weapon in our coming battle to save the homes.

Mounting Pressure to Sell the Homes

Even before the Hayes bill became law, notices appeared in Missouri, Arkansas, and Tennessee newspapers announcing that an auction for the ten projects would take place on March 15, 1945, and that all residents would be forced out by mid-May. Under the provisions of the new law, the homes and community centers in each project would be sold individually and transported to other locations by the successful bidders. The FSA would then sell the cleared

63

lands to the highest bidder. It was obvious by now that the FSA managers at the ten communities were in league with the cotton planters. For example, the manager of the South Wardell project cut off water to the homes for ten days, and another manager sold all of the furniture in vacant homes and in the project's day-care center.

This was the state of affairs in early April 1945, when Mitchell sent me to the small town of Wardell in southeast Missouri to confer with the local STFU organizer, Bill Johnson, and see how the STFU could get involved. I liked Bill immediately—he was a short man of about sixty with a face like Mount Rushmore and false teeth that occasionally popped out of his mouth. We traveled around, and he introduced me to the elected chairmen of each of the ten project councils. I was struck by their courage and quiet determination. The houses they were defending were modest wooden affairs, just a few rooms in each, often with no water inside, but generally in good repair, and certainly better than the dilapidated, planter-owned shacks where the people had once lived. I wanted to help them stay, but it was clear by now that a sale was inevitable. So between Bill and me, an idea took form. Why not try to turn this threat into an opportunity? Why couldn't the tenants be the buyers of these homes? Johnson and I drew up a petition demanding that the families receive the opportunity to bid on their homes. The idea struck a responsive chord: in two days more than six hundred residents in the ten Delmo projects had signed our petition.

I knew we'd have to keep up pressure in Washington if we were to succeed. So two weeks later, I recruited a delegation of fifteen Delmo residents to take the train to Washington and lobby the FSA and Congress. As had happened back in 1939, all food, hotel and travel expenses were covered by the STFU's National Sharecroppers Fund. Our delegation met with the FSA administrator, Frank Hancock. He proved to be very suspicious of us, but we had hardly expected anything else. We found our bootheel congressman, Orville Zimmerman, who had never met a plantation owner he didn't like, to be friendly on the surface but highly evasive. We obtained unexpected support from Senator Frank Briggs of Missouri, Senator William Langer of North Dakota, and Congressman Frank Hook of Michigan. They agreed to submit identical bills in the Senate and House directing the FSA to sell the homes only to the residents. We did not try to visit President Truman, because we suspected that he had already sided with the plantation owners.

At Mitchell's suggestion, I visited a liberal lobbyist named Gardner (Pat) Jackson at his home in Washington to obtain his advice. Jackson was another longtime New Deal loyalist, one of the few lobbyists in Washington who made it his business to look out for the interests of tenants, sharecroppers, and farm laborers in America. With a knowing smile, Jackson advised me to see Pete Hudgens, the FSA's deputy administrator, as soon as possible, because "he's the only honest man left in this agency." I and the entire delegation descended on Hudgens's office early the next morning. After hearing our concerns, he gave us neophytes some sound advice on how these things should be done. We should first form an official Delmo committee made up of men and women elected by each project. Our next task, he counseled, should be to find prominent people in St. Louis and other Missouri cities who would form a sponsoring committee to lobby Congress and the FSA headquarters in Washington. Hudgens further recommended that we ask each Delmo family to contribute $100 to an escrow account controlled by the future sponsoring committee. Money from this account, he explained, could be used to make a down payment to the FSA if the agency allowed the tenants to purchase their homes.

Back in Missouri, we followed Hudgens's recommendations to the letter. We formed a Delmo tenants' committee with two elected representatives from each of the ten projects. The elected chairman of this committee was white, the vice chairman black. The sponsoring committee was created after those of us who had gone to Washington visited St. Louis. Episcopal Bishop William Scarlett agreed to head what he named the Citizens Committee to Save the Delmo Homes and to write letters to prominent Missouri citizens asking them to join. Among the people who took him up were two liberal plantation owners, Thad Snow and Charles Coleman from southeast Missouri, who showed no small courage in siding with us. Also signing on were several public-minded St. Louis businessmen and a local poet named Josephine Johnson.

The Citizens Committee worked closely with us. On August 21, 1945, in a meeting of residents from all ten Delmo projects, the treasurer of the bishop's committee announced that 314 of the 549 resident families had already sent $100 payments to the committee's escrow account.

On the advice of Bishop Scarlett, I launched over a two-month period a modest national fund-raising campaign. I sent financial appeals to national unions, church agencies, and liberal-minded citizens of wealth, and also made personal calls. One day, after a long and dusty train ride overnight from St. Louis to New York City, I got in a Manhattan taxi and told the driver to go to the office of corporate executive and philanthropist Marshall Field. Along the way I asked the driver to stop at a clothing store so I could buy a new white shirt, which I hoped would make me look halfway presentable. Shortly after, I was ushered into Field's presence and presented him with a letter from Bishop Scarlett. Field was a large, well-dressed man with a ready smile, and he made me feel somewhat comfortable. In three short minutes I told him as best I could about the plight of the Delmo families. He asked a few questions, then sent me on my way with a promise that he would make phone calls to Bishop Scarlett and others. I was sure this was a brush-off. But a week later I received a $12,500 check from Field. Mrs. Emmons Blaine McCormick of the famous Chicago family also sent us a check, for $5,000. By the end of September we had received more than $40,000 from outside donors and our escrow account containing the tenants' $100 payments had grown to just under $35,000.

Yet despite our fund-raising successes, time was running out and omens of failure seemed to be everywhere. In early August our ally Congressman Hook received a letter from President Truman reminding him that Congress had already passed a bill stipulating that the projects must be sold to the highest bidders. In late August, the FSA made its first sale of thirty homes at the smallest white Delmo project, at South Wyatt. The buyer was a wheat-processing company. Alarmed by the sale, Bishop Scarlett met Governor Forest Donnell to solicit his support to block the sale of the other projects to companies or plantation owners, but as Scarlett later recounted to me, the governor told him that "this is the hottest political issue in the state. I will not touch it until I am completely compelled by sheer necessity."

We began to believe that our major obstruction was none other than the new president himself. We recalled that as a senator, Truman was narrowly reelected in 1940 in part because of solid support from the ruling Pendergast machine in Kansas City and from cotton plantation owners in southeast Missouri. The friendly cotton planters on Bishop Scarlett's committee—Thad Snow and Charles Coleman—told us that in early 1945 Truman, then vice president, had assured local planters that they would soon get the chance to purchase the ten projects.

But we had a few reasons to be optimistic. We got word that in cabinet meetings Commerce Secretary Henry Wallace had endorsed selling the homes to the residents. Encouraged by this news, by supportive editorials in the *Washington Post,* the *St. Louis Post-Dispatch,* and the *St. Louis Star,* and by our successful efforts in raising money, the bishop recommended that his committee make a bid, though the committee had not yet been formally incorporated. So, we submitted a bid for $143,225. We held our breath and quickly got the news we had expected: Hancock rejected our offer. He told the committee that in the future he would not consider any bid under $385,000.

In desperation, I called on a family friend, Sherwood Eddy, an aging Christian evangelist who back in 1905 had helped persuade my father to turn aside a lucrative banking job and become instead a low-paid YMCA teacher in Japan. I asked if Eddy's own Cooperative Foundation, which he had founded to support two interracial cooperative farms in Mississippi, would make a higher bid on behalf of the soon-to-be-incorporated (I hoped) Delmo Housing

Corporation. After lengthy telephone conversations with Bishop Scarlett, the foundation's board members, at Eddy's urging, agreed to place a bid for $245,000 on behalf of the future Delmo Housing Corporation. But on November 1, 1945, Hancock rejected this bid too, claiming it was below his minimum, and gave Eddy only twelve days to submit another bid. In his letter to Eddy he warned ominously that unless the bid was in by that time, "we will be obligated to take other action immediately by way of liquidation."

I telephoned our friend Pete Hudgens. Ever willing to help, he counseled that we remain calm and submit in the next ten days a slightly higher bid. After lengthy conference calls with Bishop Scarlett and myself, Eddy agreed to bid $285,000 for the remaining nine Delmo communities—$73,500 as a down payment, leaving a balance of $211,500 with a yearly interest charge of 3 percent and full payment guaranteed in eight years or less. Hearing that the bid was not much higher than the rejected one, many of us on the scene were again fearful and apprehensive. We proved to be men and women of little faith. On November 12, 1945, Hancock sent a telegram to Eddy announcing that the FSA had accepted our offer. I still have a copy of the telegram. Many years later, it still gives me a thrill to read it.

Alice and I Become Delmo Residents

At the nine Delmo communities the celebrations were long and spirited. We had won a battle against the entrenched powers that had dominated southeast Missouri for decades. The Delmo Housing Corporation was incorporated on the day before Christmas 1945. A few days later Harris Rodgers, former chairman of the State Highway Commission, became the Delmo project manager. In January 1946, the 549 resident families at the nine Delmo projects started sending Rodgers mortgage payments of ten dollars each month. They were on their way to becoming full-fledged homeowners.

Bishop Scarlett and his committee were lionized in the press soon after our victory. For my role in the battle, my denomination—then the Congregational and Christian Churches—gave me an award at its national Synod meeting in 1946. But I knew in my heart that the Delmo families were the real heroes.

Soon after the victory, Alice and I sold our trailer and moved into a house at the white Delmo project in East Prairie, Missouri. We were a real family now—with us was our baby daughter Laurel, who'd been born in Memphis in April of 1945. After eighteen months of trailer life interspersed by my constant travels, we were glad to have a real house to call our own, however modest it was. It was a white-shingled, one-story structure measuring six hundred square feet. In the backyard was a water pump and an outhouse. With the help of a neighbor, I installed a kitchen sink, ran a water line from the backyard pump to the kitchen, and put in a new pump by the sink. I also painted the exterior. Alice and I felt a bit of the thrill the families had: for the first time in our lives, we were homeowners.

We had occasional problems being accepted by the people around us. Living next door to us was the Helms family. The fifty-year-old man of the house was in failing health. His considerably younger wife, we soon discovered, was constantly unhappy and an avid gossip. After I had carelessly dropped our monthly paycheck for $125 on the road, Mr. Helms found it and promptly returned it to me, surprised, I'm sure, at how large it was. His wife, however, spread the word among our neighbors that I was getting money from a subversive church agency in distant New York City. A few months later I traveled to St. Louis to attend a board meeting of the Delmo Housing Corporation. During my absence, Alice with our baby Laurel in her arms attended a meeting in the community center across the street from our house. One of our neighbors, whom we had never met, loudly charged that I was raising money in St. Louis and putting it in my own pocket. Alice became enraged and blasted my accuser in rather a rough fashion.

With other families we formed close ties, however. Owning a car, we often drove sick residents to a hospital or health clinic. I will always remember the day I drove a five-year-old boy suffering from acute asthma seventy miles to the nearest emergency room, at the Cape Girardeau hospital. The gasping boy died in the car before we reached help there.

A near-fatal accident befell our own family in October 1946, giving us a terrifying personal dose of the hardships that the Delmo families so often endured. We were spending a Saturday night at the home of our ministerial associates, Art and Ruth Churchill, at the Lilburn Delmo project some thirty miles from East Prairie. They had a bathtub. Knowing we had none, Ruth boiled up two buckets of hot water at six o'clock Sunday morning for us to use in their tub before we returned to East Prairie for our church service early that morning. Unattended, our daughter Laurel wandered into the room pulling a play toy and fell backwards into one of the buckets, sinking up to her armpits in the scalding water. Hearing her screams, Alice and I jumped out of bed, tore off her steaming pajamas, and poured mineral oil over her burns. We hurried her to a local doctor, who did what he could to help her and then told us to rush her those seventy miles down the road to the Cape Girardeau hospital. We got her there, and during the next four days she drifted between life and death. She was saved by a young doctor at the hospital who had learned the art of skin grafting two years earlier while treating burn victims as an army doctor in Italy and France. We felt singularly blessed that Laurel survived. But another young child in East Prairie was not so lucky. The week following Laurel's accident, the young daughter of a pastor in East Prairie fell into a washing tub half full of clothes, suffered scaldings, and died two days later.

At each of the nine Delmo projects, I often helped organize community meetings, which were conducted by the local elected chairman. At these meetings, residents were informed about such things as who was sick in the project, local job opportunities, and the importance of keeping their homes well painted, the roofs waterproofed, and the home gardens planted with fruit trees and vegetables. I encouraged people to recommended ways to improve their neighborhoods. I discovered at these meetings that each Delmo project had its own share of troublemakers—drunks, bullies, adulterers, wife- and child-beaters, and complainers. But on balance, despite poverty, long periods of unemployment, and the grief caused by the local ne'er-do-wells, most of the Delmo residents were eager to buy their own homes and to live in these village communities among generally compatible neighbors.

The Delmo Homes had become something of a cause célèbre for liberals across the country, and at our home in East Prairie Alice and I were frequent hosts to visitors from afar. They included Agnes Meyer, whose husband was publisher of the *Washington Post;* labor columnist Victor Reisel; a functionary of the American Communist Party posing as a labor organizer; sixteen youthful members of a summer Quaker work camp in the Delmo project in Lilburn; and members of several churches in St. Louis that had supported the Delmo cause back in 1945. I greeted them and talked enthusiastically about the successful fight to save the Delmo Homes.

But in this period of my life I was in fact having increasing doubts about whether I was in the right place. It had begun the year before, really, as I found my ideas about pacifism changing, due to the violence that I witnessed against blacks in the South and the steady expansion of the crimes that Hitler was committing against the people of Europe. I came to feel that the war against Hitler was just and that I should find a role for myself in it. I still did not feel capable of wielding a gun, but I felt that I could provide spiritual aid to those who did. In late 1944, I applied to be a chaplain in the army, hoping to go abroad and minister to our soldiers in the field. In the mail, I received in reply a letter offering me a commission, but with the caveat that I could not go overseas due to my history of rheumatic fever back in 1934. Working on an army post in the States did not appeal to me, though, and I rejected the commission in the spring of 1945, just before the Delmo struggle began. Likely I never would have seen the war anyway—it ended in August 1945 after the atomic bombings of Hiroshima and Nagasaki. Alice and I rejoiced at the return of peace to the world, but were shocked by the use of the new weapon. My parents in particular were saddened—they had spent those long years in Japan and could vividly imagine the devastation of the cities there.

The Delmo fight engaged me entirely for the rest of 1945, but when it was over and life settled down for us in East Prairie, I began feeling restless again. I finally admitted to myself and to Alice that I did not really enjoy being a scoutmaster, a sports coach, and a Sunday school teacher. I remember one night in East Prairie when an overgrown fifteen-year-old boy banged on our front door, cursed me for no apparent reason, and challenged me to fight. I slammed the wooden door in his face more out of frustration than anger. I knew then that God had not ordained me to deal with violent youths or nonviolent youths. I felt more at home with adults. The truth was that I was restless in the rural backwoods of southeast Missouri, where somehow, despite what I was doing, I felt far from the world of important, worthy causes. By mail I shared with my father my doubts and my desire to quit the ministry and become a full-time labor organizer. He urged me to stay with the church. He tried also to buoy my spirits by writing that Norman Thomas, his 1905 classmate at Princeton, had told him that the 1945 Delmo campaign "was one of the few brighter spots for liberalism in our nation."

As I fretted about the future, our second child, a boy, was born. We named him Lyman, after Professor Eugene Lyman—once my father's professor and a distant relative of Alice. He was the minister who had married us back in 1941.

That very week, I got the news I was looking for. Franz Daniel, the South Carolina director of the Southern Drive of the Congress of Industrial Organizations (CIO), offered me a job in Rock Hill, South Carolina, as chief organizer for the Textile Workers Union of America–CIO. It is often said that you should be careful what you wish for, because you might get it. With this offer in hand, I hesitated, because Alice and I had enjoyed working together for the past four years in our joint ministry. I knew that if I became a union organizer, I would be traveling and working long days and nights away from home. Alice would be left at home tending to our two children. But in the end I accepted Franz's offer. We left southeast Missouri in July of 1947 knowing we had made a contribution to the well-being of people there, their independence and their sense of dignity. We left behind friends and took away a wealth of memories— and a semi-adopted daughter, Celia Parker, an adolescent girl from a Delmo family in East Prairie. She came to live with us later in North Carolina and Georgia. With Alice's help, she eventually became a student at Berea College, Alice's alma mater.

We stayed in touch with Delmo people over the years and found that the work we began continued, and brought major benefits to the Delmo residents. According to an unpublished book entitled *Delmo Saga,* by Wilder Towle, the senior United Church of Christ conference minister in Missouri, only three families were evicted between 1946 and 1954 for failing to send their monthly ten-dollar payments. By 1955 almost all of the original 549 families had paid off their mortgages in full.[2] The projects had been brightened by health programs, thrift shops, credit unions, and truck gardening, and by the presence of the many church-employed workers who succeeded Alice and me.

In 1995, I was invited to give a keynote address at a meeting of the Delmo Housing Corporation and the Delmo staff to mark the fiftieth anniversary of the victory. The homes were still there, looking a bit weather-worn, but forming the basis for vibrant communities of the type I remembered. Here and there I met aged veterans of the long-ago fight. We shared tales and complimented each other on a job well done.

But I have to confess that one of the nicest things I ever heard about my role at Delmo came from the mouth of a man who had been our enemy during the long struggle, Congressman Orville Zimmerman. In February 1946, I returned to Washington to thank our ally Pete Hudgens and to call on Zimmerman. The ever-affable politician sat me down and tried to charm me with claims that he'd backed the bishop's committee all along. And then, behind the closed doors of his office, Zimmerman offered me something like this: "Brother Burgess, when St. Peter at the pearly gates of heaven asks you what you did during your life to help brothers and sisters among the poor of this world, you can tell him that you helped to save the Delmo Homes for the working people living there. St. Peter will then say to you, 'Well done, good and faithful servant.' And then he will open up the gates of heaven to you."

9
Cutting My Teeth as an Urban Labor Organizer, 1947–1949

IN THE LATE 1940s, the Aragon Mill on the edge of Rock Hill, South Carolina, was the workplace for about two thousand men and women, but in some ways it more closely resembled a state prison. It was a series of dour brick buildings and an adjoining village of tiny company-owned houses, all set close together and surrounded by a tall fence with unsmiling guards at the gates. There was little foliage. The place had an overbearing feeling of drabness about it. Organizing textile workers at the mill was to be my focus for many months. It would give me my first experience and education in the travails of urban labor organizing.

The labor movement had done well in cities of the North in the 1930s, organizing workers in big industries such as automobiles and steel. The famous sit-down strikes in Detroit had been matched by similar, though less dramatic, actions of unions in other American cities, and the lives of many workers were better as a result. But the South was much less touched by the labor movement. Most workers continued to labor in hot and unsafe conditions, with no right of grievance. They depended on the largesse of their employers for wage increases, medical care, and basic safety on the job. Some companies from the North, notably old textile companies of New England, eyeing this employer-dominated system with some envy, moved operations to the South in order to escape unionization. The Second World War brought a partial hiatus in strikes, as all sides focused on turning out the goods needed to beat the Axis powers. But after the war, beginning in late 1945, a wave of strikes broke out as the CIO organizing campaign known as Operation Dixie got under way. Southern employers and their allied conservative lawmakers began a campaign of union resistance. President Truman, who, despite his feelings about the Delmo fight, favored organizing rights for urban workers, vetoed the anti-union Taft-Hartley bill, only to have Congress override his veto. Meanwhile, the legislature of

South Carolina outlawed the "union shop," a system in which all employees at unionized companies had to be members of the employer-recognized unions.

Other problems were of the labor movement's own making. Though we all used the term "union," we were not in fact united. There were multiple hostile factions, sometimes competing against each other in certification elections in which workers voted on whether to accept a particular union as their sole bargaining agent. One important group of unions was affiliated with the American Federation of Labor (AFL). Though the AFL had played an important, historic role in early efforts at collective bargaining in the United States, its unions in the late 1930s were often dominated by conservatives who failed to press aggressively for better wages and working conditions for industrial employees. I had thrown in my lot with the more militant Congress of Industrial Organizations (CIO), which had broken away from the AFL in the mid-1930s to pursue a more radical tack to benefit industrial workers.

With our two children, Alice and I moved to Rock Hill, a town of about thirty thousand people, in July 1947. The day after we arrived, Franz Daniel, director of the South Carolina CIO organizing drive, came to town to show me around. With a broad smile, he introduced me to organizer Don McKee as another of those "God-damned college graduate intellectuals." That was an allusion to factionalism within our own union, the Textile Workers Union of America (TWUA). The phrase was said to be used by TWUA President Emil Rieve about many organizers hired by his chief internal rival, union Vice President George Baldanzi, who was also the deputy director of the CIO's organizing campaign in the South. There was a certain truth to the words, as most of us were college-educated and from more affluent backgrounds than the people we were trying to organize. That day Franz also introduced me to organizer Nancy Blaine, a recent Vassar graduate and heir to part of the fortune of the McCormick family of Chicago. Our outsider status helped to bond us together, but it proved later to be a powerful weapon used by employers against us in plants we were targeting.

CIO organizers had had some initial successes in Rock Hill, one of the few South Carolina towns where that was true. In 1947 about three thousand workers at four plants in the town were members of the TWUA. So, young and energetic, we began to lay plans to expand those numbers, feeling confident we could.

The Aragon Campaign

We targeted Aragon Mill, the local flagship operation of the J. P. Stevens Company. Across the street from the mill, I rented a modest office for our team, which consisted of me and the four organizers I directed. We got to work. We stood at the gates and passed out union leaflets when the eight-hour shifts changed. Two evenings a week we held a meeting with workers who wanted to know more about the union. We persuaded some to sign a union card, and circulated a petition to the National Labor Relations Board (NLRB) calling for an election in which workers would vote, under the board's supervision, for or against our union as their future bargaining agent.

We also visited workers at their company-owned homes. After several textile workers slammed doors in our faces, we realized that the mill executives had been waging a well-planned anti-union campaign for years. We were told that when the TWUA had started an organizing drive at the Aragon Mill more than three years ago, company officials placed a huge weaving machine on a platform near the mill gate. Foremen told the workers that if they voted for the union, the company might close the plant and ship that machine and all other machinery to plants in other states or south of the border in Mexico. Three years ago the TWUA had lost that election by a three-to-two margin partly as a result of the company's campaign of fear.

With us on the scene, company officials again made threats to move the mill. Workers were also reminded that the company had the power to evict them and their families from their rented homes in the company village. In the workplace, foremen spread lies about the union and persecuted workers sympathetic to the union. On one occasion, when a pro-union worker had left his weaving machine for his lunch break, a foreman slashed the threads on the machine. When the worker returned, the foreman charged him with faulty weaving and told him he was going to be fired. Rightly suspecting that the foreman had slashed the threads himself, the worker started a fight with him. The next day the company fired the worker, charging him with "faulty work and violent behavior." He and members of his family were evicted from their home in a few days. Hearing this story, a number of workers tore up their union cards and stopped coming to meetings at our office.

In late 1948, a few weeks before the NLRB election, each worker received a four-page, single-spaced letter from the president of the Stevens Company which listed the benefits given to them by the company and portraying the TWUA as the tool of outsiders, led by people with strange foreign names who did not share the workers' values:

> Who are the men who lead this union? I will name some of the chief officers: Baldanzi, Rieve, Chupka, Genis, Jabor, Knapk and Rosenberg. Where do these people come from and where do they live? Are their backgrounds, upbringings, viewpoints, beliefs and principles anything like yours and mine? Have they ever given a cent to build

a school your children attend, or roads you drive on. Have they ever given a penny to your church?

The president ended his blast by saying that signing on with the union would bring only strikes and unhappiness.

We kept up our pressure. To protect the workers who were the targets of company action, a TWUA staff lawyer took the company to court, charging officials with illegal anti-union activity and recommending that the NLRB fine the company for those activities. But in seemingly endless court appeals, company lawyers, bolstered by the provisions of the Taft-Hartley Act, blocked the payment of the fines levied by the board. Meanwhile, the victimized workers who were fired got scant relief because the TWUA had limited funds to support them. The company in turn offered some of the fired workers a tempting deal: destroy your union cards and we will forgive you, give you back your jobs with additional benefits, and allow you to return to your homes in the textile village.

But in leaflets that we distributed at the plant gate at shift changes, day and night, we continued to outline the benefits of joining the union—better wages, health benefits, job protection, grievance procedures. We used a radio station too. In Sunday-afternoon dramas which I wrote, we portrayed such characters as an antagonistic anti-union foreman, a confused and timid worker, and a union member. Staff members and textile workers read the parts from these melodramas before a radio microphone. In addition, elected leaders of TWUA locals spoke on the radio and at our meetings in the union office by the mill, explaining how in other Rock Hill textile plants the CIO-affiliated Textile Workers Union had brought benefits to three thousand textile workers and their families in Rock Hill.

On the day of the election, a half-dozen NLRB officials set up voting booths early in the morning. Starting at six o'clock, Aragon employees cast their ballots for or against us. Two hours later, Franz Daniel came to our office and complimented all the organizers for their hard work. During the day, as the voting progressed at the mill across the street, we tried to be outwardly confident and cheery, consuming endless Cokes and hamburgers. But inwardly, both Franz and I sensed impending defeat. Throughout our campaign, I knew we had never succeeded in signing up a majority of the plant's employees or in creating a popular pro-union movement within the plant itself. At eight o'clock that night, NLRB officials came to our office and announced that the union had lost. As in the previous vote, the margin was three-to-two. We had labored in vain for months. Franz and I and some of our colleagues wept openly.

Looking back, it seems to me that two main things worked against us. One was the company's brazen intimidation of the workers. The other was the culture of the mill's workers. Many people there believed that the company was kind of a father of the family, and that it was their duty to do what they were told, just as children must obey parents. Clearly, they also realized that some of the TWUA's organizers, like myself, were outsiders, men and women of different religious, educational, and ethnic backgrounds than theirs.

Church Opposition to the Labor Movement

Many of the workers' religious leaders had shared the hostility toward us. During our campaign, I was appalled to find that taking the company's side were two local Baptist pastors, who condemned the CIO from their pulpits and during visits to workers' homes. Soon after we lost the vote, the management of the mill donated funds for a new church education building and a new parsonage. Why churches and the union movement were so often at odds in the South became a question of great concern to me. I began to read up on it. I gained some insights from a book entitled *Millhands and Preachers: A Study of Gastonia,* by Liston Pope. Raised in the South and later the dean of the Yale School of Religion, Pope in the early 1940s made a sociological study of Gastonia, a large textile-manufacturing city in North Carolina where for decades employers were in league with pastors in common opposition to organized labor. Pope traced the recruitment of farmers and their family members by mill management beginning in the late nineteenth century, their transformation into obedient textile workers, a bloody and unsuccessful strike of 1934 in the North Carolina town of Gastonia, and subsequent company efforts, with clergy support, to oppose further efforts of the workers to organize. Pope summarized the state of company-clergy collaboration in Gastonia:

> From the beginning the employers used the churches as vehicles of welfare work and have supported church programs in numerous ways. The churches in turn are proud of the responsibilities entrusted to them and set out to mold the transplanted farmers into stable, contented, sober citizens and industrial workers. Methods used in helping to convert an atomistic assembly of rural individuals into a disciplined work force, amenable to a high degree of social control, consisted of inculcation of personal virtues (stability, honesty, sobriety, industry), provision of a center of community integration other than the mill itself, and an emotional escape from the difficulties of life. Both as a disciplinarian and a safety valve, the mill church became a valuable center for the constitution of a new industrial control. . . . Thus under the employer control, the mill churches have often become the center of opposition to the growing labor movement.[1]

In May 1949, I testified before the Labor and Education Committee of the U.S. House of Representatives about the hostility that most southern clergy displayed toward CIO organizing efforts.[2] To prepare my testimony, I sent a questionnaire to CIO staff members all over the South and asked them to give me specific examples of clergy opposition to the CIO. The answers showed that little had changed since Pope made his study of Gastonia less than two decades earlier. I began my testimony to the committee by describing the pattern of employer paternalism in mills and company villages. The average pastor there is hardly free to preach the Gospel unafraid, I said. Over him is the employer who might have donated the land where the church was built, given substantially to the church building fund, paid for lights and water, contributed to the construction of the parsonage, and covered a large portion of the pastor's salary. As a result, when organizers come around, the pastor often has no choice but to speak out against them from the pulpit. In my testimony, I offered some examples of this opposition, based on recent answers to my questionnaire:

- In Easley, South Carolina, a pastor proclaimed at an employer-called meeting that the CIO was "Godless and subversive" and that any church member who joined the union would be expelled. When the Sunday school superintendent joined a union, the pastor asked him to leave the church.

- In a mill church at the Pacific Mills in Lyman, South Carolina, a Baptist minister declared in his sermon, "It's either Christ or the CIO. You can be a Christian or a CIO man but not both."

- In August 1946, during a CIO organizing drive at the U.S. Rubber plant in Hogansville, Georgia, the pastor of a Baptist church charged that the CIO was nothing more than the "Sign of the Beast" as described in the Book of Revelations. He warned that "Communism, Catholicism, and other isms are sweeping the South from the North to overthrow us with modernistic devices." He concluded with an anti-Catholic twist: "We don't need a padre to say mass on the picket line in Hogansville."

- In Cuthbert, Georgia, a local black Methodist pastor courageously allowed mill workers interested in joining a union to meet in his church. Visiting the pastor the following day, a group of white citizens including a mill's chief manager threatened to burn down the church if there were any more such meetings there.

- In Trinity, Texas, the state CIO director was scheduled to address a meeting of workers at a local Baptist church, but upon going to the church he found the doors locked. The next day the church moderator told a union state director that God had called and told him to keep the church locked. Later he confessed to the director that the call came not from God but from the local mill manager.

The list of such anti-union activities went on and on. Later in my testimony, I quoted recent resolutions of the Catholic Church and several mainline Protestant denominations affirming the workers' right to organize and to strike.

The Aragon Aftermath

We were defeated in the Aragon vote, but I believe we did bring lasting benefit to the mill's workers, though they may not have realized it. Employers often gave pay increases to employees as an inducement for them to vote against the union in forthcoming NLRB votes. In Rock Hill, I learned that employers at non-union plants sometimes matched the wage level of workers at the four unionized textile plants in the city.

The real casualties of the lost election were some Aragon workers who had thrown in their lot with us. A few months after the defeat, I stopped at a small textile town north of Rock Hill to fill up on gas. Standing in front of the station was Ken Taylor, a very loyal union supporter during the Aragon campaign. He looked sad as he walked toward me. I will always remember his words: "I love you like a brother, Brother Dave, but I don't want to see you again." He told me that he and his wife had been fired from the Aragon Mill and that they and their three children had been evicted from the company village. Now he and his wife were working at a much smaller mill, earning less than two-thirds of what they had made before. I was at loss for words. We embraced briefly and parted.

Other union members were fired on essentially false charges. Though the union showed in subsequent NLRB hearings that many workers had been discharged solely for backing the union, neither the NLRB nor the courts were able to force the company to reinstate them or pay their lost wages. Two years later, the Stevens Company was able to defeat the TWUA once again in Rock Hill, this time going after some union officials in court. The managers of the Stevens-owned Industrial Cotton Mill, which was just a mile from the Aragon Mill, brought false charges against officers of the company-recognized TWUA local there. The officers were convicted and jailed. Six months later they were released after union lawyers convinced a judge that a frame-up had occurred. But the workers at the mill were so confused by the accusations, counter-accusations, and court proceedings that a few weeks later a majority of workers voted in an NLRB election to decertify the TWUA as the bargaining agent. And so the formerly strong local died at that mill, a victim of corporate power and the skill of a union-busting law firm.

After Aragon, Franz sent me to join other CIO organizers at the U.S. Rubber plant in Winnsboro, South Carolina. Our purpose there was to dislodge a local affiliated with the Textile Workers Union–AFL, which Franz regarded as a nothing more than a subservient company union. In the first election, the TWUA got more votes than the AFL textile union, but because eighty of the two thousand workers at the plant voted to have no union at all, the TWUA lacked a majority of votes. There would have to be a runoff election. That gave the company the opening it was waiting for, and it played on racial tensions.

While we were preparing for the second vote, I saw a new example of the damage the clergy could do. A company-paid black preacher visited the homes of all 125 black employees at the plant, claiming, we were later told, that "the CIO is full of Communists. It's better to have a separate Jim Crow, Grade B black local union with the recognized AFL union than an all-in-one union with the CIO where blacks would be only a minority." Meanwhile, company officials were telling white workers in the plant that the CIO was full of Communists and was backing programs that would force the company to employ more blacks— which according to company brochures would lead to racial "mongrelization" among the plant's workers. We lost the runoff election to the AFL union by a slim margin of 150 votes.

Two months after that defeat, I was organizing workers at yet another plant, a newly constructed textile factory of the Celanese Company just north of Rock Hill. I was given the task of visiting the homes of all black employees to talk up the benefits of a vote for the TWUA. On many such visits—their homes were scattered all over the county—I was accompanied by the president of the Rock Hill branch of the NAACP. The vote came, and we were elated to find we had won by a small margin—it was one of the rare victories the labor movement enjoyed in those days in South Carolina. My home visits with the same NAACP official had clearly been a success. I later discovered that practically every black worker employed at the plant voted for the TWUA. Their vote was the margin of our victory.

The CIO in Politics

The CIO philosophy was that there was more to an organizer's job than organizing mill workers. We had also to work to remove anti-labor politicians and put sympathetic politicians into office. So in early 1948, many union members attended seven Democratic precinct meetings in Rock Hill and captured control of four of these precincts. We next asked Assemblyman

Eugene Cobb, a resident of Rock Hill, to run against the anti-labor Democratic incumbent, Congressman Dick Richards. We promised Cobb the support of union members and help with funding. He reluctantly agreed to run in the Democratic primary in August 1948, on a platform calling for better pay for teachers, better services to veterans, improved farm-to-market roads, and repeal of the Taft-Hartley Act. I wrote radio speeches for him and designed his campaign brochures. I also made a major effort to win the black vote for Cobb in the congressional district—a vote which was small but not inconsequential.

I finally persuaded the local and state NAACP leaders to campaign for Cobb among their black constituents, reminding them that at the last national CIO convention, CIO President Phillip Murray had advocated the passage of national civil rights and voting rights laws. The NAACP leaders had something to remind me of too: that in Rock Hill textile mills, blacks could get jobs only as sweepers or handling cotton bales in humid, lint-filled "picker rooms." Local cotton mill bosses had long warned white workers that no white woman was safe in any plant hiring blacks, and most whites agreed. I and the NAACP leaders talked at length, and finally they pledged their support to Cobb. They made good on their pledge, but there were not enough black voters and liberal white voters to elect Cobb. The day after the primary, Congressman Richards met me by chance on Rock Hill's Main Street. He shouted at me, "You damned Yankees with all of your CIO money could not defeat me by running your stooge Eugene Cobb." I made no reply as I walked away.

My Hero Franz Daniel

Within the labor movement, I made some lasting friends among my fellow CIO organizers in Rock Hill. Over the years, I stayed in close touch with CIO organizer Don McKee, now living in Maplewood, New Jersey, and with the late Nancy Blaine, who later left the TWUA and married Gilbert Harrison, publisher of *New Republic* magazine. Joe Glazer, the CIO troubadour, encouraged organizers and workers alike with his guitar and lively singing. But through all my ups and downs, I found my greatest inspiration from Franz Daniel, the South Carolina director of the CIO Southern Drive. Perhaps I felt a bond in particular because he too had graduated from Union Theological Seminary. One morning in 1929 in his final year at Union, a Communist Party flag was discovered flying from the pole above the entrance to the seminary. A lengthy investigation was launched, but the perpetrator was never found. Many people assumed it was Franz, though we never found out for sure. After Union, he and his wife, Zilla, taught at Myles Horton's Highlander Folk School in Tennessee, a utopian experiment that trained labor and community organizers in the South. Franz split with Horton because Franz was an avid socialist, in the old-style idealistic sense. In his union career, he was a firm opponent of the Communists. For more than ten years, he was a highly successful organizer for the Amalgamated Clothing Workers Union–CIO in the South. In 1946, CIO President Phillip Murray chose him to head the South Carolina part of the grand organizing drive known as "Campaign Dixie."

Franz was merciless in his verbal attacks on mill bosses and other exploiters, but with his CIO organizing staff he was most friendly, nondominating, and cooperative. He never faulted us for the many defeats we suffered; instead, he was always there with encouragement.

But underneath, there was an element of tragedy in him. His young asthmatic son had died in a bizarre incident in 1946, choking to death in a doctor's waiting room. Bit by bit, I began to see into Franz's inner world. I will always remember a night in 1948 when he and I were attending a CIO conference in Atlanta. That day at the conference he had strongly condemned several top CIO officials for their refusal to send their more skilled organizers to the South and to supply much-needed funds. That night Franz had too much to drink at the hotel bar. I walked him back to his hotel room. Sitting on the edge of his bed, he said to me sorrowfully, "Dave, you have an advantage over me. You believe in something, but I no longer believe." I knew that he was disgusted with the spiritual shallowness and lack of dedication of some of his union associates, a sentiment that I shared in part. He worried that some of the more committed CIO organizers were losing heart because of a chain of recent losses in representation elections. Perhaps Franz was seeking an answer to one ultimate question that southern organizers had often grappled with—where is the God of justice in the South? In the end, Franz may not have lived up to the high expectations of his union friends or even his own expectations. But he was a good human being who felt a deep kinship with rural and industrial workers. Despite his personal weaknesses and bitterness, he never lost his willingness to help others with generosity and grace.

Family Affairs and Union Affairs

During this period, Alice and I and our two young children rented a Rock Hill apartment that had only two large rooms and an adjoining kitchen and bathroom. The kids were blessed with a large yard in back and a school playground across the street. Life was a bit more normal for us than it had been in the migrant camps, but a series of family crises struck nonetheless. At age three, Lyman was hit by a car in front of our house. The driver stopped and drove him to a hospital. Rushing there, we were terrified, remembering how we'd almost lost Laurel in an accident, but his injuries turned out to be only minor. Then Alice, a twin herself, suffered a miscarriage of twins. I'll never forget that when I told the two children we had lost the babies, Lyman, then four, asked, "But Daddy, where did they go?" I had no apt answer.

And in mid-August 1949, as I was staying overnight at the O'Grady Hotel in Greensboro, North Carolina, there came a telegram from my mother that father had died, of another heart attack. After making frantic phone calls, I managed to reach my mother and tried to console her. The next night I wrote her a letter, which read in part: "I have always admired his unselfishness, his frankness, his ability to put others first, his rather naive assumption that all men and women are potentially honest and straightforward."

Throughout our stay in Rock Hill, we had a hard time finding friends outside of my work. This was in large part, I think, because I was a CIO organizer and was viewed with suspicion by many local citizens. Alice applied for a job at a nursery, but was turned down, we believed, because of my union affiliation. We attended a Southern Presbyterian church near our home whose pastor was a liberal minister named Kenneth Phifer. Ten years later Phifer told me what happened when our application for membership came before the seven-man church session that governed the church. One member stated that the church was full of such professionals as doctors, lawyers, and mill managers and that Alice and I would be much more at home at a Southern Baptist church attended by textile workers. The chair of the session then remarked, "We must not forget that Dave Burgess is a CIO organizer, an agitator, possibly a fellow traveler and secretly a member of the Communist Party. He calls himself a former minister but I doubt that he is one." The debate went on for half an hour. Phifer finally broke his silence and said, "Not all of us agree with the Burgesses on certain issues. I believe, however, that they should be welcomed here." He concluded, much to the surprise of session members, "If you reject their applications for membership, I will leave this church." He promptly left the room. After further debate, session members approved our application by a slim margin.

I have to say that I had a similar unfriendly opinion of textile executives, and it probably showed, even in church. I regarded them as the prime enemies of our campaign and, for that matter, of decency itself. It might be asked, these many years later, why we wanted to join a church that was so hostile to us. I suppose it was because we did feel like outsiders in this little southern town and wanted the occasional fellowship of other professional and educated people who called themselves Christians.

We stayed three years in Rock Hill. In the end it wasn't due to pressure from the companies or people like the session members that we left. It was old-fashioned factionalism within the TWUA. The rivalry between union President

Emil Rieve and Vice President George Baldanzi had always been there behind the scenes, but it burst into the open in early 1948, when Baldanzi announced he would challenge Rieve for the presidency at the union's national convention in Atlantic City. When Rieve soundly defeated him there, I and about thirty other people whom Baldanzi had hired for the Southern Drive—the "God-damned college graduate intellectuals"—felt our security at an end. When I returned to Rock Hill after attending the convention, I was surprised to discover that Rieve supporters from the North had already taken over the office. Convinced that I had better jump before I was pushed, I made many phone calls and wrote many letters during the next six months to find a new job. I finally accepted an offer to work in the South as a political organizer for the CIO Political Action Committee. Within a week after quitting the Rock Hill job, I was traveling all over North Carolina with a new cause: to win votes for a liberal named Frank Graham in the May 1950 Democratic primary for the U.S. Senate.

10

The Crusade to Elect Frank Graham, 1949–1950

FRANK GRAHAM WAS already in the U.S. Senate, but only as a temporary fill-in. Our job was to keep him there.

Following the death of North Carolina's Senator Joseph Broughton in 1949, Governor Kerr Scott had made the rather brave decision to put Graham in the vacated seat to finish out the late senator's term. Dr. Graham was a famous educator and an honored president of the University of North Carolina. He was also the kind of man the CIO dreamed of having in a position of power: he was a public advocate of civil rights legislation, higher Social Security payments, more federal aid for education, and U.S. support for the United Nations. During the Second World War, Graham had been a member of the War Labor Board, and later President Truman named him to a three-man United Nations panel which in 1949 helped persuade the Dutch government to grant independence to Indonesia. Truman's later nomination of Graham to serve on the new Atomic Energy Commission was condemned by Congressman Martin Dies of Texas, chairman of the House Un-American Activities Committee, who charged that Graham was a member of many "subversive" organizations. A subsequent FBI report refuted these charges, and Graham got a seat on the commission.

Predictably, Graham drew fire from conservatives in Congress. Within a few days of Graham's arrival in Washington in 1949, Republican John Bricker of Ohio, speaking on the floor of the Senate, declared that Graham's "record of collaboration with the communists should not be overlooked."[1] In reply, conservative Democratic Senator Clyde Hoey of North Carolina defended Graham as a loyal and trusted man. Senator Wayne Morse of Oregon, who had served with Graham on the War Labor Board, declared on the floor of the Senate that "Dr. Graham is one of the most Christ-like men I have ever met."[2]

Despite this rocky beginning, Graham became within a few months one of the most trusted members of the Senate, among both liberals and conservatives.

Here's a tale that is told of him: in April 1950, an aide to Graham asked conservative Senator Richard Russell of Georgia to urge Graham to take a stand on a particular bill. Russell turned on the aide and said rather tersely: "Young man, don't tamper with Graham's conscience. That's what we in the Senate love about him."[3]

However popular Graham managed to become in Washington, in North Carolina he had to contend with an upcoming primary that was going to be nasty. In January 1950 former senator Robert Reynolds announced his candidacy for the Senate seat. Then attorney Willis Smith, former president of the American Bar Association, entered the race as well. Though in reality Reynolds and Smith were identical twins in their conservative ideology, Smith for a short while tried to portray himself as a moderate between reactionary Reynolds and ultra-liberal Graham. In March of 1950, Reynolds ran out of money and dropped out of the race. Then Smith began to flood the state with brochures and billboards that today we would describe as "attack ads." One of Smith's street billboards in many parts of North Carolina had a large picture of Graham capped by these words in bright colors: "Frank Graham: Communism, FEPC and Socialism." The letters FEPC referred to President Truman's Fair Employment Practices Committee, which some conservatives saw as a servant of the Communists.

Though most politicians and newspaper editors assumed that Graham would be unbeatable in the primary, AFL President George Meany and CIO President Walter Reuther both feared that the forces of corporate power and racial bigotry might defeat him. Word came from Reuther that the CIO should lend Graham a hand in the upcoming campaign. That was how I became a full-time organizer for Graham.

During my visits to Graham's campaign headquarters in the state capital of Raleigh, I talked frequently with campaign manager Jeff Johnson and his deputy Terry Sanford (later president of Duke University and a U.S. senator). They told me that Graham had a very unconventional way of running his campaign. He insisted on writing all his campaign speeches himself in longhand on yellow legal pads. He refused to attack his rival, even though Smith had frequently lied about him. I was troubled by the fact that five months before the May 1950 primary, Graham's campaign had raised little money. Knowing that Graham was not a practical politician but a highly principled reformer, his friends went out on their own late in the campaign to raise funds from such well-heeled liberals as Marshall Field, Harold Ickes, Phillip Stern, Edgar Stern, and Ralph Gardner.

In 1950, Senator Hoey was involved in a separate race for the Senate. Governor Kerr Scott had settled on a policy of discouraging anyone from running against Hoey, thinking that this favor would encourage Hoey to endorse Graham in return. Late in the campaign, in a vague and somewhat halfhearted manner, Hoey agreed to do so, but I felt he got the better part of the bargain. Historians Julian M. Pleasants and August M. Burns, in their book *Frank Porter Graham and the 1950 Senate Race in North Carolina,* wrote about this policy and mentioned my minor role in the debate over it:

> The lack of a credible candidate against Hoey was a condition still troubling organized labor. . . . In contrast, many of Graham's associates remained convinced that his campaign would be better served if they did not promote opposition to Hoey, on the theory that the reactionaries, anticipating a massive Hoey victory, would remain quiescent and not fight Graham. But Dave Burgess, the CIO factotum, continued to stress that the decision was a tactical mistake. It suggested to the voters that Scott forces lacked strength—perhaps the courage— to challenge Hoey. Moreover, if Hoey ran unopposed, the conservative money interests would pour all of their resources into the campaign to defeat Graham.[4]

Unfortunately for Graham, the conservative forces in North Carolina did much as I had predicted.

As a CIO organizer, my chief concern, however, was not the strategy of the Graham headquarters but getting out the vote among CIO and AFL members. I met with NAACP and Urban League leaders in North Carolina to urge them to increase voter registration among their members and to encourage blacks to vote for Graham on election day. During the final two weeks before the primary, Smith stepped up his attacks on Graham, lying about Graham's stand on civil rights and fair employment as well as his alleged association with "Communist front" organizations. Some of Smith's brochures had pictures of the black singer Paul Robeson and American Communist Party President Earl Browder interspersed with pictures of Graham. Smith headquarters distributed thousands of brochures picturing the thirteen whites and fifty-two blacks who comprised the North Carolina Legislature back in the Reconstruction year of 1868. In large letters the caption read: "Will History Repeat Itself If Graham Is Elected?"

To counter Smith's racist appeals, my CIO colleague Dan Powell and I prepared a brochure attacking Smith's opposition to a state minimum wage of forty cents per hour. As owner of a large cotton mill in North Carolina, Smith had testified at a state hearing that such a minimum rate would be "hard, unreasonable and unnecessary." Our brochure had an authentic photograph of workers laboring in a North Carolina textile mill back in 1895. In the photograph, two-thirds of the workers were boys and girls who appeared to be well under the age of fourteen. Our caption in large letters on the brochure read:

"Will You Go Back to This with Willis Smith—15 Cents an Hour, 12 Hours a Day, Children in Mills?" When Graham saw our brochure, he demanded that we destroy all copies immediately, because he did not want to smear his opponent. Graham's demand dismayed us, but we reluctantly complied.

Despite Smith's lies and anti-black racial appeals to white voters, Graham received 303,606 votes in the May Democratic primary, Smith got 250,222, and Reynolds received 58,752 (he was still on the ballot even though he'd dropped out of the race). Graham had won the primary, but he was not out of the woods because he had fallen short of a majority vote by 11,269 votes. A runoff was scheduled for June 24. With this date only five weeks away, Smith escalated his racial attacks on Graham. Because Graham had nominated Leroy Jones, an honor student at a black high school, as an alternative candidate for West Point, the Smith campaign headquarters sent a photo of Jones to every white registered voter in the state. Other brochures put out by Smith's headquarters warned that if Graham were elected and a fair employment act were passed, there would soon be black foremen over white workers; and since 28 percent of the state's population was black, it was alleged, 28 percent of employees in all manufacturing plants by law would have to be blacks. Another Smith brochure contained dire warnings: "White People WAKE UP Before It Is Too Late. You May Not Have Another Chance. Do you want Negroes working beside you, your wife, your daughters in the mills and factories? Negroes beside you, your wife and daughters in buses, cabs and trains. Negroes sleeping is same hotels and rooming houses . . . Negroes using your toilet facilities. Frank Graham favors mixing the races."[5]

From the beginning of the campaign, the CIO staff hoped to use economic issues to persuade workers to vote for Graham. I continued to plead with Graham's staff, as I had done before the first primary, to get him to take the offensive, attack Smith, and stress Smith's anti-labor positions, but they would rejected my recommendations.

Convinced that mobilizing the black vote along with the labor vote was crucial, I met frequently with the state NAACP director, Kelly Alexander. I agreed to hire black precinct workers with union funds. I recruited white ministers who were members of a liberal group called the Fellowship of Southern Churchmen and willing to try to mollify mill workers' opposition to some of the liberal racial views held by Graham. I believed rather naively that liberal men and women of the cloth could effectively refute Smith's campaign of ugly racial propaganda and persuade voters to support Graham as a proven friend of working people.

The task wasn't an easy one. Though the CIO and AFL distributed thousands of Graham circulars all over the state and recruited hundreds of campaign workers for the second primary, our effort to build a statewide coalition between blacks and white mill workers was fragile from the start. The number of registered black voters was too small to be effective, and many whites didn't like allying themselves with blacks in any way. Indeed, I was cursed numerous times by some white workers for supporting "that nigger-lover" Graham. In addition, I found that in several counties the organizing campaign by labor and Graham's other supporters was chaotic and unprofessional, with Graham's campaign workers depending too often on local political hacks. And I soon became aware that the Smith forces were offering up to seventy dollars a day to workers willing to campaign for Smith. One textile worker told me that he had been promised twenty-five dollars if he would change his vote and support Smith in the runoff primary. In Lenoir County I observed firsthand that Smith's supporters were using both liquor and hard cash to buy votes.[6]

On the eve of the June 24 runoff primary, I sensed that Smith's accusations against Graham would carry the day. North Carolina just wasn't ready for Frank Graham. Attempting to cover my inner pessimism with outward smiles, I spent election day driving dozens of CIO members and their family members to the polls. That night, while at the wheel of my car headed home to Rock Hill, I heard the horrible news on the radio: Graham had lost. Almost a half million people had voted; Graham had lost by 19,325 votes. I recall feeling tremendously heartbroken and embittered. The next day CIO colleagues told me that at campaign headquarters in Raleigh the previous evening, Graham had shown his usual gracious ways, walking from one campaign worker to another the whole evening, trying to cheer them up and thanking them for their labors on his behalf.

There was endless speculation about how we might have managed things differently. Much of it concerned Graham's refusal to take the offensive, but some people focused on something that had happened in April of 1950. Graham had fallen seriously ill with a respiratory infection and became bedridden in Raleigh. For reasons I never ascertained, he refused to allow his fellow North Carolina Senator Hoey to indicate during a roll call in the Senate that if Graham were present he would have voted against closure of debate on a pending civil rights bill, a vote indicating opposition to the bill itself. According to biographer Warren Ashby, Graham opposed details of the bill, not its principles. Still, a vote against the bill would have softened his image on civil rights with anti-black white voters. Senator Hoey suggested after the second primary that if Graham had allowed him to report Graham's opposition, he might have gotten an additional 50,000 votes in the first primary. This would have made the runoff primary unnecessary and assured Graham six more years in the Senate.[7]

Later, when I was able to view Graham's defeat more dispassionately, it became clear that Graham had only one way to counteract the racial smears: to attack Smith and the economic big interests supporting him. This Graham refused to do. He rejected the use of what he regarded as his opponent's attack tactics because he deeply believed that his own lifetime of service in the state and the nation spoke for itself, particularly to the farmers, shopkeepers, and workers of North Carolina.[8]

The campaign over, Graham returned to his home in Chapel Hill. Now in his mid-sixties, he was in poor health and had little money. Despite his outward optimism, he felt deeply wounded by his defeat. According to Graham's biographer, Warren Ashby, his "hurt was greatest of all because he was rejected by the very people—textile workers, small farmers, and small business men—for whom he had lived and fought."[9]

I met Graham twice in ensuing years, and each time he lived up to my memory of him as optimistic, kind, and a noble public servant. One was a chance visit at the Washington, D.C., airport the day after Dwight Eisenhower first won the presidency in 1952. Graham greeted me with a warm smile and, knowing what I'd think of the presidential result, said, "Cheer up, Dave, the world hasn't come to an end. There will be a better day tomorrow." The second time was in 1959, when Graham was on his way to Kashmir to mediate the long-standing territorial dispute between India and Pakistan. He greeted me with that same smile, asked about the health of my family, and expressed hope he'd be able to do something about the dispute. As it turned out, India and Pakistan are still in conflict over Kashmir forty years later.

Graham died in 1972 at the age of eighty-six. A few days later, Jonathan Daniels, editor of the *Raleigh News and Observer* and former chairman of the Democratic Party in North Carolina, referred back to the 1950 campaign in a fitting epitaph for his friend: "In facile judgment it might be said that Frank Graham lived too long. In his last two decades of his life he moved as a man who had been rejected, in a political campaign of savage intensity, by people he loved the most. . . . [He] had labored for the vision of peace on earth and had seen it mocked. Yet his faith in America never wavered. He was a little man nobody pushed around in his adherence to righteousness as he saw it."[10]

11

The Fellowship of Southern Churchmen, 1942–1955

IN THE 1940s and early 1950s, Alice and I always looked forward to getting into the car and driving, sometimes hundreds of miles, to the annual conferences of a group called the Fellowship of Southern Churchmen. Founded in 1934, it was a Christian organization of white and black clergy and laypeople who opposed racial and economic injustice and got involved in early environmental causes as well. I have always felt that the Fellowship has not received its fair share of attention in the many books that have been written about the civil rights movement in the South during the 1930s, 1940s, and 1950s. Let me correct that imbalance a bit here.

Today it's hard to imagine the social environment of the South in which Fellowship members lived and how radical their views were for the time. A Communist Party member, in fact, is said to have remarked after attending one of its meetings in the late 1930s: "I felt like a conservative in that crowd." The Fellowship was publicly up against just about everything that defined the Jim Crow South: white and black schools that were separate and grossly unequal, lack of voting rights for most blacks, and the requirements that blacks sit in the back of the bus and keep away from public toilets and drinking fountains marked "white." State segregation laws enacted in the 1880s and 1890s were strictly enforced, both by the courts and law authorities and, at times, by white vigilantes.

Members of the Fellowship were also committed to the union of whites and blacks in worship and in social action campaigns. As Howard Kester, a driving force in the Fellowship and for many years its executive secretary, once reminded me: "Our one hour of worship on Sunday mornings here in the South is the most segregated hour for us good Christians." It was Kester who had written a declaration that the group issued on Christmas Day 1942. It said: "While our birth in the Kingdom of God on earth commits us to overcome these barriers that hurt and divide the human family, our democratic faith summons us to oppose these obstacles that bar the path of full citizenship."[1]

Over the years, many Fellowship members paid dearly for publicly standing by such beliefs. Alva Taylor, professor of religion at Vanderbilt University in Nashville, was fired because of his Christian radicalism. Charles Jones, pastor of the major Presbyterian church in Chapel Hill, North Carolina, was brought up on charges before a specially formed commission of the Orange Presbytery. Commission members reprimanded him for allowing students from a nearby black college to eat breakfast at his church and to attend Sunday-morning worship services. Later the commission also found him guilty of giving overnight sanctuary at his church to black and white "freedom riders" who were seeking to desegregate interstate buses in a 1947 movement called the Journey of Reconciliation. After eight years of this kind of harassment, Jones resigned from his church.

There was serious trouble too for one of the founding prophets of the Fellowship, a Southern Baptist pastor and biblical scholar named Clarence Jordan. Believing in following the example of Jesus, he and his wife and a couple named Mabel and Martin England founded in the early 1940s the Koinonia interracial cooperative farm near the town of Americus in southern Georgia. I visited the farm more than once and talked at length with this gangly man, who, though he was an advanced biblical scholar, dressed in dirty blue overalls like any other south Georgia farmer. He had a ready smile, a keen sense of humor, and the inner strength of solid Christian faith. Soon after the Supreme Court's 1954 ruling on school desegregation, hostile neighbors circulated rumors about "race mixing" and "Communist infiltration" at Koinonia farm. Two years later his local critics persuaded feed suppliers and produce purchasers to boycott the farm, and white supremacists dynamited a large produce stand the farm operated next to a major highway. Jordan commented to a *Time* magazine reporter soon after the bombing: "I was raised in this county near Talbotton. My brothers and sisters live there now. I know how the people of Americus feel. I would probably feel the same if I had not seen some of the teachings of Jesus Christ."[2]

Jordan left one other important legacy when he died of a heart attack in 1969: he had inspired Millard Fuller, a millionaire who had given away almost all his wealth and then joined the farm staff, to establish Habitat for Humanity in Americus. Formed seven years after Clarence's death, it has already overseen the construction of more than eighty thousand Habitat homes in America and in poor countries overseas.

As impressive a man as Jordan was Howard Kester, who was the driving force in the Fellowship for many years. A white southerner with courtly manners and sometimes excessive moralism, Kester was a radical from the days of his youth. He was asked to leave Princeton Seminary and the Vanderbilt School of Religion in Nashville because of his radical beliefs and frequent clashes with conservative professors. During the early 1930s he worked for the Fellowship of Reconciliation (FOR), a pacifist religious group whose leaders asked him to investigate lynchings in Mississippi and other southern states. He helped to found in 1934 both the Fellowship of Southern Churchmen and the Southern Tenant Farmers Union. From 1935 to 1940 he was the chief national spokesman for the STFU and a fund-raiser for its National Sharecroppers Fund. Kester and union president Harry Mitchell visited the White House in the mid-1930s, and soon after, First Lady Eleanor Roosevelt made a public statement about her support for the fund and her cash contribution to the fund.

Kester was a brave man and had many opportunities to show it. He was jailed by sheriffs in Arkansas and other southern states and more than once escaped violent death at the hands of cotton plantation owners and their armed agents. On one occasion, as he later recounted to me, a deputy sheriff put a pistol to his head and shouted, "You God-damned son of a bitch, you think more of a dog than you do for us white folks. I'm minded to blow your brains out right here." In 1939 Kester brought Socialist Party leader Norman Thomas to Birdsong, Mississippi, to address a gathering of black and white sharecroppers and tenant farmers. The white sheriff and many indignant white citizens shouted Thomas down as he began to speak. Uttering threats, they forced Thomas and Kester to retreat to their car and return to Memphis.

By 1939 Kester was deeply troubled by the continuing factionalism within the STFU. He was convinced that some of the union's leaders lacked integrity and were "loose livers." Mitchell told the tale years later of how Kester went to New York City to raise money and happened to stay at a hotel where Mitchell and a young woman were having an overnight affair. During the night the couple was awakened by a voice coming from Kester's room. Creeping to its partially open door, they found Kester on his knees praying loudly for the sinful couple.[3]

Though he considered himself in many ways a follower of Karl Marx, Kester actively opposed Communists in the labor movement and often said that they shouldn't be welcomed in the Fellowship either. He got his way. In 1940, after a number of alleged fellow travelers left the Fellowship, Kester became the group's first full-time executive secretary. In a 1945 letter to me, he explained his decision five years earlier: "I had lost faith in the promise of politics, unionism and the organized church. The kind of health [the South] needs will come not through politics or economic organization. There has to be an ethical orientation, a moral confrontation based on the teachings of Jesus and the principles of democracy."[4]

I last saw Kester at his home in Black Mountain, North Carolina, in the mid-1950s. He was still what he had been when I first met him—an intense but tender man who did not suffer fools or compromisers gladly. Despite his gracious southern manners, he had little time for small talk. He seemed to be carrying the weight of the world on his slender shoulders. Possibly in our troubled world his divine discontent was a necessary precondition for all who confront people deaf to the cries of the oppressed and blind to the moral demands of the Bible. I admired Kester's courage, his clarity of thought, and his devotion to the poor. I only wish that God had given him a greater measure of happiness and peace in his life before he died in 1977.

With help from Alva Taylor, then teaching at the historically black Fisk University in Nashville, I organized the first Fellowship church-labor conference in 1945. Pastors and labor organizers and workers came to the gathering, which, like all Fellowship meetings, was interracial. We discussed the chasm between churches and the labor movement in the South, that sad fact which I had come up against countless times in my years in the South. We agreed on what churches and unions have in common, and the theological basis for stronger cooperation.

My involvement with the Fellowship included writing a thirty-page illustrated brochure entitled "Trade Unions and Preachers." This 1953 brochure, which was based on my experience as a union organizer, told a fictional story about conflicts between an anti-CIO pastor and a pro-CIO one, and between anti-union and pro-union workers in a textile mill. With financial assistance from the Fellowship and the Religion and Labor Foundation of New Haven, Connecticut, the brochure was circulated to pastors, lay leaders, and union members in many southern states.

Between 1944 and 1949 the Fellowship enjoyed, in my opinion, its most dynamic period, because of the inspired leadership of a new executive secretary named Nelle Morton. She took office shortly after Kester resigned in 1944. For many years she had been a Methodist social activist. She started her job at Fellowship headquarters in Chapel Hill by writing hundreds of letters to white and black church leaders throughout the South who were fighting racial injustice. She urged them to become members of a south-wide religious coalition that the Fellowship was organizing. She skillfully edited the group's quarterly journal *Prophetic Religion*. She formed three Fellowship commissions to deal with race relations, cooperation with labor unions, and preserving the soil. As a result of her hard work, the Fellowship's membership and attendance at its annual conferences dramatically increased. These annual conferences, as Robert F. Martin accurately observes in his evaluation of the Fellowship, "deepened the members' insight into contemporary problems and fostered a badly needed sense of fraternity among a small group of radical Christians who might otherwise have labored in isolation."[5]

I have to confess, however, to being behind one of its less successful episodes. In 1948 I obtained an $8,000 grant from Nancy Blaine Harrison, my former textile union colleague in Rock Hill. The money enabled the Fellowship to purchase 385 acres of beautiful mountain land near Swananoa, a small town east of Asheville, North Carolina. My brother-in-law, David McVoy, then a professor of architecture at the University of Florida, drew up elaborate plans without charge for the construction of a conference center at Swananoa large enough to house six hundred people. Kester, who drove to the site with us to tramp around it and breathe the fresh air, dubbed the place the future "Seminary in the Cornfield." With his vision and hope, Kester launched a campaign to raise money to begin construction. But this turned out to be a cause that most church folk would not give their money to. The conference center was never built, and the land was eventually sold.

In 1957 the Fellowship held its last annual conference in Nashville. Attending were three hundred pastors and laypersons and none other than Dr. Martin Luther King, Jr. After the conference, King wrote to Kester expressing satisfaction with the gathering. Dated May 31, 1957, the letter concluded with this hopeful message: "I still have faith in the church and the Christian ministry, and if the problem [of the South] is solved the church must stand in the forefront of the struggle. Let us continue to hope and pray that the brighter daybreak of freedom and brotherhood will emerge in the not-too-distant future."[6] As it turned out, the 1957 conference was the Fellowship's last. Running out of members and money, it disbanded that same year.

In his 1991 biography of Kester, Robert Martin attributes the decline of the Fellowship to the growing weariness of some of the older members, increased reliance on conciliatory methods at a time when civil disobedience was gaining steam, the lack of a new generation of younger members, and the relatively low percentage of blacks and women in the Fellowship. Most of the committed radicals in the 1950s, Martin observed, "were devoting their energies to the more dramatically active groups that were beginning to proliferate."[7]

Ironically, the Fellowship did in fact die at the very time that Martin Luther King, Jr., was becoming a national figure in the civil rights movement. With the success of the Montgomery bus boycott, King and other leaders of his new organization, the Southern Christian Leadership Conference, rejected FOR's proposal to make the conference interracial. So the Fellowship's advocacy of interracial coalitions was not a good fit for the times. The criticism that it was mainly white and mainly male is valid, but contrary to Martin's claim that its older prophets were "growing tired," most of those with whom I kept in close touch over subsequent years remained faithful radicals for the rest of their lives. None, however, were short-term optimists. They shared a common vision of a New Jerusalem descending upon the South which would become a reality long after they had passed from the scene. I believe that in important respects, the group helped prepare the South for the civil rights movement. Its members plowed hard ground and cleared the highways to freedom for younger generations, both black and white. The prophetic record of the Fellowship of Southern Churchmen and its dedicated members speaks for itself.

12

Leading the CIO in Georgia, 1951–1955

WE COULD HEAR the men climbing the stairs now. I and a co-worker, a burly steelworker union official named Charles Mathias, tensed up and prepared for a confrontation. It was 1953, and we were standing in the door, George Wallace–style, of the southern regional office of the United Packinghouse Workers of America (UPWA) in Atlanta. The men approaching, we knew, had been sent from Chicago by Tony Stevens, the UPWA's Communist-sympathizing organizational director, and they intended to take over the office and oust the elected regional director. They soon reached the top of the stairs, and we saw them—six men in blue jeans and sports shirts, and a rather short man in a dark pin-striped suit, who it soon became clear was their leader.

I had become executive secretary of the CIO's Georgia State Council—in effect the head of the council—in 1951, and found out quickly that it was much more than a desk job. I worked in the state capital in Atlanta, addressed late-night meetings of union members, tried to build consensus among disparate unions, attempted to form coalitions with liberals both white and black, and appeared on the new medium of television to speak up for the labor side of things. It was an education as well as exhausting work for me. I had arrived in Georgia feeling that the union movement had a fair supply of idealists, but I found I spent a lot of my time dealing with overt racism and factionalism in our own union ranks.

Seeing the menacing faces of the approaching men, I wondered how we were going to stand up to them—here, after all, was a variation on the hypothetical picket-line situation in which, despite my pacifist ideals, I had always thought I'd be willing to use violence. This confrontation drew on a long-simmering fight within the UPWA. The UPWA's national president was a man named Ralph Helstein. He and his organization director, Tony Stevens, were very unhappy with McKinney, the UPWA's southern regional director,

96

who had been elected by union members in the South but didn't care for the Communist Party line. So these men had been sent to throw McKinney out, physically if necessary.

Standing at the office door with Charlie Mathias, I put on my best bold face. I shouted, in rather officious language: "We have been told by CIO President Walter Reuther to defend Director McKinney and block you from taking over his regional office. He was duly elected to his position. I command you all to leave." I looked the short man in the eye, and realized I had met him before. He was in fact a clergyman on the union's national staff. He replied to my demand by chiding me. "What right do you have, as a fellow Christian minister," he asked, "to stop me and my colleagues from obeying the directions of our UPWA leaders to take over this office? Get out of our way!" I found myself yelling: "Get the hell out of here yourself!" To my surprise, there was no scuffle. The men and their well-dressed leader turned on their heels and disappeared back down the stairs.

Even without this kind of trouble (and this particular fight went on for months longer), the CIO in Georgia had a very difficult task in advancing labor's status. A few years earlier the state legislature had passed a "right-to-work" law outlawing the "union shop," which made union membership a precondition of employment. As in South Carolina and most other southern states, manufacturers and their highly paid lawyers were doing everything in their power to weaken the unions and block their organizing efforts. Moreover, the corporate powers corrupted politics and politicians in this one-party state of Georgia. It was common knowledge that in close races in Democratic primaries, corporations sometimes contributed to both the leading candidates. Or they sometimes funded the most liberal candidate on the ballot as a means of splitting the liberal vote and electing a conservative they favored.

Across the South, the CIO had often feuded with the AFL. But during my four years in Atlanta, I teamed up with two AFL lobbyists to create the Joint AFL-CIO Legislative Committee. Our focus was repealing the "right-to-work" law, raising unemployment benefits, increasing welfare and workers' compensation, lowering the state sales tax, increasing the state minimum wage, and opposing Governor Herman Talmadge's plan to extend the "county unit" system from the May primaries to the general elections in November. Under this county unit system, each county, based on its total population, was given one, three, or six votes in an electoral body convened after a popular vote. The victor in any local, congressional, or statewide race would be the candidate who received the largest number of county unit votes rather than the largest number of popular votes. The county unit system tended to favor the election of conservatives and white racists in the many rural counties of Georgia. It essentially discounted the votes of people in cities, where most CIO and AFL union members lived.

The Joint AFL-CIO Legislative Committee also nominated union members to sit on advisory committees of state agencies, recruited and endorsed candidates for public office, and lobbied for progressive legislation. My job in particular was to prepare brochures about key legislative goals. Over the months that we representatives of the AFL and CIO worked together, I know we gained the grudging respect of Governor Talmadge and most legislators, because they knew we could not be bribed or influenced by special favors.

I soon learned that white officers and members of several CIO unions in segregated Georgia did not always walk the moral high road on race advocated by the CIO. For instance, almost all workers at the huge General Motors Corporation plant in Atlanta were white. The community had many blacks who would have qualified for the high-paying jobs there, but they were generally employed only as sweepers in that plant. Some of the union workers in this plant were also members of white supremacist groups.

One day I received a phone call from a senior official of the United Auto Workers headquarters in Detroit. He asked me to arrange a trip through the GM plant in Atlanta for a trade union delegation from India. Since my friend Charles Thompson, director of the Atlanta NAACP, had a long-standing request with me to tour the plant, I called him and asked if he'd like to go along with the delegation from India. He said yes. The night after the tour, the president of the plant's UAW local telephoned me and loudly condemned me for "sneaking that God-damned nigger Thompson into our plant."

The dispute that led to the standoff at the union's office door had racial overtones as well. When word leaked out that the men were coming from Chicago to eject McKinney, Bob Oliver, the chief assistant of CIO President Reuther, asked me to call all the UPWA unions in the South and request that they send all the money from their union treasuries to me for deposit in a special escrow account until the battle over McKinney's tenure was settled. The purpose was to safeguard the funds. But members of the group that came down from Chicago got on the phone after we turned them back and told black leaders of UPWA locals all over the South that I was a vicious white racist and they should not to cooperate with me. In the end, more than half of the unions I called sent me money from their treasuries. Most of the unions that did were predominantly white. Unions refusing my request were predominantly black.

We later lost this round of the fight. Because it was becoming clear that McKinney lacked sufficient support to win a new term in office at the upcoming UPWA national convention, Reuther's assistant told me to send back to the locals the money I had collected. Two years later, however, things turned around in our favor. At the urging of Emil Mazey, the United Auto Workers national secretary-treasurer, UPWA President Helstein fired Tony Stevens on grounds that he too often followed the Communist Party line.

Though I was officially responsible to the board of the Georgia CIO Council and its president, Bill Crawford, in reality I was my own boss, and I liked that. I traveled extensively and conducted several political education workshops in various corners of the state, working quietly to lay the foundation for a political coalition among union members, black community leaders, and liberals both white and black. Numerous defeats interspersed with a few victories made my work exciting but highly unpredictable.

Alice and I now had four children—in addition to Laurel and Lyman, son John Stewart, named after my father, was born in 1951, and our youngest daughter, Emagene ("Genie"), appeared in 1953. We had a more comfortable home life. We were living in a house we had bought in northeast Atlanta. It was graced with a spacious backyard. During our four years in the city we made many friends among our neighbors, union colleagues and their families, leaders of the black community, and liberal politicians.

The New Georgia Politics

We fitted well in Atlanta in part because this city was undergoing a political and economic renaissance. Progressive Mayor Bill Hartsfield campaigned successfully on the slogan "Atlanta is too busy to hate." Ralph McGill, a middle-of-the-road opponent of segregation, edited the *Atlanta Constitution*. Lillian Smith was writing novels and essays about the ugly underside of southern segregation. There was a very important exception to this trend toward racial tolerance and understanding, however. The man who represented the Atlanta area in Congress was the reactionary James ("Jim") Davis, who drew his support generally not from Atlanta and the surrounding Fulton County but from rural Rockland County and suburban DeKalb County. The county unit system made victory in the 1952 Democratic primary a virtual certainty for him, unless a strong candidate could be found to oppose him. In the fall of 1951, I was asked to join an unusual team of liberal Democrats set on finding such a candidate for the primary, which, in the light of state voters' tendency to favor Democrats, functioned as a *de facto* general election. Participating in this search committee were Mayor Hartsfield; Rufus Clement, president of black Atlanta University; Atlanta attorney Morris Abram; Josephine Wilkins, head of Citizens Against the Georgia County Unit Amendment; and various lawyers, NAACP leaders, and AFL and CIO representatives. After weeks of discussion, our committee chose as our favored candidate a white attorney named Baxter Jones, a veteran of the Second World War and recently named Man of the Year by the Atlanta Junior Chamber of Commerce.

Jones reluctantly agreed to run. The main points of his platform were to abolish the county unit system and streamline the federal government to save taxpayers money. Despite what turned out to be rather meager financial aid from the CIO, the AFL, and other supporting organizations, Jones ran an excellent campaign, soliciting votes door-to-door and appearing frequently on TV and radio. In the May 1952 primary, Jones received a majority of the popular votes cast. But because of the county unit system, the Georgia Election Board declared Davis the winner since he had lost Atlanta's Fulton County but had carried DeKalb and Rockland Counties and had amassed more county unit votes in the district than Jones had. Members of our committee persuaded Jones to file a class-action suit in federal court claiming that the county unit system was unconstitutional and that Davis's "victory" should be overturned. We settled in for a long fight.

Meanwhile, another front was opening in the county unit battle. Governor Talmadge placed on the November 1952 general election ballot an amendment to extend the county unit system from the primaries to the general election. He immediately launched a well-financed campaign to win support for the amendment. His brochures warned that the amendment's defeat would lead to "mixed schools, boss rule and greater organized crime." His campaign propaganda blatantly appealed on radio and TV and in the press to the racist fears of white voters. One brochure pictured an NAACP-sponsored interracial dance which took place "just two blocks away from Governor Talmadge's capitol." One of Talmadge's last brochures claimed that if his amendment were not passed, black voters in the Atlanta area "would reduce every county from its present status of active and effective representation to that of mere vassalage."

During the summer and fall of 1952, many of my labor colleagues and I became active in a group known as Citizens Against the Georgia County Unit Amendment, directed by Josephine Wilkins. We fought back with a statewide campaign that was spirited but had nowhere near the financial backing of the Talmadge operation. On election day, we were elated to find that a majority of white and black voters had cast their ballots against the Talmadge-inspired amendment.

Baxter Jones won his suit, though he had to wait a very long time. For six years, the case slowly made its way through the courts before arriving at the U.S. Supreme Court in 1958. Meanwhile, Davis was reelected to Congress three more times. Atlanta attorney Morris Abram delivered an impassioned attack against the county unit system before the Supreme Court. The justices, then headed by Chief Justice Earl Warren, ruled unanimously that the county unit system was unconstitutional. But Baxter Jones did not reap the fruits of court's decision. He never again ran for public office, and in 1961 he and his wife were killed in a plane crash at Orly Airport near Paris.

Adlai Stevenson and Southern Politics

In the 1952 general election, a great majority of Georgia voters supported Democratic presidential candidate Adlai Stevenson, who lost to Republican Dwight Eisenhower. But in the months after the vote, leaders of the National Democratic Committee began recognizing conservatives and even former Dixiecrats as the most legitimate spokespersons for the party in the South. Concerned about this trend, I wrote to Stevenson in my capacity as executive secretary of the Georgia CIO. I told him I believed he was a "man of principle" and urged him to support liberal Democrats in the South against the entrenched conservatives. In October 1953, Stevenson accepted Governor Talmadge's invitation to address a joint session of the Georgia legislature. While in Atlanta, in response to a request from me, he met with me and board members of the Georgia CIO Council for an hour and a half at the council headquarters. Stevenson struck me that day as a modest, highly articulate man with strong convictions, but at the same time as a searcher for compromise and consensus among contending factions and individuals. I felt that he highly underestimated the harm done to him by southern conservatives both before and after the national election he had lost the previous year. A week after our meeting I wrote him a letter summarizing our meeting and thanking him for his visit. I enclosed a copy of my article "Struggle for the South," which appeared in the January 1953 issue of *Progressive* magazine. In the article I called for greater loyalty to the Democratic Party among southern Democrats and warned that if Stevenson succumbed to the unfaithful Southerners and relinquished control, the Democratic Party would die for lack of a national appeal. Stevenson and other leaders of the party, I predicted, "will then become caretakers" and will soon "find themselves as undertakers of a splinter party dominated by tories."[1]

In his letter of reply, Stevenson said that he liked my article. Although I was pleased to be flattered by a man whom I admired, I was troubled that in his letter he gave no hint of how he was going to handle the southern senators, congressmen, and governors who had given him no support or at best lukewarm support in the general election of November 1952. Later I wrote him predicting that the Georgia delegates to the 1956 Democratic convention "would be hold-overs from the Talmadge regime." I complained again that progressive Democrats in Georgia "had received little or no help from the National Democratic Committee in recent years." My sentiments about many modern conservative politicians in the South were well summarized by a sentence from an article entitled "Adlai in Dixie" by Jonathan Freeman (a pen name) in the February 1954 issue of *Progressive* magazine: "The new leaders of the Democratic Party in the South don't wear galoshes, chew plug tobacco or speak slovenly English but they remain enemies of progress in the South."[2]

I've written a lot in these pages about racist feelings in the union movement, but slowly things were changing. I have always felt that one of my proudest accomplishments in Georgia was to help organize an integrated annual state convention of the CIO in a segregated state. It took place in 1953 at the Dempsey Hotel in downtown Macon. Black and white delegates ate together and stayed overnight at this hotel. Our keynote speaker was Henderson Lanham, the only liberal in the Georgia congressional delegation. Pulling this off did not come without friction, however: some white delegates criticized me for working "too closely" with the NAACP, the Urban League, the League of Women Voters, and other "do-good" organizations in Georgia.

My Recommendations to the CIO President

Unfortunately, as the key indicator of union success—victories in factory representation elections conducted by the National Labor Relations Board—the CIO's record was highly negative. During my four years in Georgia, the CIO lost far more organizing campaigns than it won. Meanwhile, starting in 1954, I was alarmed to find that many international CIO unions were reducing both their cash contributions to the CIO Southern Drive and the number of able staff people loaned to it. In November 1954, I wrote a letter of appeal to CIO President Reuther based on what I had learned in more than ten years as a labor organizer in the South. My letter to Reuther read in part:

Organizing unions in the South is not a matter of waiting for an opportune moment and then rushing in with reinforcements. It is rather a day-to-day problem of how best to train workers to organize themselves. The job of organizing will take CIO manpower—organizers who are dedicated to the proposition that the South cannot be free and democratic without a strong and progressive labor movement, organizers who are able and willing to settle down in the South for months and most probably for years before the goal of organizing is successfully reached. . . . Many of us who have been working in the South during the last several lean years have come to the conclusion that certain top leaders of the CIO have little firsthand knowledge of the South and lack at times the burning desire to organize workers in the South. As a result, we feel that we lack friends in court on top committees of the CIO who can articulate our growing concern about the increasing neglect of our organizing needs in Dixie by many of your colleagues at the CIO headquarters and at offices of our larger CIO international unions.

In my letter to Reuther I recommended that the CIO survey the movement of industry from the North to the South, investigate why so many unorganized workers in the South are anti-union, persuade international unions to increase their cash contributions substantially and lend their most skilled organizers to the campaign, and draw up a new master plan for the Southern Drive itself.

In November 1954 I attended the national CIO convention in Los Angeles. Here for the first time I met Victor Reuther, younger brother of Walter and then director of the CIO's International Relations Department. He had read my letter and said he liked it. He told me, however, that Walter was not making organizing the South a present priority because he was preoccupied with plans for the AFL-CIO merger, which was scheduled to take place in December 1955. For me Victor's words were small consolation, but at least they were an explanation. And then Victor asked a question that was to send my life off in a completely different direction.

13

The FBI Investigates Me, 1955 and 1966

VIC REUTHER'S QUESTION was this: would I be interested in moving to Burma, as the American labor attaché at the American Embassy there? Vic explained that I would be a U.S. Foreign Service Officer, but at the same time I wouldn't be parting ways with the American labor movement. I would be nominated by the CIO and in effect be its man in Rangoon, the capital of Burma. Say the word, I was told, and Walter Reuther will submit my name to the State Department.

Factional politics played a role in the invitation, I later discovered. What was to be a long and bitter rivalry between Walter Reuther and the AFL's head, George Meany, was already at full boil. The U.S. State Department and Labor Department had in effect assigned certain countries to each of them for labor attaché nominations, and now each was scrambling to get his people into the jobs. Walter Reuther's patronage brought me the nomination; later it would cause me some painful problems with Meany.

Needless to say, I was stunned by the proposal. I returned home to Alice with the exciting news, which we discussed at length. On the personal side, the idea of moving to some far-off land where we knew no one was intimidating. And I was hardly a fan of the Eisenhower administration, which had entered office in 1953 and was prosecuting the Cold War with enthusiasm. But in the end, we said yes. I was flattered to be made such an offer, to be invited into the halls of power. And after more than a decade of working in the South, both Alice and I were weary and wanted a change. I had affectionate feelings about Asia from my boyhood and relished the idea of seeing Asia again. And in the meantime Walter Reuther had emerged as one of my abiding heroes. If he wanted me to go abroad (the country to which I was to be nominated was soon changed from Burma to India), who was I to say no?

There was just one formality to take care of—a security clearance by the

Federal Bureau of Investigation (FBI). In February 1955, while still in Atlanta, I completed my lengthy application form and sent it to the State Department. I assumed I would be cleared by May at the latest and that I and the family would be leaving for India shortly thereafter. But May came and went with no reply from the State Department. In July, the family moved to Alice's hometown of Cummington in Massachusetts to await the clearance which Victor Reuther assured us was just around the corner. I packed a suitcase and went to Washington to work at CIO headquarters as a temporary staff member of the International Relations Department, headed by Victor. I roomed at the home of Victor and Sophie Reuther in Washington's upper northwest section.

Soon there were signs of very real problems. I was called to an interview with the Labor Department's assistant secretary for international affairs, a man named Ernest Wilkins, who was the brother of NAACP Director Roy Wilkins. Given my long work in behalf of labor and civil rights, I arrived at his office thinking that my visit was just a courtesy call. But on Wilkins's desk was an ominous-looking stack of files that he kept referring to during what turned into a very lengthy interview. He first explained that he would be asking me many questions to ascertain my suitability for the post in India. We talked, and then he asked me to name all the organizations I had joined since my freshman year at Oberlin College some twenty years earlier. I guessed that he wanted to know if I had been a member of any organization listed as subversive by the House Un-American Activities Committee. I wracked my brain for an adequate response and managed to name a few organizations that I had joined. Implying that I was not giving him thorough answers, he continued to consult that mammoth file on his desk, which I now guessed was the FBI's report on me. Again and again he asked to list the organizations I had joined since 1935. Since I could remember only a few of these organizations, he accused me of not being altogether forthcoming and of withholding important information from him. I left his office downhearted, convinced I had failed the test.

Looking back, it's hard to understand why I didn't see all this coming. This was, after all, just a few years past the height of the McCarthy era, when even a hint of association with a "subversive" organization could sink a career. But I had begun the application process naively, believing that everything was going to sail through thanks to the backing of the Reuthers and the CIO.

More than thirty years later, courtesy of the Freedom of Information Act, I got a look at a good part of my FBI file. After submitting a formal request to the State Department for its release, I was sent 275 pages of what turned out to be a 400-page document outlining the results of "field investigations" that the FBI did on me in 1955 and again in 1966. I later wrote several letters to the State Department asking for the missing 125 pages. But on grounds that releasing these to me might "endanger national security," State Department and FBI officials turned down all my requests.

Examining the pages of my file in 1988 was both fascinating and disturbing. It showed the length to which FBI agents in our ostensibly free society felt at liberty to pry into my private affairs and pass judgment on my political beliefs. Dozens of FBI investigators had interviewed many people in twelve states and the District of Columbia in 1955, and eleven years later additional people living in India and Indonesia. Our bank records and credit ratings were checked. Even police blotters were reviewed. All of the people whom the FBI interviewed were asked a long and standard list of questions about my appearance, political opinions, ideology, and smoking and drinking habits. They were asked about who was entertained or stayed overnight at our home, what books and newspapers I read, my sexual orientation, whether or not I had a stable marriage, and so forth. What did I think about capitalism, socialism, and communism, loyalty to the nation, and the "American way of life"? How close was I to the Reuthers and George Meany? Did I have friends in the White House and the Eisenhower administration?

Happily, I had some fans out there. Truman Douglas, head of the Board of Homeland Ministries of the future United Church of Christ, described me as fully masculine and a determined opponent of communism—attributes sure to win favor for me in the evaluation. Others described me as above average in intelligence, neat in appearance, neither a drinker nor a smoker, not a user of profane language. I was a church member, a devoted family man enjoying a stable married life, they said.

But needless to say, I had quite a few critics too. In view of who they were, I found myself taking pride in their observations more than once when I read the file. In some cases, they sized up my political beliefs correctly, I think. In others, they had me and my motivations all wrong. The names of my critics were inked out in the FBI documents, but judging by their choice of words and where they were interviewed by FBI agents, I was able to guess who many of them were.

For instance, Charles Mathias, the Steel Workers Union official who back in 1953 had helped me to guard the regional office in Atlanta from the UPWA gang from Chicago, remarked that I "crusaded too much on racial issues and worked too closely with the NAACP office in Atlanta." He believed that my ideology was "closely allied with socialism" and concluded that I should not be employed by the State Department, particularly "in Southeast Asia where the threat of communism is imminent and socialism is only a step away from communism."

Likewise, an unnamed AFL official in Charlotte, North Carolina, recommended that the State Department stay away from me. He told the FBI that my views were "socialistic in nature" and that I believed in "government control of industry" rather than the free-enterprise system.

An executive of the Industrial Cotton Mill in Rock Hill, South Carolina, which we had unionized, characterized me as "a man floundering and trying to grasp some straw of reality" and—because I had left the full-time Christian ministry—a man who has "an instability in his emotional make-up."

A high official of the Cone Cotton Mill in Greensboro, North Carolina, faulted me for walking on the union picket line one night in April 1951 with my oldest two children, ages six and four. He said that my activity during the strike against his company "was completely un-American" since I "kept walking through the strikers [that night] shouting and making speeches in an attempt to stir up the crowd to the point where violence might occur."

A Memphis minister, showing the anti-labor bias that was so common among some southern clergy, found my views were "not only socialist but extremely socialistic." He accused me of having half-baked ideas about "the government owing the poor people a living regardless of their efforts." He concluded that I had a "phobia against anyone who had everything" and accused me of wanting to be with people of another race more than my own race, since I "mixed more with blacks than with whites." This was a theme heard from other critics of mine. The file revealed that several of our nearest white neighbors in Atlanta were disturbed by the presence of black guests at our dinner table. Some of these neighbors believed the false rumor that we had planned to sell our home to a black Atlanta University professor in June 1955.

By and large, the FBI accurately tracked down what organizations I had joined or been affiliated with over the years. Among them were the Youth Committee Against War, the American Youth Against War, the American Student Union, the Southern Conference for Human Welfare, and the Coordinating Committee for Non-Violent Disobedience Against Military Segregation. Some of these organizations had been named as Communist fronts and subversive by the House Un-American Activities Committee. There was one glaring factual error in the report. Alice, whose maiden name was Stevens, was at one point falsely identified as Alice Stevens of Oneida, New York, who had been an elector of the Communist Party in the 1940 presidential election.

The file showed that as I and the family cooled our heels in 1955, there were serious doubts as to whether we would go to India at all. A high State Department official recommended in August 1955 that I be interviewed because of my "apparent radicalism" and my association with "questionable organizations."

On September 5 a State Department personnel officer wrote a memo based on my FBI evaluation to the deputy director of personnel stating: "There are indications that he may not possess the requisite objectivity to carry out the Department's policies. He failed to make a full disclosure of his affiliations officially characterized as communist. Although witnesses describe him as anti-communist, and he so describes himself, some people feel that he is not a strong advocate of the capitalist system, believing [instead] in a labor form of government and holding views which coincide with socialist philosophy."

Yet in the end, I made it through. The reason was old-fashioned politics. I became valuable to one of Georgia's senators, Walter George. He was planning to seek renomination in the 1956 Democratic primary and believed that getting me approved would be a favor to labor and help deliver to him the state's labor vote. In Washington, I had lunch with George's chief of staff, John Carlton. At Carlton's suggestion, I wrote a letter to Senator George, who was then head of the Senate's Foreign Relations Committee, outlining the hardships to me and my family caused by the delays in my appointment. After I met the senator, he agreed to support my nomination.

He made good on his promise. One day, he summoned Assistant Secretary of State Max Bishop to his office. At the senator's direction, I was shown to a seat in a room adjoining his office with the door slightly ajar. I heard Senator George giving Bishop and his State Department colleagues hell for delaying the appointment of "this Georgia boy of mine." Bishop agreed to do all he could to press my case with Secretary of State John Foster Dulles. The following week the senator sent a letter to India to Ambassador John Sherman Cooper, a former Kentucky senator, detailing his efforts on my behalf. The ambassador forwarded a copy of George's letter to Secretary Dulles.

Walter Reuther got involved too. He paid an unannounced visit to Assistant Secretary of State Robert Murphy and outlined the terms of agreement between the State and Labor Departments to allow Meany and Reuther to nominate candidates for labor attaché posts. Murphy agreed to speed things up. I was finally cleared by both the FBI and the State Department in late October 1955. I called Alice in Massachusetts, and we celebrated over the telephone line.

My own disturbing experience of being investigated twice by the FBI—it happened again eleven years later when I was nominated to be an official American member of the staff of the United Nations Children's Fund (UNICEF)—raises important questions for all Americans. I discovered that the second FBI report, in 1966, was highly critical of me, even though since entering the Foreign Service in 1955, I had been promoted from the rank of Foreign Service Officer 3 to Foreign Service Officer 2 in 1959, had received the State Department's Meritorious Service Award in 1959, and had served in posts in the State Department, the Agency for International Development, and the Peace Corps. The 1966 report, according to the written words of a top State Department personnel official, was most critical of me. It described me in terms that the Department would consider damning: "a pacifist, conscientious objector, extremely . . . liberal, socialist, racial integrationist. He is . . . undoubtedly a man inclined toward labor types of . . . government with controls of labor and management. He is reported to be a protege of Victor Reuther . . . and hand picked for the position of Labor Attache."

In a May 5, 1988 article in the *New York Times Magazine* entitled "The FBI on the Defensive," newspaper correspondent Sanford Unger concluded that in the FBI "there is still a conservative right wing mentality among some agents working for security. Paranoia is rampant. It scared me."[1] Considering the agency's continuing conservative and often reactionary bent, I strongly believe the FBI should not be allowed to evaluate the political views of candidates for appointive office and their overall fitness for government posts. Why should its views of candidates who happened to have been social activists be permitted to block them from government service? Why should the FBI remain an unanswerable judge of public virtue, the gatekeeper determining who is fit and not fit for government employment?

In 1955, if Senator George and Walter Reuther had not intervened, I am sure I would have been kept out of the Foreign Service. We have heard much talk since that the FBI no longer has the power it once did in American society, but as long as such checks are done—and they still are—I am certain that they will have the effect of barring progressive candidates from government service.

14

Return to Asia, 1955–1960

IN DECEMBER 1955, a very excited Burgess family boarded the SS *Independence* in New York City harbor and sailed for Europe. State Department people traveled first class in those days. Alice and I were both delighted and appalled at the luxury of our cabins and the dining room—we had lived the early days of our marriage, after all, in a trailer and rude wooden houses. Neither of us was really at ease with our fellow first-class passengers, either. We felt at times as if we still had dirt under our fingernails.

In Rome our son John, age four, and our daughter Genie, age two, came down with measles. A doctor told us to remain in Rome for a week or more as a quarantine measure. We couldn't bear the expense or suspense of waiting, though, so we bundled the two sick kids into shielding mufflers and coats, boarded a plane, and landed in New Delhi two days after Christmas.

The India that we reached was just eight years into its independence from British rule. It was a vibrant, pulsating society of 500 million people speaking many different languages, a place with more than three thousand years of history and religious heritage. For our first four weeks, we stayed at the colonial-era Cecil Hotel in Old Delhi. From there we ventured out for first taste of our new country of residence. There were tombs and temples, bazaars with strange foods and spices, horse-drawn "tongas," carts hauled by coolies, taxi drivers speaking pidgin English of the British variety, mobs of bicycle riders at all hours, many beggars, little girls and boys hawking trinkets and asking for candy. Alice and I saw the other extreme of Indian society when we attended our first diplomatic reception. There white-coated servants served cocktails to businessmen of substance, Oxford- and Cambridge-educated officials of the Indian Ministry of External Affairs and their well-dressed wives. That was and still is the essential reality of India—never a shortage of people, and vast gaps in wealth among them.

In mid-January 1956 we moved into a large house at 61 Friends Colony, on the south end of New Delhi. Most of our neighbors were wealthy Hindus who had fled Pakistan in the wake of the British departure and the bloody Hindu-Muslim riots of 1947. Our two oldest children, Laurel and Lyman, entered the American School. We hired servants and in ensuing years lived very well—a summer vacation on a houseboat in Kashmir, weekend trips to the Taj Mahal, and elephant rides in search of tigers in a game park are today parts of our memories. We never felt quite right about all this luxury, but it was how diplomats lived in India and I can't say we put up a great deal of resistance.

For most of what became a five-year stay in India, however, I wasn't vacationing. I spent long periods on the road. Part of my function was to become well acquainted with labor leaders, industrialists, government officials, and politicians influential in labor matters in this huge and fascinating country. Most of them weren't in New Delhi, so I traveled, and the costs of my journeys, I later learned, exceeded the combined travel expenses of the other four political officers in the embassy. I can say without exaggeration that I became one of the better-known Americans in India outside of New Delhi. I called on people at their homes, in factories, in offices. Often they would sit me down and serve me tea as old fans stirred the air overhead. I quickly found that I liked Indians. Unlike the people of East Asia, for whom formality and avoidance of overt conflict are the watchwords, the people of India love lively conversation and are free with their views.

Cold War Competition

India in the 1950s was one of the world's premier arenas of political competition between the United States and Soviet Union. Formally neutral, India was getting substantial aid from both sides, with each trying to outdo the other in winning over Indian loyalties. Both sides sent in cultural troupes, political leaders, and technology experts. They invited Indians to their capitals on all-expenses-paid visits to learn firsthand the superiority of their system. And both sides tried to form alliances in the world of labor unions. That was where I came in.

Since the end of British rule in 1947, organized labor had enjoyed very rapid growth. Loom operators, railroad technicians, tea pickers, government clerks—millions of them were now loyal union members. There were three main labor confederations, known, as labor organizations are everywhere, by their initials: INTUC (the Indian National Trade Union Congress) was the largest; AITUC (All India Trade Union Congress) was a close runner-up for the number one spot in size; and the much smaller Socialist Labor Federation of India, normally called by its Hindi initials HMS. Indian unions were quite different from American ones. Many had been created from the top down by politicians seeking to expand the influence of their respective parties, rather than by workers taking their fates into their own hands. Each labor federation or union was in effect the wing of a political party, relying on it for funding. INTUC was affiliated with the Congress Party, which had led India to independence and was in power in New Delhi; AITUC was part of the Indian Communist Party; and HMS was with the country's comparatively small Socialist Party. The unions could make few decision of substance without first consulting their politician bosses. To me the system was at odds with a key purpose of a labor movement—to give working people their own voice through organizations that were beholden to no one.

Diplomats at the Soviet Embassy, naturally enough, found their closest allies among the Communist unions of AITUC. We Americans favored INTUC, which despite its many shortcomings was the most democratic and representative of the labor federations. But we often came close to blowing the relationship. Before leaving for India, I had seen an example of this firsthand. Attending the AFL-CIO merger convention in early December 1955 in Manhattan, I heard the new president of the merged organization, the fierce cold warrior George Meany, deliver the keynote address. He denounced, by name, a number of overseas Communist sympathizers and "neutralists" (in his mind that was a terrible epithet), including Prime Minister Jawaharlal Nehru of India, President Sukarno of Indonesia, President Kwame Nkrumah of Ghana, and President Josip Tito of Yugoslavia. A leading New York newspaper reported the rumor that Meany planned to call Nehru a "communist stooge" publicly when the Indian leader was scheduled to visit the United States in 1956.

After Meany's address, Victor Reuther introduced me to a man named Tripathi who had been recently elected president of INTUC and was visiting the United States. Tripathi commented to me that Meany did not understand why Nehru and leaders of other neutral countries felt that their states' interests would be best served by steering clear of the confrontation between the Cold War superpowers. Saying that Meany appeared to be "the spokesman for the American War Department," Tripathi predicted that Meany's speech would cause INTUC and HMS, with which we also maintained friendly relations, to withdraw from the International Confederation of Free Trade Unions (ICFTU), a world organization of democratic union federations with which the AFL-CIO was affiliated.

Alarmed by Tripathi's prediction, the Reuther brothers, other CIO leaders, and I met in Walter's hotel suite. After an hour of discussion a consensus emerged among us: Walter should go to India that spring, preferably as a guest of the Indian government, to try to undo the damage done by Meany's speech, to persuade INTUC and HMS to stay in the ICFTU, and to find ways that the AFL-CIO unions could strengthen these two Indian organizations in their battles against the Communist unions. That night I realized that preparing for Walter's trip would be my first important duty as the new labor attaché in India.

So, even before I arrived in India, I was getting an education on how factional politics within the American labor movement would affect my work there. Through much of my time in India, this distraction would continue. Between the two wings of the newly formed AFL-CIO was a deep ideological rift about international affairs. On one side were Meany and his principal international adviser, Jay Lovestone, who had been a leading Communist Party member in the 1920s and early 1930s, only to become a rabid anti-Communist in his later years. Both had close ties with the State Department, the CIA, and other U.S. intelligence agencies. They were enthusiastic defenders of our government's military Cold War policies and were not averse to the idea of using government funds to weaken and sometimes remove foreign labor leaders whom they regarded as anti-American. I learned that Meany and Lovestone had access to classified U.S. government memoranda and cooperated with a network of bureaucratic insiders in the U.S. national security establishment.[1]

On the other side were the Reuthers—Walter, who was now one of the new vice presidents of the AFL-CIO, and Victor, his major international adviser—and presidents of several of the more progressive AFL-CIO unions. This group was philosophically opposed to close collaboration with U.S. government agencies abroad, but unlike Meany and Lovestone, they lacked a large network of sympathetic government officials in Washington and overseas.

Soon after his return to India, INTUC President Tripathi visited Nehru and recommended that Walter Reuther be invited to India as an official guest of the government. Nehru quickly agreed, and that same day I informed Ambassador John Sherman Cooper at the embassy and the State Department about Nehru's decision. I recommended that the Department voice support for Reuther's visit, but key Department officials remained silent, I believe, out of fear of Meany's disfavor.

In early April 1956, Reuther stepped off the plane at the New Delhi airport and was greeted warmly by a huge crowd. I had the privilege of accompanying him on an eleven-day whirlwind journey to New Delhi, Bombay, the steel town of Jamshedpur, the textile town of Ahmadabad, and eighteen other major cities. His energy was phenomenal—according to my tally, he gave 118 speeches in those eleven days. Each speech was translated into Hindi or one of the eight major regional languages by a local labor leader. Walter called at factories, union meetings, workers' homes, and the offices of industrialists and government leaders. Everywhere he went, he wore the Gandhi independence cap and closed each speech with the Hindi words "jay hind," which mean "strength to India."

In most of his speeches, Reuther declared that he strongly disagreed with Secretary of State John Foster Dulles and Meany on foreign policy, and that he sympathized with India's desire to be non-aligned in the Cold War. In private meetings, leaders of INTUC and HMS recommended to him ways that the AFL-CIO could strengthen the non-Communist labor federations in India. Over the course of his visit, Walter persuaded the leaders of INTUC and the HMS not to withdraw their organizations from the ICFTU.

On the last day of his trip, Reuther had a closed two-hour meeting with Prime Minister Nehru. He told me later that he had tried, without success, to convince the prime minister that for the good of India, labor federations should not be tied to political parties. They talked about Meany's verbal blast against Nehru and other neutral heads of state, about the policies of Secretary Dulles, and about the desired warm relationship between the two nations and their labor movements.

As I saw Reuther off at the airport, I had the feeling that he had made a real impact for the good. Three days later a captain of the Indian National Security Guard, which had served as Reuther's round-the-clock bodyguard during his stay, told me that this foreign visitor "had received the warmest reception of any American traveling in India since India's independence in 1947."

The Meany faction, of course, could not allow Reuther's popularity to go unanswered. In the fall of 1956, Irving Brown, Lovestone's chief deputy, arrived in India to address the annual conference of INTUC in the city of Surat. Meeting him for the first time, I found him to be a pleasant conversationalist and an expert on international labor affairs. But when he addressed the INTUC delegates, he suddenly became a shouting preacher, warning them about the growing influence of the Soviet Union in India and other developing nations. I was sitting on the speaker's platform at the time and was appalled at what I was hearing. Beside me was Kundabiah Desai, a former president of INTUC and at the time the national labor minister in Nehru's cabinet. He whispered to me amidst the din, "Reuther's approach is the correct one. He told us what the American labor movement does and what the American people have achieved in economic growth since the Second World War. At the same time he gave the leaders of INTUC and HMS some tempered and useful advice. But Brown spends little time telling us about the American labor movement. Instead he gives us a lecture as if we were completely ignorant." Later that afternoon Desai whispered to me, "The Russians are successful in India because they use the Reuther approach."

Shortly after Brown's visit, I sent the State Department a long classified memorandum analyzing and contrasting the foreign policies advocated by Meany and Reuther. I stated that Nehru and the democratic unions preferred Reuther's sympathetic approach, and added that I did too. I wrote this with the full knowledge that Meany, Lovestone, and their assistants were allowed to see such reports. In my State Department career I would later pay a high price for my undiplomatic bluntness.

Long after he returned to America, Reuther kept up his interest in India by becoming deeply involved in programs to strengthen India's steel industry. India was very anxious to acquire world-class steel-production capability, both to help in development and to stoke the pride of Third World citizens who were anxious to have smokestack industries. The United States and the Soviet Union, to no one's surprise, were in a contest to be India's chief helper in this endeavor. Moscow had sent to India large numbers of steel technicians and were training five thousand Indian steel technicians in plants in the Soviet Union. So Reuther urged officials of the United Steel Workers Union and the Rockefeller and Ford Foundations to back a program to train five hundred Indian steel technicians in the United States. In January 1957 in his conversations with Secretary Dulles, Reuther stressed the need for this program. Later, President Benjamin Fairless of U.S. Steel Corporation, other steel executives, and U.S. government officials traveled to India to explore its feasibility. They concluded the program was worthy of support. By July 1957, plans were set: 115 Indian steel technicians would arrive in New York City in early August, a second group of 85 would come in December, and 300 more would arrive at later dates. The training program began with help from the Ford and Rockefeller Foundations and was jointly run and financed by the American Iron and Steel Institute, the United Steel Workers Union, and six training universities in Pennsylvania, Illinois, and Ohio.

Much of the American steel effort in India focused on helping the Tata Steel Company double its annual production in the city of Jamshedpur. I visited the town, which was dominated by this large steel mill, and was welcomed by Michael John, president of the local INTUC union. He told me that the Communist AITUC federation had opened an office in Jamshedpur and in effect was trying to muscle in on INTUC territory. To respond, he said, he needed twenty-five to fifty trained Indian organizers—trained in India—to strengthen his operation in Jamshedpur and to try to form INTUC locals at a Soviet-financed steel plant in Bhilai in Madhya Pradesh state, at a British-built steel mill in Durgapur, and at a West German–built plant at Roukela.

I reported these recommendations to our new ambassador, Ellsworth Bunker, and to the Reuther brothers. It was crucial, I told them, that American labor unions reach out to help John and strengthen INTUC's organizing capabilities. I was dead set against the use of U.S. government money, however, for this type of program because there was always the chance it would be U.S. intelligence agency money, coming with strings attached. In 1957, a man at the embassy whom I knew to be a CIA officer asked me if I would be willing to distribute "walking-around money" to INTUC and HMS leaders in the state of Kerala, where an important state election pitting the Congress Party against the Communist Party was coming up. Not wanting to become a briber using U.S. government cash, I flatly refused the offer. That year the Communist Party won the Kerala election and took over the state government.

My concern that U.S. unions must do more for democratic labor unions in India was magnified when I visited the huge Soviet plant in Bhilai. I discovered that the Russians were winning over the Indians not by ideology but by one-on-one friendships. From the beginning of construction, the Russian engineers refused to take prime responsibility for building the plant. Unlike the West Germans or the British, who turned over fully constructed steel plants to the Indian government in turnkey fashion, Russian engineers made it clear that they were there to help rather than to manage. They successfully positioned themselves as "fellow Asians" rather than supervising foreigners. Moreover, Indian technicians who had gone to the Soviet Union insisted that this nation gave the very best in foreign training. Two of them told me they had never heard politics discussed during their fourteen-month stay. Of great significance to these two technicians was the fact that the Soviets allowed them to operate machinery in steel plants in the Soviet Union, not just to watch, as often happened in the training program for steelworkers in the United States.

I kept in close touch with Walter Reuther throughout this period, both by mail and, in 1958, during a visit to his house outside Detroit when my family and I were on home leave in the United States. I was surprised to find that his home was surrounded by a tall electrified fence with a guard tower at each of the four corners. This, and ever-present bodyguards when Walter went out, was the legacy of a 1948 assassination attempt that severely wounded him. We talked at length that summer evening, and again I was impressed with Walter's charm and grasp of the facts. He assured me of his continued support for the additional labor resources I was requesting for India. He and his brother Victor, he told me, were backing a plan to establish in India a permanent trade-union training center to counter the Communist unions. Unfortunately, and much to my sorrow, it soon became clear to me that Reuther's proposals were falling on deaf ears at the State Department and at AFL-CIO headquarters in Washington. Meany and Lovestone had already opened such a training center in the Philippines, but Nehru and the heads of democratic unions in India were deeply suspicious of it because it was staffed by Meany and Lovestone appointees and possibly subsidized by the CIA and other U.S. government intelligence agencies. In the end, nothing came of Reuther's plan to open a trade-union training center in India. It was Meany's era now. The Reuthers simply lacked the clout and contacts to make it happen.

Looking back, I am surprised at how often the U.S. government managed to misread what the Indians would value. Even personal relations were often mishandled. In 1957, for example, Nehru visited Washington and New York City. Eleanor Roosevelt had arranged a small dinner for him at her New York City apartment, to which Chester Bowles, Adlai Stevenson, and Walter Reuther were invited in order to have a down-to-earth chat. But the anticipated chat, Reuther told me in a letter, never took place because the State Department insisted that stripe-panted diplomats also be present that evening. As a result, the dinner was all formality and protocol. Absent was the anticipated down-to-earth chat.

The American government sometimes erred in its sponsored cultural exchanges as well. It tended to bring in upscale performers such as opera singers to entertain wealthy audiences in the large cities. In contrast, the Soviet Union brought folk troupes to small communities, accompanied by Russians whose flawless Hindi was the talk of the town for weeks afterward.

In my final years in India the two sides escalated their efforts. In 1959, President Eisenhower paid an official visit to India; in 1960, Nikita Khrushchev flew in. In the end, the Soviets, in my opinion, won the competition. The Indian Communist Party never came to power, but India became a *de facto* client state of the Soviet Union, relying on it for development aid and military equipment and voting with it in world diplomatic forums. This was partly the result of geopolitics. Like the Soviet Union, India shared a border with China and, after losing a brief border war with it in 1962, was worried about China's military might. When the Sino-Soviet split took place for real, it was natural that India took the Soviet side. But I felt it was also because of American mismanagement and at times a conflict between the interests of our country and those of poor India. During my five years in India, I concluded that most of the leaders of rich America never managed to convince the government leaders of poor India that America had India's concerns at heart.

India and My Personal Development

During my many travels, I was often preoccupied with official meetings with leaders from unions, companies, and government. At times I put from my mind the fundamental fact that most cities in India were full of hungry and homeless people. An experience in Bombay gave me a dramatic reminder that poverty was all around me. Late one night I had checked into a dusty, second-rate hotel on the edge of a huge park. From my fourth-floor window, I looked out and saw that the park was full of trees and footpaths. The ground looked dark and lifeless, but now and then I saw faint silver glimmerings. Weary, I went to bed. The next morning, just as dawn was breaking, I looked out the window and saw that literally thousands of men, women, and children were sleeping in the park. The silver light during the night had been the reflections of the moon off their clothes and other meager possessions.

In India I had the good fortune to meet some remarkable people who were trying to do something about the nation's abiding poverty. In the fall of 1958, I visited a small village in the poverty-stricken state of Bihar as a guest of a man named Jaya Prakash Narayan. I spent two days at his ashram or spiritual center. It was eighty miles east of the town of Gaya, where in the fifth century B.C. the great Buddha experienced nirvana sitting under a banyan tree. In a letter to my mother I told her about my visit:

> Jaya Prakash Narayan, or J.P. as he is popularly called, is raising up a new generation of young rural leaders prepared to preach the triple gospel of self-sufficiency, village self-rule and mass distribution of unused land to the poor. . . . Essentially he and his disciples seek to plant in the hearts of lowly villagers a sense of responsibility and power. . . . After seeing him among villagers, most of whom are untouchables or tribal folk, I was deeply moved by his simplicity, his courage, and his devotion to the common people. What attracted me to J.P. was not so much his wisdom and dedication, but his presence and the depth of his spirituality.

> Back in 1953 Prime Minister Nehru had tried to persuade Narayan to become the deputy prime minister. J.P. refused the offer. Recently he resigned from the Socialist Party of India and declared that he was done with parties and political power. But the people of India—both high and low—will not leave him alone. Everywhere people of all ages gather around him when he visits a village or a city. The President of the Congress Party had recently invited him to come to New Delhi to consult with him about what he calls Prime Minister Nehru's "declining influence." Many of J.P.'s countrymen believe that he is the only man with national influence who should be Nehru's successor.

As it turned out, when Nehru died in 1964, Narayan was so preoccupied at his ashram with following in the steps of the independence leader and ascetic Gandhi, distributing land to the landless under Vinoba Bhave's guidance and shunning politics, that he did not offer himself for the post. At the American Embassy in New Delhi in 1958, most of my colleagues regarded Narayan as a mere dreamer and an impractical idealist. They and some State Department officials believed that in my favorable judgment of Narayan, I had taken leave of my senses.

One thing that forever concerned me in India was how this country of so many dynamic, educated, and skilled people could be stuck in a cycle of poverty and be so slow in developing true representative democracy. During my fourth year in India, I offered some answers in a long dispatch to the State Department titled "Can Hinduism and Hindu Culture Provide an Ideological Foundation for Democracy in India?" I answered this question in the negative, because I had reached the conclusion that current Hinduism had no social ethic, no prophetic ethic, and no concept of a meaningful history. Hinduism is summarized in the Hindu affirmation that "Brahma is real: the universe is not." Because traditional Hinduism instructed believers to stay within the confines of their own caste—the social group into which they were born and which determined most everything about their future—Hinduism in its present form was inimical to the development of democracy in India. I knew that most of my English-speaking Indian friends in government were tolerant, pragmatic, and generally moral people, but they were doing little to reform Hinduism. In the days to come, I concluded, their morality and philosophy of life would be sorely tested as the institutions of caste started to crumble and increased urbanization began to destroy the old securities of the village while providing little security for new city dwellers in the future. The needed reformation of Hinduism in a nation that professed to be an emerging democracy was simply not taking place. If India were to save herself, she would have to find a new soul and her own democratic faith.

I spun out the same theme in a letter to my old family friend Jerry Voorhis, who, after leaving Congress in 1947 following his loss to Richard Nixon in a congressional election, had become the head of the Cooperative League of the U.S.A. I claimed that the great curse of India was its people's dependence on the authority of their superiors—whether the superior was the landlord, an employer, or a government official. The joint family system, the prevailing caste system, and centuries of colonial rule were the root causes of this condition. In labor relations, national political leaders were inclined to believe that curbs on the right to strike and the teaching of so-called "voluntary discipline" were the best ways to persuade the working people to cooperate with the latest Five-Year Plan. What they forgot was that average industrial workers felt like a cogs in a giant machine, that they probably hadn't heard about the Five-Year Plan, and even if they had heard about it, they saw no connection between it and their tedious work each day in the factory. It was my conviction that the latest Five-Year Plan would not be a success without the willing cooperation of workers; and workers could not be concerned about the future of India unless they were encouraged to join unions of their own choosing and to work for the good of the nation through their unions.

After five delightful years in India, the Burgess family—now seven strong after the birth of our last child, Steve, in 1957—said farewell to that country. It was November 1960, and more than fifty friends, both Indian and American, came to the New Delhi airport to see us off. I boarded the plane feeling sad, but my heavy heart was offset by the welcome news that had come from America that same day: Senator John F. Kennedy had won the presidency. Republican rule was soon going to end. We rejoiced all the way home.

15

Leading the Peace Corps in Indonesia, 1963–1964

IN EARLY MAY of 1963 I flew to Iowa State University to meet eighteen young Americans. Three were women and fifteen were men, many with the crew cuts and wise-cracking optimism that were common in those times. We shook hands all around. They were all Peace Corps volunteers, training for duty in Indonesia, and I was their newly appointed boss, the country director for that Southeast Asian nation. At the university they were studying the history and culture of Indonesia, as well as the policies of the Kennedy administration and the Peace Corps itself. They also spent long hours learning the Indonesian language.

Much of the euphoria over President Kennedy was over now, more than two years after his inauguration, but the Peace Corps stood apart as a genuinely innovative creation. Founded in 1961, it sent thousands of young American volunteers abroad to work closely with local people in developing countries, living in local housing, eating local food, speaking local languages—just as some young Russian technicians had done in India.

These eighteen would be the Peace Corps' first volunteers in Indonesia, a country of over 100 million people. It was ruled by President Sukarno, a charismatic strongman of windy speeches, several mistresses, and grandiose development plans. From the day of his nation's independence from the Dutch in 1949, he had been kept in power by an uneasy alliance between the Communist Party of Indonesia (PKI) and the generally pro-Western armed forces. On a visit to Indonesia in 1961, I had listened as Sukarno, wearing his trademark dark glasses and Muslim fez, harangued a huge crowd in the capital, Jakarta, for almost three hours in an Independence Day speech. Despite the fact that his country was more than three thousand miles from east to west and made up of at least as many islands, he vowed to build unity and conformity in this new nation. Toward that end, he and his minions had already abolished freedom of press and outlawed several rival political parties. As had happened in India, his country was teetering between East and West, receiving substantial aid from both the United States and the Soviet Union.

Sukarno (like many Indonesians, he used only a single name) was by nature a bombastic man who sometimes tried to strengthen his own authority by stirring up national crusades. In the early 1960s he trained his sights on Malaysia, a new country recently formed next door from a union of Singapore, Malaya, and the Sarawak and Sabah states on the island of Borneo in East Malaysia. Sukarno asserted that the creation of Malaysia was an imperialist plot of the British, who had been the colonial masters of the various parts of Malaysia. He claimed the Borneo portions as Indonesia's own. The Indonesian military began launching sporadic raids into them. In speeches, newspapers articles, and on TV, Sukarno was trying to build up hatred against Britain. As Britain's closest ally, the United States naturally felt some of that ire as well.

The director of the Peace Corps, Sargent Shriver, wanted to send volunteers to Indonesia, and Sukarno was willing to have them come, but in what capacity? There was a feeling in both Washington and Jakarta that the volunteers should stay out of activities such as economic development and community organizing, which might smell of a secret political agenda. But sports was another matter. Sukarno and the Indonesian people at large were sports-crazy. The government was organizing an international mini-Olympics called the Games of the New Emerging Forces in 1963, using Sukarno's term for the newly independent Third World. The Soviets, ever quick to recognize a client's wishes, had stepped in and built a huge sports complex in Jakarta. The Peace Corps, it was decided, would get in on the sports boom too, offering famous American expertise in the athletic arts. The Indonesians agreed. Thus it happened that, with the exception of one English teacher, the eighteen volunteers I met at Iowa State were all coaches, skilled in such sports as track, basketball, and swimming.

For the previous two years, following my return from India in late 1960, I had already been working to assist Indonesia in the U.S. Agency for International Development, popularly known as USAID. Hopes I'd nurtured for a senior job in the Kennedy administration hadn't materialized. I was told by Ralph Dungan, a special assistant to Kennedy, that the ever-powerful George Meany had vetoed my appointment to any senior position in the Kennedy administration. Walter Reuther protested to the White House, but to no avail. That result wasn't entirely a surprise, given my long association with the Reuthers and the undiplomatic dispatches I'd sent from New Delhi. So, for the next two years I became chief of the Indonesia-Burma division in USAID.

In that capacity, I made two extended trips to Indonesia. One was with a team of Americans given the task of recommending ways that the mammoth Indonesian armed forces could launch civic action programs, such as building roads and bridges, constructing health centers, and clearing land for agricultural production. Our team traveled to many parts of Indonesia and talked with high-ranking government officials and army generals. We concluded with regret that neither Sukarno nor leaders of the armed forces appeared motivated to put our recommendations into effect. There was only one real reason for that: they were preoccupied with sending paratroopers to attack East Malaysian villages in the states of Sabah and Sarawak.

My other trip to Indonesia was with a team of five American economists. We went for the purpose of developing a future U.S. foreign assistance policy for Indonesia. At the request of Walt Rostow, chairman of the Policy Planning Department of the State Department, I recruited the economists and served as secretary of the delegation in Indonesia. We didn't know it at the time, but the report we delivered to the U.S. and Indonesian governments in 1962— recommending substantial U.S. help in such areas as education, agriculture, public health, and industrial development—became the foundation for U.S. foreign aid policy in Indonesia for the next three decades.

It was not my most happy time professionally, however. From 1961 to 1963, I was becoming increasingly suspicious of U.S. foreign policy in the poor Third World nations. The Vietnam War was getting under way, and Deputy Secretary of State Chester Bowles, a very decent man who had become a mentor of sorts for me, had been allegedly demoted by President Kennedy in November 1961 to the position of ambassador-at-large, reportedly after he had opposed the buildup of our armed forces in Vietnam.

My eyes were opened to the effects of many U.S. policies on developing countries when in the spring of 1963, I and other senior officers in USAID and the State Department were required to attend a two-week course on the Kennedy administration's counter-insurgency plans in poor nations. I learned there how our government in its campaign against the Soviet Union in poor nations was often seeking to undermine and even to destroy progressive reform movements benefiting the poor. None other than Attorney General Robert Kennedy gave the keynote address at this seminar. He was then an enthusiastic supporter of counter-insurgency in developing countries, though he later condemned President Johnson's counter-insurgency policies in Vietnam when Kennedy was campaigning for the Democratic Party presidential nomination in 1968. Two of the most interesting lecturers at this were CIA officials who had recently returned from Vietnam. In a private conversation with me and two other USAID colleagues, they asserted that the United States was losing the war in Vietnam.

The Vietcong, they said, had gained the confidence of most peasants, who now regarded the United States as a white imperialist power that opposed the interests of common people in poor countries.

When in January 1963 a call came from Sargent Shriver asking whether I'd be interested in heading up the first Peace Corps program in Indonesia, I said yes in short order. I was happy to work for an agency that was far from the world of counter-insurgency.

Following their training in Iowa, the seventeen Peace Corps volunteers (one had washed out) got a White House send-off. President Kennedy greeted them in the Rose Garden and in a gracious ten-minute address urged them to work hard, learn about the culture of Indonesia, and identify themselves with the common people of this very important nation.

Alice attended the White House reception, but I did not. I was already in Jakarta preparing with other Peace Corps officials for the volunteers' arrival. We were quite nervous. Leaders of the PKI were publicly condemning the volunteers' impending arrival and organizing a protest demonstration at the airport for when they landed. There was a real danger, I felt, that PKI gangs would physically attack the volunteers there. With help from my deputy, Alex Shakow, who spoke the Indonesian language fluently, and Dr. Don Wackow, resident Peace Corps physician, I persuaded the minister of home affairs and the police chief of Jakarta to ring the airport with soldiers and police. It turned out to be a wise precaution. As the plane landed on May 30, the airport was already filled with unruly crowds of well-coached PKI protesters, who shouted in English, "Yankee go home" and "Down with imperialist pigs." The soldiers and policemen surrounded the volunteers as they left the plane and escorted them to a large van which took them to a hotel in Jakarta. Here they were welcomed by Sports Minister Maladi. It was not the kind of start we wanted, but we felt it was necessary not to be cowed.

The next morning, U.S. Ambassador Howard Jones greeted the volunteers at the embassy. Within a few days each volunteer shipped out to an assigned town in Indonesia where he or she was assigned to live and work for the next two years. For a while all went smoothly, though we did have the odd crisis such as the six-foot, ten-inch volunteer who lost ten pounds because he couldn't find potatoes in the market. Since potatoes were virtually unknown in Indonesia, we persuaded him to eat rice instead. I and my two staff members visited each volunteer frequently and met the local sports officials and Indonesian families with whom the volunteers lived.

But political and military events soon intruded. Almost daily, over national radio and in press conferences, Sukarno cursed the British for ceding Sabah and Sarawak to the new nation of Malaysia and threatened to send more paratroopers to attack villages in these two states. Following Sukarno's lead, commentators on government-controlled radio and editors of major newspapers sounded the same message.

In October 1963 things came to a head. I watched from the roof of the Hotel Indonesia as PKI-organized mobs stormed and burned down the British Embassy, located just across a traffic circle from the hotel. Eyeing the violence, I was fearful for my own safety and that of my family, who had arrived from Washington several months earlier. I asked the education minister, whose house was next to the hotel, to let me ride a ministry limousine from his home to mine. He agreed. At his suggestion I lay down on the back floor of the limousine all the way home. That night, PKI-organized crowds burst into many British-owned homes around Jakarta and other cities, carting off the furniture and other household goods and burning them in the street. A gang appeared in front of our home too, but went away after our servant went out and convinced the would-be attackers that our home was American-owned. The Peace Corps volunteers later informed me that in their towns PKI members had tried to disrupt their sports programs but had never physically threatened them.

Happily, things settled down after that. But then in November came a sad and memorable event during a two-day conference at a hill retreat with all volunteers and staff members attending. On the first day, each volunteer outlined what he or she had accomplished in the coaching programs and planned for the next six months. I told the group that fifteen more coaches would arrive the following January and that the Peace Corps program was likely to expand beyond sports because eight other Indonesian ministries had requested doctors, geologists, industrial trainers, laboratory technicians, and agriculture experts.

But the next day our high hopes turned to sadness when a volunteer arriving late from Jakarta informed us that President Kennedy had been assassinated in Dallas the previous day. The group became silent. Then some of volunteers wept quietly. Alice and the volunteers recalled the warm reception they had received in the Rose Garden just a few months earlier. Back in Jakarta, President Sukarno surprised us by proclaiming three days of official mourning. He stated in a nationwide radio address that Kennedy was the first American president who really understood Indonesia. As a result of Sukarno's proclamation, the churches and mosques of Jakarta and other Indonesian cities were filled with mourners. The depth of the tragedy was made more real to me and the volunteers when in January of 1964 Robert Kennedy and his wife visited Jakarta. His face was drawn, his eyes distant. He appeared to me to be in a continuing state of mourning. He spoke to the embassy staff and some volunteers, openly sharing with them his grief and his hopes for the future.

In late November 1963, most Peace Corps coaches and staff attended the

Games of the New Emerging Forces in Jakarta. Taking part were athletes from fifty-one countries, including Indonesians trained by Peace Corps coaches. I attended several of the events, staged at the Soviet-built sports complex. It was all quite exciting, though the judges were often openly partisan. The Chinese, as expected, dominated the games. Indonesia and the Soviet Union were practically even in second place, but far behind the Chinese.

The second group of coaches arrived in January 1964. But because of the continuing political instability, Shriver was reluctant to recruit volunteers for other positions requested by the Indonesian government. Meanwhile, Communist Party leaders were publicly advocating that Indonesian troops seize East Malaysia. Indonesian generals, however, were sharply divided on the wisdom of such a mass invasion. The British threatened to use their own military might against Indonesia if Sukarno persisted in sending in raiding parties.

Then, in late January 1964, these threatening foreign affairs became academic to me. I received a telegram bearing Shriver's signature instructing me to fly to Washington immediately "for consultations." I had no idea what the purpose was until I reached Peace Corps headquarters in Washington. Here I was told that because of Alice's drinking problem I and the family had to return to the United States immediately.

That she had a serious alcohol problem was a very painful fact of my life, one that I had long tried to push to the side, just as I have delayed mentioning it in this narrative. She had begun drinking near the end of our five years in India. It's clear I contributed to her unhappiness by being away from home for long periods and being obsessed with my own work. Alice had welcomed the return to America from India and had pleaded with me that we not move to Indonesia. But we did anyway and in Jakarta her drinking continued. Word got back to Washington. Whether this was the real reason I was being recalled was not clear to me. In Washington, Shriver assured me that he felt I had been a very successful country director in Indonesia, but I have long looked on my recall as caused by some of Shriver's deputies who were jealous of my close relationship with him and unhappy with my assertive work, feeling I was pushing too hard to get more volunteers into a potentially dangerous environment. I talked at length with Shriver, but he would not be moved. So in late March, Alice and I and our three youngest children arrived back in Washington in the midst of a driving snowstorm. The education of our younger children was rudely interrupted, and my future in the Peace Corps became most uncertain. To this day, more than thirty-five years later, I cannot recall this episode without feeling a twinge of anger.

Despite the excellent leadership of my successor, Alex Shakow, all was not well in Indonesia with the expanded team of thirty-two Peace Corps coaches. Tensions between the PKI and the military's Generals Council were growing. Sukarno's precarious balancing act between these two contending forces seemed less and less tenable. So the State Department in 1965 sent Ambassador-at-Large Ellsworth Bunker to evaluate the work of the volunteers and recommend whether or not they should remain in Indonesia. In his report, Bunker praised the coaches for hard work and popularity, but concluded that because of the potential threats to their safety, they should leave Indonesia. So in mid-1965 the coaches said farewell to their many Indonesian friends. Some returned to America, while others joined Peace Corps programs in other Asian countries. Thus a modest but highly successful Peace Corps program came to an end.

A few months after the coaches' departure, the long-predicted explosion occurred. It began when Communist Party agents murdered six Indonesian generals and threw their butchered bodies down a well near Jakarta. The armed forces under General Suharto quickly counter-attacked and crushed the PKI, killing some of its leaders. During the next few weeks, an estimated 400,000 to 500,000 mostly innocent people were slain mercilessly by the military or by roaming gangs of youths given weapons by the army. President Sukarno was forced out of office. In 1967, General Suharto was proclaimed the new president. Some Indonesians gained in wealth during Suharto's ensuing thirty-one-year rule, as their nation became one of the "tiger" economies of Southeast Asia. But most Indonesians remained poor, and none enjoyed elemental democratic rights. In May of 1998, President Suharto, who had enriched his family and his many cronies over the years, was finally forced from office in the midst of an economic crisis, widespread looting, and concerted demands by students and ordinary people for democratic rights.

My story of Indonesia and subsequent tragedies in this the fourth-most-populated nation in the world would not be complete unless I closed with a tale of love triumphing. In 1963 a volunteer-coach named Bob Dakan was posted to a small town in central Java. Within a few months he had fallen in love with the daughter of a major PKI leader in central Java. When the Peace Corps pulled out of the country in 1964, Bob moved to another Asian nation. Just before the Indonesian army began arresting and in some cases executing leaders of the PKI in the fall of 1965, the young lady, accompanied by her Dutch-born mother, fled to Amsterdam and met Bob. There the young couple married and flew to America. Later, Bob, accompanied by his wife and their children, worked with refugee families in Laos. Next he was appointed the USAID director in Belize in Central America. I always admired Bob's friendly nature and devotion to his wife. His marriage to this wonderful Indonesian lady was one of the happy results that came out of the Peace Corps' all-too-brief presence in Indonesia.

16

Opening Up the Peace Corps to Blue-Collar Workers, 1964–1965

WORKING AT PEACE CORPS headquarters in Washington in the spring of 1964, I cast about for a new project and quickly found one staring me in the face. In examining the list of young men and women who had been recruited by the agency since 1961, it struck me that there was a very firm policy that most volunteers should have a college degree. The makeup of the 8,358 volunteers abroad in May 1964 strongly reflected this bias: 84 percent had college degrees, and 13 percent had some college education. Only 3 percent had never gone to college at all.

I sought out a high official of the Peace Corps' Selection Division and asked why we were sending so few skilled industrial workers overseas. Most host governments, he explained, wanted volunteers with B.A. or B.S. degrees who could teach English as a second language. He also said that volunteers without college degrees generally had difficulty mastering the language of the host country. Moreover, he declared, they tended to be poor ambassadors for the United States because they knew little about the history of their country and were intellectually less equipped to appreciate foreign cultures. It seemed clear to me that this elitist view of American society reflected class prejudices at Peace Corps headquarters. Many members of the staff, I discovered, were from university faculties, and many had doctorates. The same was true of most country directors—they tended to be well-educated people with little experience in the industrial world. It seemed to me that this "college graduates only" policy worked against the goal of meeting the pressing needs of peoples of poor host countries. I was convinced that they needed volunteers with manual skills who knew how to produce cars, steel, and industrial chemicals and to repair jeeps and farm machinery. These potential volunteers, clearly, would best be found in factories and construction projects, not on college campuses.

I concluded that the Peace Corps headquarters needed a division of industrial recruiting. So I drew up a formal recommendation to the Peace Corps' director that he create such a division, put me in charge, and assign as my deputies two recently returned volunteers. To my great surprise, he agreed quickly and enthusiastically with my recommendation.

I got down to work in this new job. At my suggestion, Shriver wrote letters to 350 top corporate leaders asking them to grant leave and carry over seniority, pension, and other benefits to any employees who joined the Peace Corps. He also recommended that companies grant them automatic reemployment rights when they returned from their assignments abroad. Many companies were already granting former employees reemployment rights after military service. Shriver later told me that he had received positive replies from about two hundred of the company executives. Only eight replied negatively.

Despite my past differences with AFL-CIO President Meany, I asked to see him to discuss the program. He received me in his office in Washington, and the famously gruff man was in fact quite cordial to me. He asked me to address a meeting of the AFL-CIO Executive Board about our recruiting efforts. When I did so, most board members seemed favorably impressed. After the meeting, several told me they would insist upon a "Peace Corps clause" in future labor-management contracts guaranteeing reemployment rights to former employees who served as volunteers. Meany appointed Joseph Beirne, then president of the Communication Workers of America, to chair an AFL–CIO–Peace Corps liaison committee.

For thirteen months beginning in May 1964, I and my two deputies traveled around the country to recruit skilled workers. We went to New York City, St. Louis, Peoria, Pontiac, San Francisco, Seattle, and Los Angeles, to name just a few cities. Our method of recruiting was rather unusual. We set up headquarters at an accessible hotel or motel. We appeared on local TV and radio and spoke to newspaper reporters. We called on company executives and obtained their permission to address gatherings of their workers on all three shifts. We visited union offices. Union leaders usually let us address their executive committees and meetings of union members and shop stewards. We often encountered hearty support on the part of city officials. In Baton Rouge, for instance, the mayor declared a "Peace Corps Week" and gave me the key to the city.

I was very encouraged when one company executive said to me, "Two years ago, anyone from the Peace Corps could not have gotten beyond the guard at the front gate." But we had made a good enough impression that we were now free to recruit there. Another executive was so supportive that he agreed to pay employees who served in the Peace Corps a substantial bonus upon their return. Meanwhile, Shriver informed all of the agency's country directors about our work and asked them to spread the word to host governments that skilled industrial and construction workers would be available to serve in their countries.

One of our most successful efforts was at a Caterpillar plant in Peoria, Illinois, where the United Auto Workers was the sole company-recognized bargaining agent. I and my two deputies addressed shifts of fifty to one hundred people on the production floor. Often the production line was stopped while we talked. The workers were genuinely curious. They had lots of practical questions: what would happen to their seniority, to their pension? One man with fifteen years' experience approached me and asked about work in repair of cars and earthmoving equipment. All told, we made thirty-eight speeches and came away with eighty-four applications from the plant's employees. After our visit, labor columnist Victor Reisel published a flattering article declaring that a "Blue Collar Peace Corps" had been launched. He called our efforts to recruit industrial workers "a Rhodes Scholarship Program."

By June 1965, my deputies and I had recruited more than twenty-two hundred skilled workers, mostly from manufacturing firms. We were all very optimistic. Unfortunately, we declared victory too soon. At headquarters, the staff of the Selection Division remained lukewarm and in some cases were openly hostile to our recruiting efforts. They were not pleased when a United Auto Workers team traveled to the African nation of Guinea-Bissau at the union's expense to survey whether twenty-five to fifty future Peace Corps volunteers from UAW plants should be sent there. Meanwhile, the Selection Division turned down requests from the Nigerian government for sixty volunteers with mechanical skills. The division also opposed sending fifty industrial-arts instructors to Malaysia, whose government had requested them. To make matters worse, the applicants for the industrial slots were required to pass the same written tests given to candidates with college degrees. The division also insisted that wives of skilled workers have manual skills themselves if they were to accompany their husbands abroad.

That spouse policy effectively torpedoed the plans of many would-be industrial volunteers, such as the man I'd met in Peoria. His wife was a schoolteacher, but that wasn't good enough for the Selection Division. He wouldn't go without his wife, so his application was scratched. As a result of this kind of obstruction, only a handful of industrial volunteers actually went abroad. In the spring of 1965, only 133 Peace Corps slots in the entire world were officially designated as open to industrial workers.

In a final report to Shriver in June of 1965, as I was finishing my two-year term with the Peace Corps, I praised the assistance given by company executives, by the AFL-CIO, and by Shriver himself. But I told him that people we'd signed up from the factories were getting suspicious. It would be hard, I said, for us to return to places like the Caterpillar plant in Peoria unless we could show that we were actually sending substantial numbers of blue-collar applicants abroad as Peace Corps volunteers.

Though our industrial recruitment program did not live up to my high hopes, I believe that over time it helped change the mind-set of the Peace Corps. We created some excitement among industrial workers about the possibility of serving their country and humanity in foreign countries. After I left the agency in 1965, it became more common for developing nations to ask not just for English teachers, but for skilled workers in manufacturing and construction, and to get them. Though today the Peace Corps remains largely a college graduate's haven, I look back on our work as an important accomplishment in sharing with our friends abroad a bit of the blue-collar know-how that made America a great industrial power.

I continue to believe strongly that the days of Peace Corps elitism in democratic America will end. This will happen only when leaders of this agency realize that thousands of young Americans and older Americans without college degrees but with manual skills and a desire to share their skills with workers in developing nations can be successful ambassadors of our nation overseas.

17

With UNICEF in East Asia, 1966–1972

IN THE MIND of the average person in Thailand, one of the most solidly Buddhist countries anywhere, leprosy was taken as a sign that the victim had lived an immoral life. That's not so far from fundamentalist Christian views of reaping what you sow, but the approach to treatment of leprosy and other diseases was a world apart. The Thais believed that a Buddhist doctor should not become too closely involved with a leper, or care too much for him or her, because this kind of caring and bonding is at the root of human suffering. In Buddhism, spiritual salvation comes through cutting oneself off from fellow human beings, suppressing all desire and love and becoming one with the higher power.

A Thai doctor in charge of leprosy control programs for the whole country explained this view to me one day in 1967, when I was visiting a leprosy hospital in the city of Chiengmai. He lamented the negative impact this approach had on programs to cure the disease. Given the religious doctrine of Buddhism, it was not surprising that the facility we were visiting, Thailand's oldest leprosy hospital, bore a Western name, McKean, and had been established by Christian missionaries, in 1905. And the man who showed us around that day in 1967, the hospital's director, had been raised a Buddhist but later converted to Christianity. I came up against this kind of spiritual gap often during my six years in Southeast Asia, where I worked in various senior capacities for UNICEF and in cooperation with other United Nations agencies concerned about health, nutrition, and education of mothers and children. Eastern religion was taking root in the United States at the time, but I have to confess that even after living in a Buddhist culture for so long, it had next to no impact on me. Like Hinduism in India, Buddhism in Thailand seemed to me to produce no joy and optimism among its adherents. I also had trouble too with its obsession with the individual. Believing Christians identify not with themselves but with the people to be served. They put their ultimate faith in a forgiving and loving God who resides within the world and within the hearts of all men and women.

My Own Spiritual Renewal

During the journey to Thailand in the summer of 1966, I had undergone a rather unusual spiritual revival. There was much loose talk in the 1960s, as today, about a man's midlife crisis as if it were always a catastrophe. But for me this crisis brought a greater understanding of myself and the higher power of God.

After I had left the U.S. Foreign Service in 1966 and was en route to a UNICEF job in Thailand, my spiritual breakthrough began on a ship that was taking me and my family across the Atlantic and the Mediterranean. Perhaps the trigger was my professional trauma of the previous three years, the enforced idleness of an ocean voyage, or the natural questioning that comes with aging. Whatever the cause, I was able for the first time as an adult to take a fresh look at my past, the quality of my present daily life, and my plans for the future. Suddenly, I was able to appreciate the wisdom of a close friend who had recently said to me, "You still regard yourself, Dave, as a young man in a hurry as you approach your fiftieth year. You are anxious to get things done. You are more concerned about plans for tomorrow than about the wonderful reality of each swiftly passing moment today. You are so preoccupied with doing that you neglect being."

On shipboard, as I sat on a deck chair or lay in my cabin, I found myself withdrawing inwardly to contemplate, to review my life and record my findings in my diary. I became aware that my past concentration on the future, combined with my daily anxieties, often drained my life of much joy. Too often I had lived with my eyes on a distant horizon. The result was that my life had turned into a form of sleepwalking, full of half-heard sounds and half-seen faces of strangers and loved ones alike. Now and then I had experienced the reality of God's world and fellow human beings, but then the fog of confusion would descend and I would be left walking on shifting sands with only the light of distant horizons to guide me. Amidst the flux and changing scenes of each day, I knew that even in my mortal life there was an eternal reality for which I had long yearned. I hoped to catch a glimpse of the eternal in a sunset, a smile, a loved one's comforting word, a sudden and often unexpected burst of joy. I sought, and to an extent found, a God-given illumination of the spirit when, figuratively speaking, the clouds would lift, the gentle winds would blow the fog away, and a rich, verdant valley leading to the future would stretch out before me.

Before our ship docked at Haifa, Israel, I wrote in my diary: "I feel that I will soon be in the right calling as a UNICEF representative. Considerations of rank, prestige, upward mobility, and what others think about me are now minor concerns of my life."

The following April in Thailand, two months before my fiftieth birthday, I wrote: "Suddenly and unexpectedly I have felt a new awareness, a new sensitivity, a new opening, a melting of the walls which have sometimes prevented me from seeing beyond the four walls of my own cramped self. I am now more calm and refreshed, ready to enjoy petty events and big events in the company of my fellow human beings. For the gift of this new and more joyful life, I am deeply grateful to God."

On June 15, 1967, the day of my fiftieth birthday, I wrote in my diary: "I am enjoying life more. I have found a proper niche in UNICEF. I am still ambitious, still anxious to assume greater responsibilities. But today I am striving in a more relaxed manner. I feel that my efforts to live a more meaningful life have just begun. My spiritual engine is now operating on all cylinders. My heart is calm."

During my spiritual crisis, I realized that I owed much to both of my parents, particularly my father, who had died in 1949. On the twentieth anniversary of his death, I wrote to my aging mother: "What Dad gave me was the conviction that people are far more important than causes—no matter how noble the causes may be. He helped me to listen to others and to put myself in others' shoes. I knew some of his students who were willing to share their troubles with him. I knew that some of his foes took advantage of his trusting nature and his willingness to give others the benefit of the doubt. In the end, however, with a few exceptions, he was able to win over his adversaries. I don't think that I will ever be as trusting and good as Dad was, but I will try."

Looking back, I realize there was something I could have given more consideration to—Alice's continuing problem with alcohol. She had been against our coming to Thailand, but again I had prevailed on her to come anyway. Her drinking had not let up, and it continued to be a major trial for her and for our family members during our six years in Thailand.

A New Life in a New Country

The journey ended with us stepping off a jet plane into the tropical heat of Thailand. This Southeast Asian kingdom was ruled by a close-knit group of military officers, civil servants, landowners, and business executives. At the top was the king, dressed in white, symbolizing both goodness and authority. In Thai society, I soon discovered, proper attitudes and actions toward one's superiors and one's inferiors are the acknowledged signs of virtue, both in government and in private life. A pair of military strongmen then ran the government, becoming fabulously wealthy along the way, but their actions generated no real popular opposition. There was little democracy as we know it, though there were elections, courts, and a parliament. An American missionary friend who had spent ten years in Thailand put it this way to me: "The spirit of democracy is dead in Thailand, but the empty forms of democracy are all around us."

Thailand was unique in Southeast Asia in having escaped colonial rule by a European power. It had accomplished that in part by opening its borders to foreigners. From the middle of the nineteenth century, it welcomed American missionaries who established schools and medical centers as well as foreign businessmen who created companies and trade. Thailand welcomed them provided they did nothing to undermine the hierarchical structure of Thai society.

In 1966 when we arrived in Thailand, the new guests were American military personnel, in very large numbers. Bangkok was a major rest and recreation center for GIs posted at a half-dozen air bases in Thailand and in Vietnam, where the war had reached its full intensity. Many Thais, strongly anti-Communist and with historical suspicions of Vietnam, favored America's military role in the region and in their own country (U.S. funds and weapons were being used against Thai Communist insurgents). But Thai people greatly resented the appearance of thousands of free-spending, skirt-chasing GIs in their midst. Many Thais also accused top American diplomats and generals of poking their noses into Thai government affairs. I remember the words of Kukrit Pramoj, a prince and later prime minister of Thailand, when I paid a call on him at his home in Bangkok: "The trouble with you Americans," he said in a not unfriendly way, "is that when you visit a Thai home, you want to peek into every room. You don't realize that sometimes we Thais like to keep certain rooms strictly private."

When I arrived in Thailand in July of 1966, I had just left the State Department and it felt good. One reason was that I wanted nothing to do with the Vietnam War and my country's military interventions in Vietnam and other Third World countries. The other reason for my change was that I had known for a long time as a Foreign Service officer that if there were places in the U.S. government where I did belong, the State Department was not one of them. There had been many warning signals since I joined the Department back in 1955: the long-drawn-out FBI security clearance in 1955; a CIA official at the embassy in New Delhi who asked me rather rudely soon after my arrival in 1955 (possibly after reading my FBI file), "How in the hell did the Department let you in?"; a prediction from a friendly State Department official in 1961 that I would probably not last in the Department unless I found a highly placed patron to protect me as a "controversial person"; word from a well-meaning friend that in the opinion of the Department I was both "over-identified" with the poor of India and "a reluctant defender of American capitalism abroad"; and finally, AFL-CIO President Meany's continuing opposition to my appointment to any senior position in the Kennedy administration and subsequent ones.

From September 1965 to the summer of 1966, after leaving the Peace Corps, I had returned to the State Department to work as member of its Board of Examiners, the group that vets applicants to the Foreign Service. Sitting on a three-member panel, I listened to many young people tell why they deserved a job in the Department. I was struck by how bland and unoriginal most of them were. Many seemed almost devoid of moral convictions. They assumed, with a degree of accuracy, that the Department was the establishment, peopled with faithful and hard-working conformists who were eager to defend the status quo and fearful of the winds of change blowing through the poor nations of the world. I had conflicting feelings as a member of the Board of Examiners, as I was functioning as a gatekeeper to the Department.

Apprehensive that I was a controversial person who might be "selected out" of the Department, I began casting about in the fall of 1965 for a job outside the Department. I was advised by a friend to see Louis Martin, publisher of the *Chicago Defender,* a leading black newspaper. Martin was then deputy chairman of the National Democratic Party. In my interview, we spent a few minutes reviewing possible jobs for me in the Johnson administration. Suddenly he changed the subject and began criticizing Dr. Martin Luther King, Jr., for condemning President Johnson for escalating the war in Vietnam. King, he claimed, was neglecting his campaign to increase black voter registration and to deal with other domestic needs of the black community. Suddenly he turned to me and asked if I, as a fellow ordained Christian minister, would be willing to visit Dr. King and do what I could to persuade him to silence his opposition to the war and turn his attention back to pressing domestic issues of concern to blacks. If I succeeded, Martin assured me, a job in the Johnson administration might be found for me. I was confounded by his proposal. Two days later I diplomatically rejected it, since I was in full agreement with King's opposition to the war. I could only assume that Martin was under pressure from the White House to shut King up. Now I knew with certainty that the corrupting poison of the Vietnam War had affected even members of the civil rights movement in America.

In April 1966, I was officially informed by a State Department official that I would probably be selected out of the Department in 1966 or 1967. Fortunately, I was able to make an important connection just a few days later. At the recommendation of Chester Bowles, the Department's ambassador-at-large, I visited the New York office of Henry Labouisse, former director of the Agency for International Development and then the recently appointed executive director of UNICEF. During a conversation in his office, he offered me the job of chief of UNICEF programs in Thailand, Malaysia, Singapore, and Hong Kong. My office would be in Bangkok. After receiving Alice's reluctant approval, I accepted the offer. This time my FBI security clearance took only four months. When the chief United Nations physician refused to clear me, given my history of childhood illnesses, United Nations Secretary-General U Thant intervened at the urging of Labouisse and the physician promptly gave me medical clearance. It was nice to be wanted.

The UNICEF Mission

My major concern at UNICEF was the welfare of poor children, youths, and mothers in three Asian nations—Thailand, Malaysia, and Singapore—and the British colony of Hong Kong. My professional associates shared my interests and were truly an international group: at the regional UNICEF office in Thailand we had staff members from Canada, the Netherlands, Turkey, Iran, Egypt, Brazil, and the United States, as well as many Thais. We worked in pleasant buildings set right on the side of the Chao Phraya River, which wound gracefully through old Bangkok.

Having come to Thailand to get my humanitarian concerns back on track, I was surprised to come into contact with glamour in the form of royalty and Hollywood stars. Among the major supporters of UNICEF were members of the Thai royal family. King Bumiphol Adulyadej—foreign-educated, a skilled saxophonist, and fluent in English—frequently took part in charitable events to raise funds for us and other agencies benefiting children. In 1967 he was the guest of honor of UNICEF at the Lido Theater in Bangkok where in a fund-raising event we showed the film *Oliver Twist* and a UNICEF film about our work during the recent deadly drought in the Indian state of Bihar. I greeted him at the entrance to the theater. Alice made a curtsey she had practiced and offered him a corsage. Another avid supporter of UNICEF was the Queen Mother. A spunky woman getting on in years, she played in UNICEF's annual charity golf tournaments. She visited the poor, the blind and the crippled all over Thailand. As a former nurse, she was particularly concerned about the welfare of mothers and children. I could see that her humanitarian concerns had rubbed off on her son, the king.

I was also host to a number of celebrity supporters of UNICEF. By far the most interesting was the actor Marlon Brando, who came to Thailand in 1967 after visiting UNICEF projects in Africa and Asia, including ones aiding victims of the drought in the Indian state of Bihar. Taking him around to visit UNICEF projects in the Bangkok area, I found him to be intense yet unassuming and likeable, a man in search of a life purpose. We had long talks about hunger and disease. He told me about a starving young boy who had literally died in his arms in Bihar. Resting after a game of squash one day, Brando talked of his life and his recent realization that the many dollars he had earned as an actor were nothing more than "the ashes of success." He was a gracious man, to the point of joining a family lunch for my daughter Genie's fourteenth birthday.

After his departure, I was pointedly told by New York headquarters of UNICEF that Brando had been traveling to Africa and Asia at his own expense. It turned out that he wanted to be named an official "ambassador" of UNICEF around the world, but headquarters had refused. I wrote to UNICEF headquarters recommending that we take him on, recounting how he had visibly moved the Thai press corps in his descriptions of the Bihar drought, despite a deeply ingrained prejudice against India and Indians in Thailand. But my pleas fell on deaf ears. In time, I came to realize that his controversial image wasn't the stamp that UNICEF's top leaders wanted, but I always felt that we lost out for not making Brando an ambassador for UNICEF.

The entertainer Dinah Shore came through as well, and we visited a number of schools and other UNICEF projects. In 1971, Danny Kaye arrived in town for a similar round of visits. At each site he put on a humorous mime act to the delight of children and adults alike. At his request, he and I visited the king. Kaye recounted to him the story of his early life in Brooklyn as a member of a large Jewish family of modest means. The king, in turn, told Kaye about his years in Cambridge, Massachusetts, as the son of a Thai doctor. They exchanged several jokes. Seeing how easily Kaye got on with members of society high and low, I left the palace that evening with a greater appreciation of why he had been UNICEF's global ambassador for so many years. He was effective and at the same time uncontroversial. He continued to work in this role until his death in 1990.

The standard image of UNICEF—the initials originally stood for United Nations International Children's Emergency Fund—is of tireless aid workers handing out food and medicine to children in a zone of war or natural catastrophe. We did some of that in East Asia, but for the most part the reality was quite different. It was what is known in the development trade as "institution building." We worked with inefficient, underfunded, and sometimes corrupt government bureaucracies with poorly paid staff to put in place programs that over the years would lead to a better life for children, youths, and mothers. In Thailand we supported grammar schools, trained teachers, and helped the government establish a vast network of rural health centers staffed by UNICEF-trained doctors, nurses, health aides, midwives, and nutritionists. We supported a well-digging project, as well as health programs furthering family planning and combatting malaria, smallpox, leprosy, and other prevalent diseases. UNICEF did very little in these countries by itself, for both political and financial reasons; rather, we worked through the local governments. I was pleased to know that for every dollar we gave to a project in Thailand, the host Thai government gave the equivalent of four dollars in its own currency to cover the salaries of local employees and other costs.

In my role as director for four countries and later deputy director for the whole East Asia twelve-nation region, I found myself alternately befriending members of the local governments and then facing them down. By chance, we had a wonderful connection to the upper levels of the Thai government in the form of my secretary, Suwimong, whose husband happened to be an army captain and special assistant to the deputy prime minister, General Sawaeng Senanarong. Together, the captain and I called on the general and helped persuade him to back construction of a large new building to house the East Asia UNICEF Regional Office, and at no cost to UNICEF. The large and beautiful building donated by the Thai government was completed in 1972 after I had left Thailand.

At other times, I played the role of tough cop in dealing with the Thai government. Representatives of Thai governments agencies tended to look on UNICEF as a Santa Claus that would give gifts and then fade away. But I insisted that in budget presentations to us, ministry officials give a clear statement of priorities and justify every item for which they requested UNICEF assistance. I would not authorize the funding for school laboratory equipment, for example, until I knew that the ministry had set aside money and that the schools actually had the electricity that the equipment would need. I refused to send new UNICEF jeeps to the Health Ministry until I got a report on the condition of vehicles we had formerly given. When once I discovered that UNICEF-donated powdered milk had found its way to the black market in Bangkok, I cut off supplies to the Health Ministry until officials had seized the illegally sold milk. Holding back milk shipments was not a pleasant task in a country with more than its share of malnourished children, but it had to be done.

As always, I spent much of my time on the road. I visited Malaysia, Hong Kong, Vietnam, Cambodia, East and West Pakistan, and Singapore, checking in on a host of UNICEF-funded programs. As in Thailand, they included midwife training, family planning programs, well digging, school improvements, distribution of nutritional supplements, and building community centers. At times I put UNICEF money to a use that would have surprised the people in America who drop coins into those boxes at Halloween—control of venereal disease among prostitutes. The arrival of the GIs in Bangkok had contributed to soaring rates of VD. Penicillin, a prime drug for treating it, was a very valuable commodity, and UNICEF's supply had a tendency to be "borrowed" before it reached its intended recipients. So one day, the Thai deputy minister of health and I paid a call on a senior U.S. general in Bangkok and explained the problem: the American soldiers who got VD were quickly treated, but the Thai prostitutes who gave it to them were not, guaranteeing that other GIs would get it before too long. The general listened, then agreed to donate to us a stock of military penicillin sufficient to treat all prostitutes in and around Bangkok.

The Fight against Leprosy

Of all the programs we pursued against disease, the one aimed at leprosy victims in Thailand made the deepest impression on me personally. I will never forget a two-week trip I took in 1967 to visit leprosy programs in several provinces of northeast Thailand. One day I went out with a mobile treatment team. We turned off a paved highway onto a narrow dirt road, and stopped at a large tree surrounded by bushes and far from public sight. Then I saw them—forty lepers squatting in the shade of the tree, patiently awaiting their turn for examination. They were of all ages. An old woman, chewing tobacco with a mouthful of decaying teeth, complained to us that the anti-leprosy pills she took five times a day gave her headaches. On the exposed rear of a little baby boy were marks that looked like leprosy, resulting perhaps from his daily contact with his leprosy-infected mother. A rather negative foreign medical worker among us kept up a stream of complaints that the Thai workers weren't up to the job and were keeping bad records. My mind was on the lepers, however. They had a quiet dignity about them, living with unspeakable physical and psychological suffering. They were scarred in spirit as well as body, it was clear.

At a nearby village, however, the mood was quite different. Here leprosy victims managed to live a relatively normal life among healthy people. The monthly exam by the mobile team was almost like a village fair, with just about everyone turning out to watch the doctors conduct head-to-toe examinations of leprosy victims. A young child was stripped naked so workers could look for lesions; an old man removed his shoes so that the doctor could see and touch the bottoms of his ulcerated and toeless feet; and a doctor examined the ample breasts of a woman for signs of leprosy. The spectators laughed openly at times, though it wasn't a cruel kind of laughter. The Thais often laugh at what to Westerners seem inappropriate times, but in this case their laughter put everyone at ease. I was told by other members of the leprosy team that there was genuine rejoicing when a leper in that village came to the end of the long treatment. Here, clearly, was a successful program—the disease had lost its social stigma, and its victims were getting needed treatment.

On this trip I met a young Irish doctor named Michael O'Regan. He examined countless people with leprosy as they sat in a chair before him, drawing smiles as he bantered with them in the local language, Lao, or cajoled them to be more diligent in taking their anti-leprosy pills. In patience, humor, and dedication he was to me everything a leprosy worker should be. I was saddened when he and his Thai wife and their four children left Thailand for Geneva, Switzerland, a year later.

Mission to South Vietnam

I was glad during this period to have nothing to do with the role of the U.S. government in the war in Vietnam, but I was able to play a minor role in alleviating some of the suffering there. South Vietnam was a member of the United Nations, and as such had UNICEF programs that were under my purview. I traveled there in the summer of 1967, as did our son John, then sixteen, who had ambitions to become a international newspaper correspondent. I arranged the trip, sending him to stay with the UNICEF representative there, a Swiss citizen named Bernard Klausner. John was nearing draft age, and I felt it would be a good experience for him to see the place firsthand. And see it he did—from the top of a building in downtown Saigon, he watched jets flying low and dumping napalm outside the city. He visited a hospital in the town of Quang Ngai where young American Quakers worked with Vietnamese amputees sleeping two to a bed. Back in the States, the war affected the life and views of his older brother Lyman as well. Firmly opposed to violence, Lyman, like his father three decades earlier, successfully sought conscientious objector status. He worked for two years as an orderly in a psychiatric hospital in Washington to fulfill his draft obligations.

I visited Saigon myself again in November of 1967 and found Klausner to be most critical of the war and U.S. policies in general. He faulted America for indiscriminate bombing in South Vietnam, for creating so-called "free-fire zones" where American gunmen in helicopters could shoot, in the words of a U.S. army general, at "anything that moves." Klausner predicted that the Vietcong would soon attack Saigon and provincial capitals. The Tet offensive of January 1968 proved him right. Bringing the fighting deep into virtually every major city and province capital in South Vietnam, it caused great suffering among civilians. Klausner's response to the emergency included asking the Thai government to ship to Danang tons of dried milk and blankets for civilians. At

Bangkok harbor, I and other UNICEF officers later helped to load these goods on to a U.S. Navy ship bound for Danang. No doubt the shipments helped people there, but they could have been no more than a minor salve in that terrible conflict, which would drag on for seven more years before Communist forces secured their victory in 1975.

It took a short time for me to see positive results in our UNICEF programs, and at times there were setbacks, but I considered my years with UNICEF in Asia to be among my most rewarding. Most East Asia nations were beginning an upward curve of economic growth in the 1970s. We at UNICEF played an important role in assuring that some of that prosperity reached to where it was most needed—to poor children and mothers in the city slums and distant villages.

18

The Painful Birth of Bangladesh, 1970–1972

THE YEARS 1970 and 1971 brought epic suffering not once but twice to a place in the world formerly knew as East Pakistan. First, in November 1970, a tidal wave rolled in from the Bay of Bengal and killed as many as half a million people in low-lying farm areas along the coast. The following year came human-made disaster. The Pakistan army cracked down on the dominant political party of East Pakistan, the Awami League, later triggering a brutal war of independence and one of the largest refugee exoduses of the twentieth century. Both tragedies took a horrible toll on children and mothers, so UNICEF quickly got involved. Our staff delivered food and medical supplies to the afflicted, often at great risk to themselves.

Before the tidal wave hit, I had made working visits to both East and West Pakistan, the divided wings of a single nation. They lay on either side of India, separated by more than a thousand miles. Even in normal times, rank poverty was the order of the day in both wings. In comparison, countries like Thailand seemed positively rich. Many Thai villagers could go to rural health centers when they got sick, but in such times Pakistani villagers had nowhere to turn. The illiteracy rate in Pakistan as a whole stood at 85 percent in 1970. Out of 100 children of first-grade age, only 45 entered school and only 9 of these 45 completed what was supposedly a standard six years of primary education. Most rural women lived in subjugation to their husbands, while men worked hard in the fields, often believing that life would never get better. UNICEF funneled money and technical experts to programs of health, grammar-school education, and rural cooperatives in both wings of Pakistan, but progress was very slow.

In November 1970 the tidal wave struck East Pakistan in the middle of the night. A radar warning system, one of the few pieces of modern technology in the country, was out of order at the time. Generated by a strong storm in the Bay of Bengal, a huge tidal wave swept many miles inland from the Bay of

Bengal at the height of rice-harvesting season, a time when thousands of farm laborers slept in the fields. Entire villages disappeared with all their residents. Roads built on causeways between the fields were washed away, and countless farm animals drowned. The next morning the whole area was a terrifying sea of bodies and destruction. UNICEF's regional director for East Asia, Yahya Darwish, flew immediately to Dacca, the capital of East Pakistan, and gave officials a substantial check for relief supplies. Other UNICEF officials rushed to the stricken area and were shocked at the thoroughness of the devastation. At our urging, UNICEF headquarters in New York City launched a worldwide appeal for $2 million to feed and shelter the survivors and help them return to normal life. Britain's Royal Air Force flew in blankets. I spent days at the port of Bangkok with UNICEF colleagues loading pumps, fishnets, kitchen equipment, blankets, and corrugated roofing into large ships bound for East Pakistan. More UNICEF field workers meanwhile converged on the emergency zone. With the roads gone, many came in boats, bringing with them food, medicine, and emergency shelter materials.

The other catastrophe was much slower building, and in retrospect we in United Nations agencies should have seen it coming. Its roots went back to 1947, when Pakistan was created as a homeland for the Muslims of the Indian subcontinent. From the start, West Pakistan was the senior partner in the divided nation, with almost all of the richest and most powerful families living there. The army was dominated from the ranks of general to private by West Pakistani men. With lighter skin and a higher standard of living, West Pakistanis tended to regard themselves as superior to the darker-skinned, shorter, and generally poorer Muslims of East Pakistan, as well as the many people there who were still of the Hindu faith.

Over time, Pakistan evolved into a military-run state. In 1969 the army put down civilian protests in East Pakistan with considerable bloodshed. The president, a general named Yahya Khan, immediately imposed martial law in both parts of the country, but promised elections soon. On December 7, 1970, less than a month after the tidal wave struck, the vote took place. Much to the chagrin of President Khan, the Awami League of East Pakistan captured 167 of the 169 seats allotted to the east wing of the country. In West Pakistan, the remaining 156 seats were split among six contending parties. Sheikh Mujib Rahman, the dynamic leader of the Awami League, assumed that he would be the nation's next prime minister.

His hope was dashed the morning after the election, when President Khan voided the election results and canceled the scheduled convening of the new Constituent Assembly in March. In response, the Awami League organized nonviolent protests, in the tradition of Mahatma Gandhi's fight for independence from the British. I saw one such protest march during a visit to Dacca. It was a peaceful parade of hundreds of people with high spirits, waving banners and chanting slogans. Schools and university and government offices in East Pakistan shut down as protests mounted in ensuing days. The army retaliated by killing several hundred protesters, including many students at Dacca University. The Pakistan government warned diplomats, United Nations personnel, and their families that since the armed forces "could not guarantee their safety," they should leave East Pakistan. Many did. About sixty UN staff members flew to Bangkok with their families. From them we learned more about the continuing suffering caused by the tidal wave and the brutality of the armed forces, who were largely viewed by citizens of East Pakistan as occupiers.

In mid-March 1971, with the army's violence unabated, President Khan flew to Dacca, allegedly to negotiate with leaders of the Awami League. After many hours of talk, he rejected all the League's demands, canceled the negotiations, and returned to West Pakistan. In a nationwide radio address the next day, he declared that military force was the only way to end what he called an open rebellion in East Pakistan. He announced that Awami League leaders would be tried and sentenced as traitors and common criminals. Then the army struck again, on a scale never before seen. Troops attacked Dacca University, killing hundreds of students and professors there. Their bodies were loaded into trucks, dumped in prepared trenches, and burned with gasoline. Many citizens were shot in the streets. Women were raped and then murdered. Hindu temples were torched. One night at Dacca's St. Gregory Catholic Church, a priest named Father Paul Gomez and about eight hundred of his mainly Hindu converts crowded into the church sanctuary. They met a quick death when the army set the church on fire. Troops hunted down and executed a number of Awami League leaders who had been elected to the Constituent Assembly.

I flew to Dacca several times during these troubled days. Armed soldiers were on patrol everywhere, and people were afraid to talk openly. The city exuded the feeling of oppressive military occupation. In Dacca I had conversations with Bagat El-Tawi, the special representative of the UN secretary-general, with other UN officials, and with American missionaries who, despite the perils, had not left. The Pakistani head of the East Pakistan Council of Churches told me he had good reason to believe that the army generals were determined to eliminate all Hindus in East Pakistan and all leaders of the Awami League. Since the Khan regime tended to regard all university students as potential enemies, this church official said, the parents of university students sought to protect themselves by burning their children's university textbooks.

Another purpose of my trip to Dacca was to determine if General Khan's army was diverting UNICEF supplies. This is a common occurrence amidst civil strife—relief food that the world ships is an asset that the dominant military power often wants to control, both to feed its own troops and to weaken its enemies by withholding it. Such diversions have since happened in such places as Cambodia, Somalia, Bosnia, and Kosovo. Our UNICEF staff told me that troops in East Pakistan were in fact off-loading UNICEF food and other goods meant for tidal wave victims and using these for the army's purposes. The army was also commandeering UNICEF jeeps at the port of Chittagong close to Dacca. We protested through official channels. Meanwhile, two brave members of the UNICEF staff took matters into their own hands: they entered the parking lot of Chittagong port late one night and removed key engine parts from the jeeps in order to make them inoperable.

By mid-1971 the conflict had developed into open warfare between the West Pakistan army and most of the citizens of East Pakistan. Army units swept across the countryside burning villages, firing on civilians, and rounding up people in an effort to stamp out the Awami League. In huge numbers, people began deserting their homes and fleeing to refugee camps which the government of India had constructed in the Indian states of West Bengal and Assam. President Khan meanwhile established so-called "peace committees" and hired young men known as *razakars* to seize the properties of local Hindus and any other families who had fled to the refugee camps in India. By November of 1971 an estimated 8.6 million East Pakistanis were living in camps in the two Indian states. During the war, an additional 5 million people in East Pakistan, I was told, lost almost everything they had.

In the meantime, the Awami League formed groups of young freedom fighters known as the Mukti Bahini. Many were students from Dacca University who had escaped the army's murderous sweeps there. They began dynamiting bridges, planting land mines, destroying power lines, and in a few instances assassinating those who had collaborated with the Khan regime. Many got training in the refugee camps in India, probably by instructors from the Indian government.

In response to the war's brutality, UN agencies launched another campaign to assist the victims. The UNICEF Regional Office in Bangkok shipped in 45,000 blankets and tons of alcohol for the manufacture of cholera vaccine, as well as tugboats and boat engines. The UNICEF Executive Board gave $11 million to the refugee camps in India. Other UN agencies dispatched medicines and tons of food, while the UN General Assembly created the United Nations Emergency Relief Organization of East Pakistan (UNEPRO) and sent several teams of relief workers to East Pakistan.

Official U.S. government policies toward the events in East Pakistan were far from helpful to the civilian victims. For years, and particularly after Richard

Nixon became president in 1969, Washington had been "tilting" toward Pakistan in that country's continuing confrontation with India. The U.S. government continued to ship arms to the Pakistan military during the war in East Pakistan. I learned that National Security Advisor Henry Kissinger had castigated the U.S. ambassador to India, Kenneth Keating, for publicly taking strong exception to claims by the Pakistan government that the conflict was only an "internal affair" in which other nations should not interfere. This scolding of Ambassador Keating, in my opinion, may have resulted from something we learned later: that at the time Kissinger was seeking help from the Pakistan government to make a secret trip to Beijing in July 1971 to plan Nixon's historic meeting with Chinese leaders there the following February. To Kissinger, I believe, the coming détente with China was far more important than the plight of people in East Pakistan.

Sending blankets and food to victims was essential, but I decided to take some action to try to influence my government's policy toward Pakistan. I wrote a letter to Republican Senator John Sherman Cooper of Kentucky, who had been the U.S. ambassador in India during my first six months in the embassy there in 1956. I enclosed newspaper articles detailing the suffering of the people of East Pakistan and predicting that the conflict might bring a famine there. I also enclosed statements by Americans, citizens of East Pakistan, and UN officials who had fled East Pakistan, describing in some detail the bloody actions of the army. In my letter to the senator, I wrote:

> To date the West Pakistan regime has conducted a rather successful public relations campaign to convince the world that all is peaceful in East Pakistan and that the horrible killings by the army there never happened. To date only the Governments of the Soviet Union and India have publicly voiced their horror about the slaughter in East Pakistan. The Government of China has pledged its allegiance to the Government of Pakistan and has warned India to stay out of "internal struggles" within Pakistan.

> To the best of my knowledge, President Nixon has made no public statement to date condemning the army killings in East Pakistan. I have come to the conclusion that events in East Pakistan can be changed only (1) if members of the U.S. Senate and House and the American press condemn the army killings by the Pakistan army in East Pakistan and (2) if the U.S. Government and the other nine members of the Pakistan Consortium—consisting of the United States, Japan, and certain industrial nations of Europe giving economic and/or military assistance to Pakistan—are willing to call an immediate meeting of the

Consortium and in this meeting threaten to cut off further economic and military assistance to Pakistan unless a quick settlement is made and the fighting and killings in East Pakistan cease. . . . I hope that you can encourage President Nixon to take moral leadership by calling a meeting of the Pakistan Consortium and putting pressure on President Khan to end the killings in East Pakistan.

I never found out what effect my letter had on Cooper or his Senate colleagues, but judging by newspaper reports in Washington and New York City and even in Bangkok, a growing number of American lawmakers were becoming openly critical of conditions in the Indian refugee camps, Nixon's continuing aid to the Pakistan armed forces, and the growing brutality of those forces. Senator Edward Kennedy went with a team of nutritional and emergency relief experts to examine conditions in the refugee camps in India after Pakistan authorities refused to grant the team visas to visit East Pakistan. A friend and former USAID director in India, John Lewis, later gave me a copy of the team's final report, which he had written. Regarding our nation's policy, the report concluded: "To be arrayed along with China as the principal apologist supporting a regime that willfully undertakes and persists in one of the bloodiest repressions of recent history, is not particularly helpful to [our nation's] foreign policy."

As time went on, it became increasingly clear that the crisis was going to end in war between India and Pakistan, which had already fought each other twice since the British departed from the Indian subcontinent in 1947. Indian troops were massing for an attack. Formal hostilities began in early December of 1971 when President Khan, apparently believing that a threat of Chinese intervention would stay India's hand, ordered the bombing of Indian air bases. With active support of the Mukti Bahini, the Indian army then invaded East Pakistan in a classic "blitzkrieg" operation beginning on December 4. The Chinese government protested loudly but did not intervene. During the invasion, on December 14, Nixon sent the nuclear-powered aircraft carrier USS *Enterprise* into the Bay of Bengal. It did not intervene in the conflict, but Indian Prime Minister Indira Gandhi clearly regarded the carrier's presence as a threat to India.

Indian forces advanced down the roads toward Dacca. This was a perilous time for the six UNICEF staff members who remained on the job in Dacca. Two of them were almost killed one day when Indian planes strafed their car near the city. Happily, the war didn't last long. In two weeks, Indian forces entered Dacca and Khan's forces surrendered. The next day, as commanded by President Nixon, the USS *Enterprise* left the Bay of Bengal.

The leaders of a government-in-exile, living in the Indian refugee camps, came to Dacca and in December 1971 proclaimed that East Pakistan was now the sovereign nation of Bangladesh. Sheikh Mujib, released from a Pakistani prison, became its first prime minister.

The UN responded quickly to help repair damage resulting from the months of conflict. In early January 1972, UNICEF Executive Director Henry Labouisse became the first head of a UN agency to visit the new nation. By the end of that month, all UNICEF personnel and UN relief workers had returned to their work. In February 1972, the new government authorities in Dacca estimated that Bangladesh needed a $600 million grant for reconstruction. In response to an appeal for such funds from the UN secretary-general, member nations pledged $500 million within a few weeks. UNICEF's financial needs in Bangladesh came to about $30 million. These funds were quickly pledged by several industrial nations, including the United States.[1]

It would be encouraging to say that with the liberation and the end of the war everything ended happily for Bangladesh. In reality, its history has been one of turmoil ever since. Sheikh Mujib was killed in a coup by his own army officers in 1975. The nation of Bangladesh remains to this day one of the world's poorest. But through it all, UNICEF has been on the scene looking after those who are often the first to suffer in times of conflict—children and mothers. I am proud to have played a minor role in helping these victims during this country's time of greatest trial.

19

The Voice of UNICEF in North America, 1972–1977

FEW EXPERIENCES ARE more humbling than becoming a small fish in a big pond. In 1972, after six years as an area director and then as the deputy director of East Asia for UNICEF, I was assigned to UNICEF's New York headquarters. It was a large organization with many people heading in their many different directions, and I found it easy to get lost in the shuffle. In his always kind and understanding manner, Henry Labouisse, the agency's executive director, steered me into a new assignment that got me out of the office, which was always where I was more happy. He appointed me as chief spokesman for UNICEF in both the United States and Canada.

The main job before me was to change that old image of UNICEF as an emergency relief agency passing out milk and high-protein food to starving children. It had done this in its founding days in Europe after the Second World War, but as I had learned so well in Asia, UNICEF now had a much broader mission of bettering the long-term health and education of children, youths, and mothers in poor countries and improving their general quality of life. The agency was a crucial resource in training such persons as doctors, nurses, health workers, teachers, and well diggers. So I set out to get this message across to the American and Canadian public, as well as to stress the need for much more money to underwrite these projects. I soon discovered that UNICEF had a huge network of dedicated volunteers and donors across the two countries who worked long and hard selling greeting cards and distributing Halloween collection boxes. But even they were often in the dark as to what UNICEF actually did in developing countries. So I began traveling. During my five years in this job, I talked with hundreds of grammar school and high school students, addressed students and faculty on seventy-five college campuses, and spoke before numerous service clubs, church congregations, and groups of

UNICEF volunteers. I appeared on radio and TV shows. I spoke at meetings of the Canadian UNICEF Committee and the U.S. Committee for UNICEF.

I enjoyed these sessions and was often impressed with people's generosity and willingness to part with money and time to assist faraway children whom they would never see. For the most part, they were, like me, white and middle class, enjoying the bounty of life in a world that was predominantly non-white and poor. Trying to make vivid the trials of daily life in these other countries, I sometimes presented an imaginative story written by economist Robert Heilbroner. In his book *The Great Ascent,* Heilbroner described what it would take to transform a typical American house and its resident family of modest means by American standards into a family living in a poor village of rural India. The American family would have to

- Take out all the furniture, leave a few old blankets, a kitchen table and chair.

- Take away all the clothing except for the oldest dress or suit and a shirt or blouse for each family member. Leave one pair of worn shoes for the man of the family.

- Empty the pantry except for a small bag of flour, some sugar and salt, a few old potatoes for tonight's dinner, plus a handful of onions and a dish of dry beans.

- Throw out all bank books, stock certificates, pension plans, and insurance policies, and leave the family with five dollars in cash for each family member.

- Take the house away and instruct the family to move into a toolshed.

- Cancel all subscriptions to newspapers and magazines, since your family is now illiterate.

- Lop off twenty-five to thirty years in the life expectancy of each member of the family.[1]

Some people in the audiences I addressed were put off by the thought, while others were humbled. In any case, it tended to provoke discussion.

Before varied audiences I made the point, as stated by the international economist Barbara Ward, that the economic power of the United States and its ability to better the lives of children and youths around the world were unique in many ways: "To hold in [America's] hands the living or dying of half million children, to be the only power capable of beginning the building of grain reserves, to be the chief state with power and wealth enough to rise above the narrow temptations of naked market power—here is the challenge unequal in history."[2]

I then reminded my listeners that few prosperous citizens of America and other wealthy nations were contributing their wealth to the poor in Third World nations. As a result, there was a growing bitterness among the poor and forgotten toward affluent individuals and nations. In such a world of gross inequalities and a widening of the chasm between rich and poor nations, I reminded many audiences, UNICEF can give us all a channel for our energies and compassion for children of poor nations suffering from diseases, without education, and with slender faith in their own futures. Through UNICEF we can become active participants in a worldwide campaign to bring joy and strength and hope to millions of children, youths, and mothers in the poorest nations of our world.

My second major task was to help the U.S. Committee for UNICEF to get a better handle on its main purpose of existence, which was raising funds for UNICEF. The committee simply wasn't going after many of the big-money sources in America. Instead, it was relying on small gifts, often less than a dollar, from large numbers of people. That was an important way of making people feel involved, but at the same time, corporations, foundations, and other agencies were contributing big money to charity, and UNICEF was getting virtually none of it. I helped the staff of the U.S. Committee to craft a master fund-raising program. By the end of 1973, with the assistance of an able consulting firm, the committee had created a much larger, computerized mailing list and launched a successful nationwide mail appeal for funds. To help things further, I called on some potential big donors myself. I was able to tap many of my former contacts in the labor and church worlds. The United Auto Workers, for instance, agreed to grant $95,000 to purchase and distribute vitamin A pills in Bangladesh to prevent blindness among children. I got substantial funds from agencies of the United Methodist Church and other church agencies in America and Asia. In most cases each grant went to support a specific UNICEF project in a specific country selected by the donor.

An unusual gift to UNICEF was provided by the Nippon Steel Corporation of Japan at the urging of the Metal Workers Council of Japan, a union group. In 1974 I went to Japan with Danny Kaye, who was scheduled to appear in a national TV program there for UNICEF. Before leaving on the trip, I asked Victor Reuther for an introduction to the Metal Workers Council of Japan. In meeting with council officials, I succeeded in getting them interested in UNICEF. They later prevailed on Nippon Steel to donate a large quantity of pig iron to a UNICEF-supported project that manufactured water pumps in Bangladesh.

In another case, I encouraged UNICEF volunteer Deirdre Bonifaz of Chadds Ford, Pennsylvania, to found a group called Artisans for UNICEF to sell to Americans handmade goods produced by cooperatives run by poor women in the U.S. South and a few Latin American countries. In 1980, the artisans group, by then separated from UNICEF but still directed by Bonifaz, was operating stores in Chadds Ford, Philadelphia, Ardmore, Boston, and Nantucket. Its total sales that year exceeded $500,000. I was happy to know that through the help of UNICEF volunteers, poor women in America and overseas who made the goods received some much-needed income.

In my opinion, UNICEF remains today the most flexible and effective aid organization within the large and often bureaucracy-bound United Nations family. It is closest to the governments and peoples of developing countries, especially at the grassroots level. Politically, it is the least controversial agency, as no reasonable person can take issue with the goal of bettering the lives of children. UNICEF bettered my life as well. While working for it, I had the privilege to worry not about the security of my prosperous nation, but about the welfare of the most vulnerable people in some of the most impoverished nations on earth. My eleven years at the agency left me more compassionate toward humanity, and at the same time more angry about the social causes of poverty.

There was other good news for me and my family in this period: Alice finally won her battle against alcoholism. In 1972, shortly after our return from Thailand, she spent four weeks in an alcohol recovery center in eastern Pennsylvania and came home a changed person. For the next eighteen years, as we lived in the New Jersey town of Montclair, she worked to help other women do the same. First she was a volunteer, then a staff member at a recovery center. Later, she opened a halfway house at our own home, helping scores of women battling alcoholism to follow her on the path to full recovery.

I was getting close to UNICEF's mandatory retirement age of sixty now. The events of later life were creeping up on me. My mother died in 1974, leaving me sad, conscious of my own mortality, and appreciative of how much we had meant to each other. In her papers I found decades of my letters to her, all neatly arranged in chronological order. By now all but one of my own children, Steve, had grown up and moved away, and we had many grandchildren. I continued running two miles each morning before breakfast, but I was running no faster.

I retired from UNICEF on July 1, 1977. I packed up my things in my office at the headquarters building and headed out to our home in Montclair. I knew I wasn't going to stop working, though. It was just time for something new.

My father and me, age four.

My mother with my brother Vinton, and me age six.

My father, John Stewart Burgess (1883–1949), ca. 1930.

My mother, Stella Fisher Burgess (1881–1974), ca. 1956.

Alice and I were married on Thanksgiving Day, 1941.

A farm laborer on her way to work in the blueberry fields in Whitesbog, New Jersey, leaves her children with Alice, who is in charge of the nursery in the summer of 1942.

En route to work in the blueberry fields of Whitesbog, New Jersey, I
discuss plans for a youth recreation program that evening with a fellow
staff member.

Alice and I in front of our one-room house, with many children whose parents work in the large Seabrook Farms plant near Bridgeton, New Jersey, in July 1943. Alice starts her 12-hour shift in the plant at 6 A.M., six days a week. Next to the building is our 1932 Ford.

The open sewer next to our one-room house just a few yards from the Seabrook plant near Bridgeton, New Jersey, in July 1943.

162

Outdoor cooking for us and our white migrant neighbors.

Tent city is home for hundreds of migrants from the South and from Jamaica working at the Seabrook plant and in the fields.

All day Saturday, members of a training school sponsored by the Southern Tenant Farmers Union (STFU) near Cotton Plant, Arkansas, in December of 1944. Present were F. J. Betton, vice president of STFU, and STFU organizer George Stith.

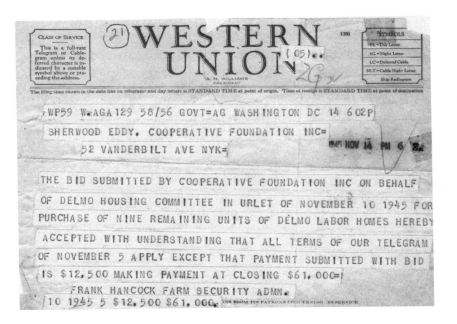

WP59 W.AGA129 58/56 GOVT=AG WASHINGTON DC 14 602P

SHERWOOD EDDY, COOPERATIVE FOUNDATION INC=
52 VANDERBILT AVE NYK=

1945 NOV 14 PM 6 2

THE BID SUBMITTED BY COOPERATIVE FOUNDATION INC ON BEHALF
OF DELMO HOUSING COMMITTEE IN URLET OF NOVEMBER 10 1945 FOR
PURCHASE OF NINE REMAINING UNITS OF DELMO LABOR HOMES HEREBY
ACCEPTED WITH UNDERSTANDING THAT ALL TERMS OF OUR TELEGRAM
OF NOVEMBER 5 APPLY EXCEPT THAT PAYMENT SUBMITTED WITH BID
IS $12,500 MAKING PAYMENT AT CLOSING $61,000=

FRANK HANCOCK FARM SECURITY ADMN.

10 1945 5 $12,500 $61,000.

Telegram from Frank Hancock, Director of the Farm Security Administration, to Sherwood Eddy, representing the Delmo Housing Corporation, announcing the acceptance of the corporation's bid for the purchase of 549 farm labor homes in nine Delmo project locations in southeast Missouri, November 14, 1945.

Tenants Pool Funds, Become Landowners

When Congress ordered the FSA to sell houses like these in the Delmo Labor Homes Project in Southeast Missouri, tenants got together and decided they would be the highest bidder. They were. And now the tenants are landowners.

By ROBERT JOHNSON
Press-Scimitar Staff Writer

They were the homeless, tired of wandering, weary of the shotgun shacks, the mean, weatherbeaten hovels in which they had lived, hungry for just a little good to lighten their wretched lives.

Farm Security Administration came, and for a time there was hope. Someone was interested in them, wanted to help them, went about it in a concrete fashion.

At last they had homes—not mansions, but trim, cheap, neat houses in which they could find contentment of a sort they had not known before.

But one by one the FSA experiments ended.

And after four years the 2000 men, women and children of the Delmo Labor Homes Project in Southeast Missouri got their notice. The FSA advertised for sale the 580 houses in the 10-farm labor community projects.

Wardell . . Kennett . . Lilbourn . . Gray Ridge . . Morehouse . . East Prairie . . Wyatt.

It Didn't Seem Right

Beat again. They sat in their snug living rooms and talked in strained voices. Back to their leaky, rotten, tumbled down shacks. Back to the misery from which they had been lifted, only this time it was to be worse because they had seen a little better times and knew what it was like to have a home. It just didn't seem right that in this richest country in the world a man willing to work couldn't even have a decent cover for the heads of his wives and kids.

Petitions were circulated, meetings held. The Southern Tenant Farmers Union began a fight to save the homes.

And now there's happiness in the Delmo homes again.

On Nov. 15 the FSA accepted a bid of $285,000 for the Delmo Project. The families which lived in its 549 homes for $6.50 a month rent won't be tenants any more.

$800 Per Home

They're landowners now.

According to H. L. Mitchell, pres-ident of the Southern Tenant Farmers Union, the total cost of each individual house, lot and furniture is estimated at $800 with interest of three per cent plus upkeep of community facilities.

"Each family raised $100 for the first payment and sent it in to an escrow agent in St. Louis," Mr. Mitchell said. "The balance of $700 will be paid out in monthly or semi-annual payments over a period of eight years."

All but 100 of the houses were taken when the FSA accepted the bid. Since then, all but about 25 have been spoken for.

The farm labor families themselves raised a total of $40,000. Interested men thruout the country, including Marshall Field, publisher of the Chicago Sun, and Alfred Baker Lewis of New York City, secretary-treasurer of the National Sharecroppers Fund, contributed to bring the fund up to the required $73,000.

Pooled Their Funds

Actual bid for the homes was made by the Co-Operative Farm Foundation, of which Sherwood Eddy is chairman, using the funds pooled by the farm families. Field work in raising the funds was done by W. A. Johnson, union organizer of Wardell, and Rev. David S. Burgess, Congregational minister working with the union.

An idea of how important possession of these homes was to their new owners can be obtained from the fact that the $100 down payment represents more than one-fourth of the average worker's yearly income.

Each house is on from a half—to a full acre of what Mr. Mitchell terms "fair land." The nine communities each have a community building, community showering and clothes washing facilities. At Kennett there is a building used as a school.

Four to Five Rooms

The houses vary from four to five rooms. Each has a large combination living and dining room, a small kitchen and concrete cellar. Six of the communities are for white families and three for negro families.

An alfalfa mill bought one of the communities at Wyatt outright for about $1000 each home to house its employes.

What the homes mean to their new owners is perhaps best explained in the words of Mrs. Oscar Thompson of Wardell, mother of five children, who told The Press-Scimitar at the time it seemed as tho they would lose their homes:

"It used to be while we were living in tenant houses that the landlord would dig us out and make us work for him for from nothing to 75 cents an hour—or get out of our house. Here, they can't order us around. Here we can hire out for any price we want to."

Our home at the Delmo project in East Prairie, Missouri, from December 1945 to July 1947.

Some of our youthful neighbors in the East Prairie project.

The staff of the Textile Workers Union-CIO and the Southern CIO Organizing Drive in Rock Hill, South Carolina, on January 28, 1948. *From left:* me, Marjie Geier, Harvey Mayo, Don McKee, and Mike Smith.

Family picture in Atlanta, 1954. *From left:* Lyman, Genie, me, Alice, Laurie, and John.

Walter Reuther and I lay a wreath on the grave of Mahatma Gandhi in New Delhi, April 1956.

172

Pictured at the government of India's reception for delegates to the Asian Conference of the International Labor Organization (ILO) in New Delhi are me, my labor attache prececessor Henri Sokolove, U.S. Deputy Assistant of Labor Leo Werts, and Indian Prime Minister Jawaharlal Nehru in mid-November 1957.

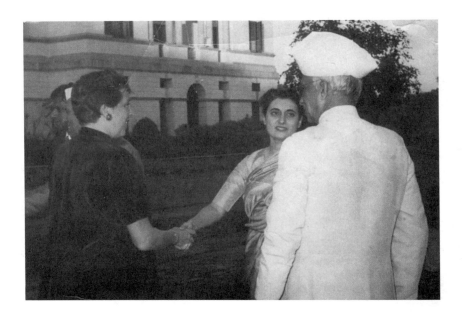

Daughter of Jawaharlal Nehru and future Prime Minister Indira Gandhi shakes hands with a very pregnant Alice while greeting Indian President Sarvepalli Radhakrishnam at the government of India's reception for the ILO delegates at the Asian Conference.

Three of my colleagues at the U.S. Embassy in New Delhi in 1958: Secretary of the Labor Section Barbara Griffith, Economic Officer Terrance Todman, and Indian Assistant in the Labor Section P.V.K. Krishnan. Todman became Assistant Secretary of State for Latin American in 1977. Later he was appointed U.S. Ambassador to Costa Rica and then Ambassador to Denmark.

American Ambassador to India Ellsworth Bunker gives the State Department's Meritorious Service Award in December 1959 in New Delhi.

In the courtyard of our home at 61 Friends Colony in New Delhi, the seven members of the Burgess family gather in December 1959. *From left:* Alice, Lyman, Genie, John, Steve (born November 24, 1957 in New Delhi), Laurie, and me.

Present at my swearing in as a U.S. Foreign Service Officer II in June 1961 are, *from left,* Victor Reuther, Edwin Martin (then China Desk Officer and later Ambassador to Burma), Genie, Alice, Steve, John, Lyman, and Under Secretary of State Chester Bowles.

Accompanied by Deputy Premier and Minister of National Development and Mom
Kraideb, a UNICEF staff member from the Royal Family, I give a UNICEF check to Her
Royal Highness the Princess Mother of the King of Thailand.

Alice presents flowers and greets the King of Thailand at the UNICEF showing of the film *Oliver* in Bangkok in 1969.

September 1969.

On the occasion of the visit of Henry R. Labouisse, the Executive Director of UNICEF, all members of the East Asia Regional Headquarters in Bangkok were asked to gather so that a memorial photo could be taken with Mr. Labouisse, who is seated in the middle of the front row. The photo was taken in December 1971, when Mr. Labouisse was on his way to Dacca to visit the leaders of the newly created nation of Bangladesh, following its liberation from the nation of Pakistan.

Montclair in 1979.

Starting on the steps of St. Stephan's United Church of Christ in Newark, supporters of the Ironbound Committee Against Toxic Waste march to City Hall to protest the construction of a huge garbage burning plant in the Ironbound in 1986.

In May 1987 the Newark Housing Authority, with funds given by the Federal Department of Housing and Urban Development, destroy four high-rise buildings in Scudder Homes containing 812 apartments for low income families. Mayor Sharpe James and eight of the nine members of the Newark City Council praised the demolition and were present to see the destruction at a time when 10,000 families were on the Housing Authority's waiting list.

Members of the Newark Coalition for Low Income Housing protest the lack of construction of new homes for low income families in late 1988 by the Newark Housing Authority. The poorly constructed homes in the background were later destroyed in a windstorm in 1990. Between the demolition of 812 Authority apartments in 1987 and 1993 not a single new unit was built by the authority.

Standing in front of the altar at St. Stephan's United Church in Newark on August 30, 1989, my last day as minister of this church, after ten and a half years.

20

Finding a New Direction at Newark's Zion Church, 1979–1986

DOUGLAS VAGIE, ELECTRICIAN and council member at Zion Church in western Newark, New Jersey, put a friendly but tough question to me as we sat over coffee one evening late in 1978: "I see from your résumé, Brother Burgess, that you have lived a most interesting life, both in America and abroad. You have met diplomats, cabinet ministers, business executives, and other people of power and influence. So why are you interested in becoming pastor of a struggling working-class church in this poor city of Newark?" I had known this question would be asked, but still I was at a loss for an immediate answer. After a moment of silence, I answered something like this: "Yes, I've worked in many places and rubbed shoulders with important people, but I've often been at a level removed from the people I was trying to help. The time has come in my life when I want to work with individuals on a one-to-one basis." I added: "Since I've never served an established church with a sanctuary, I have a hell of a lot to learn." Vagie listened, and I wondered if he liked my answer.

Life after UNICEF had been more tempestuous than I had expected. I hadn't thought it would be easy to start a new career at age sixty, but still I wasn't prepared for how rough things turned out to be. There were constant emotional ups and downs as I put my name in for various jobs, without success. My hopes for a position in the newly elected Carter administration never panned out. I did find a position for nine months in 1977 and 1978 as head of a Cambridge, Massachusetts, agency at Harvard University called the Latin American Scholarship Program of American Universities (LASPAU), which helped professors from Latin America obtain graduate degrees at American colleges and universities. From the beginning, however, I knew I was not a good fit for this job, because I had never worked in Latin America and spoke neither Spanish nor Portuguese. But I decided to see if I could succeed in this new calling.

Perhaps the high point of my time at LASPAU was a trip I took in late 1978 to Recife, Brazil, where I spent a few hours with a remarkable Catholic archbishop named Dom Helder Camara. For decades he had been a defender of the urban poor and landless peasants. Many of his priests had been tortured and a few killed by agents of the Brazilian government. He had turned the magnificent archbishop's mansion into a home for the homeless, while he lived in two small rooms adjoining an ancient and crumbling church. Receiving me at his simple residence, he spoke of the challenges of being an advocate for the poor in Brazil. He faulted the U.S. government for almost always taking the wrong side in Third World countries. National security, he said, had become almost a religion for policy makers in Washington. I will never forget him, because I found him to be a truly courageous saint battling worldly superiors in the Catholic Church and the ruling principalities of Brazilian society. The archbishop died in 1999.

On returning to Cambridge, I found that some of my senior staff members were in revolt against my leadership. One of my deputies told me that "the head does not fit the body" and that I should therefore resign. I believed that he and other staff members had overlooked my success in tapping my old contacts at the U.S. Agency for International Development in the fall of 1977 to raise considerable funds for LASPAU at a time when it needed these funds desperately. In the course of all this, I discovered that my two predecessors had been ousted by the senior staff without effective objections from the LASPAU board of directors. So, convinced that I wasn't meant for this job anyway, I resigned and returned to Montclair.

I didn't automatically find peace there, however. Our youngest son, Steve, now in his late teens, had developed signs of schizophrenia. Alice and I spent long hours working with him and consulting with various doctors. During the next five years he was frequently hospitalized, but gradually he bravely fought back against his illness. With the assistance of skilled doctors and counselors and with proper medication, he pulled himself back to mental stability. A quiet, empathetic person, he lives today in a small town in upstate New York State.

Cooling my heels in Montclair, I often despaired of finding a new professional calling. Then came an unexpected inquiry: two struggling blue-collar churches of my denomination in Newark, Zion United Church of Christ and St. Stephan's United Church of Christ, were looking for a joint pastor. Would I be interested? The pay wouldn't be much. The hours would be long. I gave the offer lengthy consideration and, after consulting with Alice, decided to put in my name. Perhaps the disappointments of the previous months were a signal to me: it was time to leave the world of big organizations and devote myself to a simple ministry. Thus I found myself meeting with Douglas Vagie and other members of the ruling councils of the two congregations. Evidently, I answered their questions to their satisfaction. I was offered the two jobs and on January 1, 1979, began a new phase of my life.

Now all I had to do was figure out how to be a pastor. I had remained very active in churches in the thirty-two years since I had left the formal ministry, by teaching adult Bible classes and occasionally delivering sermons at the request of pastors. But now I felt I was starting from scratch. I sought advice from many people. I reviewed the yellowed notes I had taken in 1943 and 1944 during a preaching course at Union Seminary. It had been taught by Dr. Harry Emerson Fosdick, longtime pastor of New York's Riverside Church and often called the greatest American Protestant preacher of the first half of the twentieth century. I still recall vividly his advice about preaching. It boiled down to this: Start with a paragraph stating in simple words the central theme of your sermon. Then make three illustrative points to clarify your theme, and close with a brief summation of your sermon's theme. Before you choose a sermon theme and readings from the Bible, imagine in your mind and heart the faces of the men, women, and children you will be preaching to. Recall what you already know about their fears, hopes, faith or lack of faith, their joys, doubts, and sadness which you have discovered during your visits to their homes and your conversations with them elsewhere. Be keenly aware of your own fears, hopes, faith, or lack of faith which are often parts of your life experiences. Try to keep your sermons to twenty minutes or less. In order to have continuing eye contact with your congregation as you deliver a sermon, preach from an outline rather than reading the text.

Elsewhere, I found good advice that sermons aren't everything. I will long remember the words of the late mythologist Joseph Campbell to journalist and author Bill Moyers during a TV interview: "People err trying to talk people into beliefs. Better they reveal the radiance of their own discovery" in the quality of their daily lives.

Zion Church, today known as Zion United Church of Christ, was founded in 1898 in the Vailsburg section of western Newark. It began as a congregation of recent German immigrants and their families. And so it remained, even after the "white flight" of the 1970s following the street rebellion of blacks in 1967 radically changed the racial makeup of the neighborhood around the church. In 1970, less than 6 percent of families living in Vailsburg were black; in 1980, in the three census tracks nearest to Zion Church, 80 percent of the residents were black. Yet in early 1979, when I became pastor, there was not a single black face in the Zion congregation.

When I arrived, the church had fewer than one hundred members. They were mostly white working-class people getting on in years. Some were openly racist and distrustful of blacks, while others wanted to find some ways to open the church doors to our black neighbors.

I began my ministry with an ambitious plan: I would visit the home of every Zion member in Newark and the suburbs. I would also visit all families—white, black and Hispanic—living within a quarter-mile radius of the church. Meanwhile, in sermons and meetings with the church council, I sounded the theme that Zion Church would never grow or prosper unless its present members agreed to open its doors to all families in the neighborhood, irrespective of race. It was our duty as professing Christians, I said, to welcome members whose race and culture were different from ours. I continued to believe, and do so today, in the ideal of integration. But my years in Newark were a lesson to me of just how difficult it was to end old patterns of the races going their separate ways in churches and programs of community improvement.

In August 1980 I won an important initial victory toward the goal of outreach: the Zion church council agreed to my recommendation that we hire a young man named Kenneth Cumberbatch, a black student from Brunswick Seminary, as a student assistant minister. Kenneth and I spent many hours knocking on doors in the neighborhood. A few of the people who opened their doors to us were hostile. Most were cordial, though often they were puzzled as to why a white and a black minister were visiting their homes on behalf of an all-white church. Said one skeptical black man as he stood at his doorway: "Zion has been run by a handful of white folks ever since it opened. I wouldn't have much of a voice there if I joined." A black woman complained about the slow and solemn hymns at Zion. She preferred the joy of singing gospel songs in a vibrant black church. Now and then we found that the families we visited had very real and immediate needs. We did what we could, which often wasn't much, to help a man with terminal cancer, a wife beaten by her drunken husband, a pregnant fourteen-year-old, a drug-addicted man, and a deeply depressed black woman who wrote poetry. During these visits I sometimes questioned if I could ever provide adequate spiritual guidance to black people, whose lives seemed so different from mine in many ways. Unlike most of my black neighbors, I had never been penniless, hungry, homeless, or the victim of race prejudice. Over time I reluctantly accepted the fact that I had a limited ability to help our neighbors. But as I became more pastoral, less judgmental, and a more careful listener, I began to understand better the needs of our black neighbors and how to minister to these needs.

Slowly we began to have some success in revitalizing the church. Initially, it came through children and young people. While most black adults in the neighborhood weren't interested in joining Zion, they liked the idea that their children and youths would have a structured, safe place to go. So we offered school-related tutorial classes on Saturday mornings and afternoons and Sunday school classes on Sunday. We recruited a number of tutors and Sunday school teachers from the neighborhood and in time had thriving programs going in the multi-roomed church basement. In fact, we sometimes had difficulty getting children in the tutorial classes to leave to make way for the next classes.

Our next black student assistant minister, Fred Marshall, was older than his predecessor. Fred was a good preacher and an excellent organizer. He added to our outreach programs by starting a youth fellowship for teenagers which met on Sunday afternoons. The fellowship put on plays, musical events, and fashion shows for the congregation and our neighbors. Here and there black adults began to join the church, because they had reason to believe that some Zion members now cared about the future of their community. Among the first black members were a retired autoworker, two surgical nurses, an interior decorator, and an employee of Jersey Bell.

Some white members of the congregation were disturbed by these developments. They began to tell me I was neglecting them. They complained that occasionally the teachers and students of the youth programs did not clean up the rooms before they left, and that black Sunday school teachers were not attending the worship service which began well after Sunday school was over. But far more important than such petty faultfinding was the undeniable fact that many whites feared black crime. One night when I was pastor at Zion pastor, the chairman of the church council was mugged on his doorstep by several black youths; a few months later, his wife was held up in her own kitchen by a young black man wearing a ski mask. Until we installed an alarm system, the church basement was regularly burglarized. The thieves even stole food intended for children in the day care center at the church.

In conversations with me, some older white members at Zion harkened back to the "golden days" before black people had moved into Vailsburg. One elderly white woman told me, "Years ago we never kept our front door locked. We could walk down the streets in the day or night without fear of being mugged."

Still, as the youth programs grew and more blacks joined the church, I decided that assistant minister Fred Marshall should be my successor. I broached the idea to church council members, and—not surprisingly—a majority of them rejected it. Fred soon heard the news. One day during the following week, much to my dismay, I learned that he had met with Sunday school teachers and members of the youth fellowship and told them that after three years at Zion he was sure that key white leaders would "rather see the church burn down than see it taken over by blacks." He told the fellowship members that "Zion will never be your church home." I was further saddened when Fred told me the next day that he would resign soon. His frustrations were understandable, but I was sorry to lose the services of a devoted friend and a talented leader.

Fred left in mid-1984, as did all the black Sunday school teachers, but the unexpected happened the week after Fred's departure. I met a young black woman named Loretta Smith. A former schoolteacher, Loretta was then a senior at Drew Seminary in Madison, New Jersey. I persuaded her to take Fred's place. Taking charge of the outreach programs and Sunday school, Loretta soon gained the confidence of teachers, tutors, children, and youths. She had a classic pastor's skill for bridging differences—she also won over a majority of church members—and we soon got back on track. More blacks joined the church, and contributions from several suburban churches in our denomination enabled us to pay Loretta's part-time salary.

Despite continued grumblings and misgivings, many white members were now willing to establish closer links with the neighborhood. In 1983, many helped to found the Alexander Street Block Association to fight crime. In 1985, fifty Zion families joined the national agency called the Self Help and Resource Exchange, popularly known as SHARE. This agency had established a wholesale purchasing system in which a member family contributed twelve dollars at the beginning of each month and received at the end of the month food worth thirty-six dollars or more. Today thousands of Newark families receive such groceries from SHARE.

The transformation of the church continued. To supplement the United Church of Christ hymnal, we purchased the Methodist *Songs of Zion* hymnal, which was full of black spirituals and gospel songs. Our elderly white choir director was succeeded by two black brothers who were both organists and piano players. Black women and a black man joined the choir. In early 1986, Reuben Jeffrey, an African American, was elected president of the church council. I began to feel that it was time for me to take my leave. Two weeks later, I announced my intention to resign on the coming Easter Day of 1986 and recommended that Loretta Smith be elected as my successor. It had taken seven years, but I felt that Zion had become an interracial church, due to the dogged persistence, long-term vision, humor, and faith of a majority of church members.

The congregation did vote to make Loretta their future minister, but that wasn't the end of the story. After that vote, I talked with her frankly about some concerns I had for the future. I was troubled that she had once said to me privately that certain white members "were beyond redemption" and that the spiritual traditions and expectations of white and black members were so different that a harmonious blending of worship could probably never be achieved. I reminded her that a substantial majority of the white members had opened the church to people of every race and had invited her to be their pastor. I told her I hoped she'd continue to foster Zion's interracial growth. She could do that, I suggested, by making a special effort to "pastor" the white members, mixing traditional Protestant hymns with black gospel hymns, limiting the length of Sunday services, keeping her prayers short and nonrepetitious, continuing the Saturday tutorial classes, and visiting white and black members and all potential new members. Loretta listened with good grace, though I knew she was her own person and would put her own stamp on the church after I left.

Over time, however, the many tensions of interracial worship did prevail at Zion. Seven years later, after I had moved away from Newark, I was disappointed to learn that Zion had become essentially a black church with only a handful of white members. But I retain the satisfaction of knowing that for several years, blacks and whites joined hands and worshiped alongside each other on Sunday mornings.

21

St. Stephan's Church, 1979–1989

As a piece of architecture, Zion Church was bland and conventional. The other church I pastored in Newark, St. Stephan's, was a century-old jewel of a building that was on federal and state lists of historic landmarks. It opened in the city's Ironbound section just before Christmas Day of 1874, the creation of a group of recent German immigrants who had broken away from a nearby Presbyterian church. Over the years, the members put no small amount of love, sweat, and hard-earned money into caring for and improving the Gothic-style edifice. In 1903, thirty-eight magnificent stained-glass windows were installed. Ten years later, a huge organ weighing ten tons and making music from 1,127 pipes was placed in the sanctuary.

As Newark grew in population, so did St. Stephan's, particularly during the forty-two years (1897 to 1939) when a pastor named Edward Fuhrmann led it, in a most determined and paternalistic German fashion. Fuhrmann was known to meet steamships from which German immigrants were disembarking at Ellis Island. He talked with these new Americans and urged them to choose Newark as their home and St. Stephan's as their church. The church offered services in the German language until Fuhrmann's death in 1939.

Between his passing and my arrival forty years later, Newark underwent drastic economic and ethnic changes. In the Ironbound (so named because the area was surrounded by railroad tracks), many factories closed down. The large Ballentine Brewery, for instance, which had employed many members of St. Stephan's since early in the century, closed forever. Many sons and daughters of St. Stephan's members had to find work outside of the city, and in many instances moved out of the Ironbound for good. The racial rebellion in 1967 sped the departure of some of the older white residents from the Ironbound. Replacing them in the Ironbound were not American blacks, however, but a new generation of immigrants from Spain, Portugal, Brazil, and other Latin American nations.

When I arrived in 1979, the remaining members of the church—about one hundred, most all of them white—quite literally felt under siege. It was not, however, due just to the ethnic changes in the community. Rather they felt abandoned by their own denomination. A few weeks before I became pastor, the area minister of the United Church of Christ met with members of the church's ruling body, known as the Consistory, and bluntly told them that because of the changing ethnic character of the neighborhood, St. Stephan's "had no future." Predictably, this announcement angered many in the congregation, many of whom had spent long hours refurbishing the church's magnificent interior. Moreover, church members had already begun reaching out to the changing community of the Ironbound. Since 1970, a Pentecostal congregation called the Maranatha Assembly of God, made up mostly of recent immigrants from Brazil, held weekly services in the church. The group's pastor operated a Portuguese-language radio station on the church's third floor, and he and his family members had rented the St. Stephan's parsonage since 1978. Also, in 1976 the church had permitted the city to open a large preschool center at the church for the multiracial children of the Ironbound. It was considered one of the best such centers in all of Newark.

Despite these positive developments, I felt that St. Stephan's had a major problem in the form of inertia and complacency. Church leaders, I discovered, were reluctant to visit or telephone non-attending members or call on neighbors who might be persuaded to join. The Sunday school was dying. I established as an early goal the revitalization of the Sunday school, knowing that this was often a way to draw parents to a church as well. But try as I would, I couldn't recruit Sunday school teachers. A church in such a condition, I was convinced, had little to attract its neighbors, whether white, black, or Hispanic.

Under these circumstances, I felt that my first duty was to strengthen the church from within, to keep those members that we had and try to get them more involved, and to worry later about finding new members. So, I started to visit the homes of practically all members, whether they showed up on Sunday or not, to reaffirm that I was there for them, that I cared.

I quickly learned from my visits that being white in Newark by no means guaranteed a comfortable life. I called on our oldest member, a frail woman of nearly one hundred years, and a disturbed woman who was afraid to close her eyes in sleep for fear she would never wake up again. There was a man still suffering from shell shock from the Second World War, and a Vietnam War veteran afflicted with deep depression. Over time, I think, my frequent visits to parishioners—particularly to those who were sick or bedridden—were crucial to keeping the church together.

Serving the many elderly members of the church gave me a fresh sense of the brevity of life. In their living rooms, these parishioners would show me to a chair and then share with me their life stories—their joys and often secret sadnesses, their guilt and stoical fatalism (often masked in public by smiles), their love for absent sons and daughters, and their faith that God was preparing a place for them and their loved ones in a future home in Heaven. These visits were by far my most memorable experience at St. Stephan's.

Often accompanying me on trips to visit our church members in hospitals or bedridden members in their homes was the elderly Art Auer. He recited the Lord's Prayer and other prayers in German when I offered communion to the sick. Art and I shared a lot together, including the experience of being mugged. One afternoon Art remained in my car while I was visiting the grave of the late Pastor Fuhrmann to clean off the weeds. Suddenly a young black man hit me with a two-by-four from behind. He snatched my wallet. Another youth held a knife to Art's throat and told him in no uncertain terms not to honk the horn of my car. Our two assailants and other members of the black gang who were lingering nearby then ran away.

Art had little respect for blacks. Though I could not agree with his views, I began over the months to understand some of the reasons why he felt as he did. Every Sunday morning I drove him to and from church. Passing by the West Side High School, where he was once the chief janitor, he remarked to me Sunday after Sunday, "Look at those dirty half-opened windows, those sloppy shades. That's what happens when the blacks take over high schools and city hall. Before the war, when whites were in charge, the streets were lined with beautiful trees. We were all safe. Everyone had a job. Everyone was happy." That was his view of the world; I was sorry I was never able to persuade him to see things differently. I was very sad when faithful Art died in 1989.

During my ten years as St. Stephan's pastor, I spent many long hours preparing sermons. Following Fosdick's advice, I never read a sermon, but rather preached from a rough outline on the pulpit. I selected passages from the Old and New Testaments and tried to make my sermons relevant to my parishioners' daily lives. But I had a lot to learn. In my first year, after I had delivered a particularly harsh and judgmental sermon, a gentle churchwoman of my own age advised me: "You must remember, pastor, that most of us come to church to pray, to be comforted, to get ourselves together for a rough week ahead. We don't want to feel guilty. Rather we want to leave the church feeling cleansed. I hope you will always close all of your sermons with some words of cheer and hope." During the next nine years, I tried to follow her sage advice.

By tradition, members of St. Stephan's put their pastors on quite a high pedestal. At first they seldom addressed me by my first name, but called me "pastor." I believed that they all thought I was more holy than they and had none of the usual human weaknesses. Then came an unsettling experience that changed my relationship with some of the members. One night when I was fast asleep, I experienced a violent epileptic seizure that fractured my backbone in two places. It was the fourth such seizure of my life, caused this time by bad advice from a neurologist that I should stop taking my antiseizure medication. During two weeks of recovery and absence from my two churches, I discovered that someone had spread the rumor in both my churches that I had fallen down my basement stairs in a drunken condition and that this was the real reason for my absence. The fact was that I had always been a teetotaler. To counter the rumor, I decided, after some hesitation, to make a full disclosure to my congregations about the history of my seizures. Upon my return, I explained that sleeping sickness at the age of thirteen had injured my nervous system, which had resulted in the four subsequent seizures. I assured my parishioners that my present medication would prevent a recurrence. Within a few days I sensed that my disclosure had created new bonds of understanding with many church members. Some were soon calling me "Dave" rather than "pastor," and they no longer kept me on that pedestal. They now knew that I, like any lay member sitting in a pew, was subject to human illnesses, and maybe foibles as well.

My conservative strategy of merely trying to hang onto existing church members changed in the spring of 1987, when I was looking for a new student assistant minister. I received a telephone call from a cheerful woman who introduced herself as Judy Vasile. In her mid-forties, she was white, a second-year honor student at New York Theological Seminary while at the same time holding down a high full-time managerial position at the nearby national headquarters of the Hartz Mountain Corporation. In my first meeting with her, I shared my hope that someday a new Sunday school would be started and that black, Brazilian, Hispanic, and white children would be recruited from the Ironbound. These children might encourage their parents, I said, to become members. She responded positively, and I knew then that I had found the right person to be the assistant pastor.

For eight years, I had had little success in recruiting Sunday school teachers. But Judy came onto the scene and quickly charmed many members into taking on that considerable responsibility. Twelve women and one man soon signed up to be Sunday school teachers. Judy had endless ideas. In May and June of 1988, as a recruiting method for the vacation Bible school, we organized a children's circus with professional clowns, first at our church, then at a public school playground next door, and finally at a large public housing project where many black and Hispanic families lived. In the summer of 1988, seventy children—black, Hispanic, and white—came to our two-week vacation Bible school. When regular Sunday school classes commenced in September, it was clear that Judy had succeeded—where I had failed—in resurrecting the Sunday school as a vital part of our church's mission to the community.

Drawing in young people did bring their parents too. Judy and I organized programs for these newcomer adults. She drew on her many connections at the New York Theological Seminary, bringing to our church speakers to teach parenting skills and other means of coping with the stresses of life in the Ironbound. Hearing about our successes, the United Church of Christ headquarters in New York City, which had ignored our church for years, sent a special media crew to make a video about our new programs. The film, widely circulated to churches of our denomination, showed once and for all that contrary to the words of that former area minister, St. Stephan's did have a future. That future was in many ways due to Judy's rare ability to work with people of many ages and many races. And, no doubt, the fact that she was white reassured the older white members of St. Stephan's that their customs and ways of worship weren't going to be forgotten.

Impressed with Judy and her rapport with the congregation, I resigned in September 1989 and turned over the pulpit to her. Three years later, after obtaining a Master of Divinity degree with honors at New York Theological Seminary, she was ordained and installed as pastor of St. Stephan's. The church remains solidly multiracial to this day.

22

Newark: A Tale of Two Cities, 1979–1990

FROM ALMOST THE first day I began working in Newark, it was clear to me that there were really two Newarks. The first, a very comfortable place, was the realm of executives of the Prudential Life Insurance Company, their associates in banks and other big corporations, and black politicians who were allied with them. This city consisted of new office towers and luxury apartments and condominiums. The other Newark was occupied by ordinary people, including the many poor—welfare mothers, crackheads, AIDS victims, the homeless with shopping bags stuffed with their meager belongings, jobless youths hanging around abandoned houses and apartment complexes. In many American cities, the affluent fled the downtown core in the postwar years. In Newark, however, one of the richest parts of the city was its office complex smack in the middle of downtown. It had been built as a grand redevelopment scheme in the 1980s and 1990s, but was surrounded by a ring of blighted areas.

Often the city's principalities and powers collaborated to serve common interests. The city council, for instance, routinely granted tax abatements and other subsidies to real estate developers and corporations. With the connivance of Mayor Kenneth Gibson and his successor, Sharpe James, the burden of taxation was being shifted from the rich to middle-class and poor residents. Aided by this kind of corporate welfare, real estate developers gentrified certain areas of the city and, in their own words, "land-banked" vacant lots with an eye toward future construction. As a result of these various developments, hundreds of poor families were forced to abandon rented apartments and homes and move to poorer areas of Newark or to other towns.

According to the 1980 U.S. Census, Newark was the poorest large city in our country (a large city was defined by the Census Bureau as any city with a population of 100,000 or more residents). In the late 1980s, unemployment in the city stood at 20 percent, while the jobless rate among youths was almost

40 percent. Among the causes of joblessness were a 50 percent dropout rate in the many dilapidated public schools (the average age of school buildings was seventy years), lack of public transportation between the inner city and places of employment in the suburbs, drastic reduction in job-training programs after Ronald Reagan became president in 1981, and the continuing departure of manufacturing plants from Newark. Between 1970 and 1985, total employment dropped 28 percent in Newark, the most populated city in New Jersey, while total employment in the state as a whole rose by 37 percent.

Crime increased with unemployment and the rise of drug addiction. At times, the Newark police seemed unwilling or unable to curb the flow of drugs to playgrounds, street corners, parks, and crack houses scattered all over the city. Many addicts, meanwhile, contracted AIDS by sharing needles. During the 1980s, Newark ranked fourth in the nation in the proportion of its citizens infected with AIDS, and second only to New York City in incidents of pediatric AIDS. In an editorial in the August 11, 1990, issue of the *Newark Star-Ledger,* Dr. Robert Hummel, director of New Jersey's AIDS Division, was quoted as saying that "people are being infected because they are battered by poverty, battered by drug use. They are living in conditions which are inherently unhealthy. They simply don't have access to medical care. . . . AIDS has become less and less a disease of sexuality per se and more and more, especially in New Jersey, a disease of poverty."[1]

Understandably, most poor residents of Newark did not believe the repeated claims of city and corporate leaders that the city was merely going through a difficult but necessary transformation from a smokestack town to a place that would have ample opportunities for rich and poor alike in the future. Meanwhile, poor families were sharply divided along racial lines. Many low-income whites, like some of the members of my two churches, complained that the city had been taken over by corrupt and white-hating blacks. The poor blacks often distrusted all whites as well as the few blacks who had climbed the corporate ladder. In Newark, most Hispanics believed—with some justification—that they had been pushed to the bottom of the totem pole by both whites and blacks. Sadly, this racial hostility further sapped the physical and spiritual energies of people who already faced a daily struggle for survival—finding work, paying the rent, meeting medical bills, and putting bread on the table for their family members.

So what should a minister do to work with these people, and at the same time retain a moral vision and sense of humor, not to mention basic sanity? Most ministers in Newark, I discovered, retreated into their churches, focusing on such issues as congregation finances and the spiritual welfare of their parishioners. Others were filled with genuine compassion and confronted the ruling powers, but they often concluded that efforts to improve life in poor neighborhoods were futile and sank into despair. A few ministers remained faithful to the teachings of the Old Testament prophets and Jesus Christ, who I believed were on the side of the poor and forgotten.

In my twin ministries in Newark, I sought to pursue a middle course. I tried to be a caring pastor for all of my parishioners. At the same time, I tried to battle the oppressive powers dominating the city, though occasionally my church members opposed this. Much of my time in activism went to the Newark Coalition for Neighborhoods, made up of fifteen neighborhood agencies demanding more police on the streets, prosecution of arsonists-for-hire (buildings were often torched for the insurance), and reduction of tax abatements for corporations and developers. Knowing that Mayor Gibson's support of affirmative action programs was a sham, I testified before the city council and demanded enforcement of city ordinances stipulating that 50 percent of employees on new construction projects be black or Hispanic. I urged the city council not to give corporations and developers tax abatements unless they followed these already-existing employment guidelines.

I worked closely with what I regarded as the most effective community organization in Newark, the Ironbound Community Corporation. I urged St. Stephan's members to support this organization's campaigns to reduce airport noise, oppose the construction of a huge industrial waste–burning plant within the Ironbound, and force the city council to deny permits to companies wanting to produce toxins in the Ironbound or transport these toxins through it.

Everywhere I looked, new examples seemed to abound of how the ruling powers robbed ordinary people of the Ironbound of basic dignities. Here is an example of such robbery concerning the demolition of the Ironbound swimming pool and bathhouse, built during the First World War just a block away from St. Stephan's. For decades, it was a true godsend for Ironbound residents. It provided the year-round comfort of hot showers for people who had no hot running water in their homes, and the cooling experience of swimming. Thousands of children and adults learned to swim in the pool, which was also the scene of many school swimming meets.

But in the spring of 1978, Mayor Gibson shocked the Ironbound community when he announced, without offering any explanation, that the bathhouse and pool would soon be shut down. Predictably, within forty-eight hours of the closure, robbers had vandalized the place, ripping out and carrying away plumbing and most fixtures, even the toilets. The community organized to fight the decision. I took part in several protest meetings at our church organized by the Ironbound Community Corporation. I spoke at rallies in front of the abandoned pool and bathhouse, as children in bathing suits were sprayed by water from fire hydrants, now the only way they could cool off. Despite these protests, Mayor Gibson in 1983 sent back to Washington $600,000 of federal funds specially allocated to rehabilitate this pool and bathhouse. Several years later, the city sold the complex to a private developer who quickly dynamited the structures and constructed in their place a high-rise building with offices and condominiums. Although we couldn't prove it, my friends and I suspected that the developer had greased the palm of city officials. When Sharpe James was elected mayor in 1986, he promised Ironbound residents that the city would soon build a new Olympic-sized pool near the neighborhood's sports stadium. But a few weeks later, municipal engineers discovered that the site was filled with toxic wastes. To this day, blueprints for this new pool languish on drawing boards in city hall.

During my eleven years working in Newark, as suburban whites blamed blacks for urban decay, I became aware of some of the real reasons for this problem. One cause was a national tax system that encouraged industry to migrate from cities to rural areas or foreign countries. Another was the fact that the federal government built high-rise public housing projects for the poor, giving ample benefits to banks and construction companies along the way, but committing only minimal funds for property maintenance and police security for tenants after the projects were built. But the most important cause for urban decay, in my opinion, was the lack of a comprehensive vision of urban renewal by successive Democratic and Republican administrations—a vision conceived to benefit the poor and to free them from the domination of city and state officials anxious to monitor and control all funds coming from Washington.

Churches of Newark affiliated with mainline Protestant denominations have done little lately to combat urban decay. As their white members moved from Newark to the suburbs, the denominations' interests moved along with them. In the 1960s and early 1970s, these denominations had sent ministers of many races into poor areas of Newark and other slum-filled cities to work with people through their churches or with inter-church organizations such as the Metropolitan Ecumenical Ministry. But over the last three decades, with mounting corporate and conservative opposition to the prophetic mission of these ministers and their sponsors, denominational executives have removed some of the most effective pastors from their inner-city assignments. They have reduced the urban missions' funds drastically and have shifted denominational spending to helping the construction of new churches in more affluent areas. Growth in the membership rolls of these new churches has too often become the benchmark of ecclesiastical success for denominational executives and ministers.

I am convinced that if the long-neglected poor of the urban slums are to experience hope and spiritual renewal, the mainline Protestant denominations must join hands with the many black, Hispanic, and Pentecostal churches in the decaying cities of America. The denominations must play an important part in a moral and spiritual transformation. Dedicated pastors of all races and faiths, I believe, could build the spiritual foundation of an urban rebirth in Newark and elsewhere if they would accept the hard truth that this rebirth can take place only when the oppressed people become empowered and take command of their own destinies.

In recent years, it's not only the urban poor who have been demoralized. Those of us who have labored in urban ministries have suffered from multiple forms of spiritual burnout as well. In our frustrations we have too often cursed the darkness, but in our more lasting moments of faith and hope, we and our parishioners have lit a few candles of hope as we have stood side by side and dedicated ourselves to the mission of social healing, uplift, and empowerment of the poor.

23

Heading Up the Metropolitan Ecumenical Ministry, 1981 and 1984–1990

SOMETIMES I WONDER how I ever got any sleep during the eleven years I worked in Newark. I had two churches, plus I agreed to take on another professional calling that often seemed like a full-time job in itself. For seven of my eleven years working in Newark, I was executive director of a multi-denominational organization called the Metropolitan Ecumenical Ministry (MEM). Leading it was a real-life lesson in how churches can join together to accomplish community goals that would be impossible alone. Occasionally, though, it taught me too how infighting, mismatched objectives, and the tendency of some reformers to ignore real-life concerns such as balancing the books can foil the best of intentions. I sometimes found myself feeling tired or emotionally wrought-up as I sought a few solutions to the seemingly unsolvable problems of Newark.

The year after the 1967 racial rebellion in Newark, church groups conducted a citywide social survey. State and local church leaders concluded that some type of ecumenical agency was needed to help inner-city churches and the poor of Newark and nearby cities in Essex County. In the wake of the assassination of Martin Luther King, Jr., in April 1968 and urban revolts that followed it in many American cities, the leaders of several mainline Protestant denominations made a commitment to underwrite the salaries of several new inner-city pastors skilled in community organizing. Thus the Metropolitan Ecumenical Ministry in Newark was formed in 1969. Its initial board of directors was made up of two local representatives from each of five major Protestant denominations: the United Church of Christ, the United Methodist Church, the Presbyterian Church, the Episcopal Church, and the American Baptist Churches. MEM got off to a strong start, but during the early 1970s, as awareness of poverty and memories of the violence of the 1960s faded, the national denominations scaled back their financial support.

After coming to Newark in 1979, I soon became a member of the MEM board as a representative of my denomination. MEM's executive director at the time was a man named Art Thomas, who had been in the job since 1974. He was an energetic leader, an ordained Methodist minister who had once worked for an interracial cooperative farm in Mississippi and later for the New Jersey Department of Education. He was white; his wife was black. Art had quickly become known as an enemy of city hall and the corporate moguls of Newark. I was impressed with his ability to make limited resources go a long way. He obtained federal funds to start an adult literacy program called Project Read. He did the same for Project Schools, a program aimed at increasing parent participation in public schools. He gathered substantial funds for another MEM program called Project Go to provide free transportation to the elderly and to disabled citizens.

In December 1980, to everyone's shock, Art was stricken with a fatal heart attack. He was only forty-nine. Two days after his death, the MEM board asked me to serve as interim executive director. Aware of my responsibility to my two UCC churches, I reluctantly accepted the position. A few days later, as I went through financial records at the organization's office in downtown Newark, I discovered that the socially dedicated Art Thomas had made a mess of the finances. MEM was deeply in debt. During the next six months, with the help of several churches in Newark and its suburbs, we raised more than $45,000 to cover all the outstanding debts. Heading MEM at that time was a complex and sometimes thankless job, so I was happy in early 1982 to hand the reins over to Frank Gibson, urban coordinator of the Newark Presbytery. As a full-time executive director. Frank brought back some of MEM's old vitality over the next two years. He persuaded several leaders of the Catholic Archdiocese of Newark, the Newark–New Jersey Committee of Black Churchmen, and two additional Protestant denominations to join MEM. But Gibson had a hard time with fund-raising. He was handicapped by President Reagan's love of cutting social spending. Twenty-two Vista volunteers who had been assisting MEM projects left in 1982 because of federal budget cuts. Federal support to most other MEM projects was reduced. Because of this uncertain financial status, several key staff members resigned. The future of the organization seemed very much in doubt.

After Gibson resigned in late 1983, I was very surprised when the MEM board asked me to be the new executive director. With some hesitation—again—I agreed, though I believed that an African American should have gotten the job. When I started work, I told the board members that I was going to put my weight behind recommendations made by a special committee that had sought a new direction for the organization: that MEM should become more advocacy-centered, keep good financial records and a separate bank account for each MEM project, recruit more lay participants, and develop closer relations with local churches and national denominations.

Three MEM Projects

We managed to achieve many of these goals over the next six years. The Project Schools campaign blossomed in the fall of 1984 after I appointed Steve Jones, an African-American who was an experienced community organizer, as its new director. After just six months on the job, Steve had raised money equal to half of MEM's total budget. Well aware that any good social activism program starts with having adequate cash, Steve recruited parents and community leaders and coached them on how to improve public schools and how to monitor the monthly meetings of the Newark Board of Education, where decisions crucial to their children's futures were made. He wisely placed policy decisions in the hands of the Project School's senate, a body made up of about fifty parents. In a clever bit of coalition building, Steve helped patch together the Newark Council of Educational Priorities, which brought together representatives of this senate, the local Urban League and NAACP, and a strong Hispanic community organization known as Aspira. It felt good to watch Project Schools emerge as a solid winner. Jones truly proved himself. As a result, when I left Newark in 1990, he became MEM's new executive director, with the unanimous approval of all MEM board members.

Another major focus during this period was the MEM Housing Task Force. Founded in 1980, it had two simple goals: to save low-cost housing, both private and public, from demolition crews, and to organize tenants both in public housing projects and in privately owned apartment complexes. In the 1970s, in the name of urban renewal, close to fifteen thousand homes and apartments had been razed in Newark, a figure which according to the state's Department of Public Advocacy represented more than one-tenth of the city's entire housing stock. In the early 1980s, the rate of demolition increased. The city was losing housing units at twice the rate that new units were being built. By the mid-1980s, the ratio of demolition to construction had increased to three to one. This trend was pushed by the skyrocketing of real estate prices in Newark and its suburbs in the 1980s and by the fact that owners of apartment complexes knew that they could make more money by turning low-cost rental units into high-cost condos for urban professionals. So owners were often paying off their federal Department of Housing and Urban Development (HUD) mortgages as quickly as possible so they could evict poor tenants and rent their apartments to more affluent families.

The joint chairs of the MEM Housing Task Force, Nancy Zak and Frank Hutchins, helped residents of forty privately owned apartment complexes to organize a tenants association. Task force members met with city and federal officials to voice the tenants' many complaints, such as owners' raising rents, neglecting repairs, and evicting residents for petty and sometimes wholly invented offenses. In many public meetings, our people spoke up about the root causes of the growing lack of affordable housing, the past conversion of private houses and apartments into high-priced units, and the threatened further destruction of public housing.

On this issue, our main opponents were not private developers, but leaders of a city agency called the Newark Housing Authority (NHA). From 1950 to 1970, the NHA had quite successfully managed in Newark twenty-seven public housing projects with apartments for twenty-eight thousand low-income families. But starting in 1970, newly elected Mayor Kenneth Gibson appointed a string of NHA directors who allowed public housing to deteriorate rapidly. Though incompetence or design, these NHA directors forced hundreds of families to vacate their apartments in public housing buildings. They also reduced expenditures for maintenance and police security, with disastrous results. Uncollected garbage piled up in the hallways, and the absence of guards made muggers, drug dealers, and prostitutes feel safe to ply their trades in the projects. The worsening of conditions soon resulted in a series of highly negative editorials and news stories in the *Newark Star-Ledger.* The newspaper's editors and various corporate leaders soon called for the immediate destruction of all public housing as a means of curbing crime and drug traffic.

The director of the NHA and his staff were only too pleased to comply with such demands. Officials stepped up their eviction of tenants in buildings already marked for demolition. In May of 1987, with funds from HUD, the NHA dynamited four public housing buildings called the Scudder Homes, where 812 low-income families had once lived. The very concept of public housing in Newark appeared doomed. The situation worsened when in late 1988 Mayor Sharpe James announced that eight more high-rise buildings housing more than 6,500 families would soon be demolished and replaced in some instances by corporate offices and high-priced condos. The announcement came at a time when 10,000 families were on the NHA's waiting list for housing and an estimated 12,000 families in Newark were homeless.

News of the mayor's announcement brought a swell of anger among public housing tenants and their supporters. Organizing soon began. With my encouragement, the co-chairs of the MEM Housing Task Force gathered representatives of various organizations which had supported public housing, including the New Jersey Office of Legal Services, the NAACP, the Urban

League, the Ironbound Community Corporation, a few AFL-CIO unions, and public housing tenants. We found an ally in Councilman Donald Tucker, who was the sole city council member opposed to gutting public housing. Soon we had formed the Newark Coalition for Low-Income Housing.

Deciding to pursue the struggle in the federal courts as well, we found pro bono lawyers to file a federal class-action lawsuit against NHA and HUD. The coalition demanded that NHA abandon its plans to demolish the 6,500 units, that it rehabilitate an additional 2,500 long-vacant NHA apartments, and that for every public housing unit destroyed in the future a new one be built, as was already required by the 1988 Omnibus Housing Act signed by President Reagan. After eight months of intensive negotiations under the watchful eye of a sympathetic federal district judge and a court-appointed mediator, leaders of the NHA, HUD, and our coalition signed an out-of-court settlement under which the NHA agreed to all three of the coalition's demands. It was a sweet victory for public housing tenants and their advocates.

Assisted by the Washington-based Center for Community Change and a few friendly foundations and corporations, I was able to raise $75,000 to enable the Coalition for Low-Income Housing to employ an experienced full-time monitor, Steve Finn, to ensure that the NHA lived up to the settlement in ensuing years. With success for several years, he carried his assignment of keeping the Newark Housing Authority honest.

I wish we had managed such a win with the MEM Toxic Waste Task Force, which was headed by a very dedicated young woman named Madelyn Hoffman. The task force's major *raison d'être* was to oppose the proposed construction of a mammoth dioxin-producing, waste-burning plant on a site in Newark's Ironbound neighborhood. City officials didn't seem to care that close to fifty thousand people lived in crowded Ironbound. Hoffman's job was made all the more difficult by two factors: few Ironbound people knew of the future dangers to public health brought by the huge waste burning plant, and the Ironbound was full of unregistered illegal immigrants who were reluctant to draw public attention to themselves.

But Hoffman kept at it, organizing a series of public protests. One day I joined Ironbound residents who assembled on the steps of St. Stephan's, eager to rally against the construction of the waste-burning plant. Other times we marched from St. Stephan's to city hall, where we presented petitions noting that the future plant would create deadly by-products, that trucks going to and from it would ruin local roads, and that residents of the Ironbound had never had an opportunity to vote for or against the plant's construction. Hoffman and I also testified before the city council and the Essex County Board of Supervisors, in sessions that were often jammed with hundreds of Ironbound residents. At one session, I reminded the lawmakers that Ironbound was thickly settled and already had dozens of chemical, paint, and other manufacturing plants creating tons of toxic substances. Over the years, in fact, the area had been turned into an illegal dumping ground for hazardous wastes. We could see the stuff in abandoned warehouses and vacant fields all over the Ironbound. A recent health survey had found that Ironbound citizens suffered 32 percent more deaths from cancer, leukemia, and respiratory and heart diseases than people living in other parts of New Jersey. We believed that the presence of toxins was a major reason why.

In 1985, shortly after newspapers in Newark and New York City reported the existence of old dioxin deposits in the Ironbound, New Jersey Governor Thomas Kean visited the site, wearing a protective white suit like a suit worn by an astronaut walking on the moon in 1969. Soon after the governor's visit, state trucks hauled away some dioxin from the abandoned Diamond Alkali plant and from other facilities.

Alas, this admission of the presence of dioxin in the Ironbound did not mean we had won the battle. With the cleanup of the deposits allegedly completed, the state declared the problem solved and as a result construction of the huge waste-burning plant got under way. State authorities, of course, promised strict controls. The waste-burning plant began operation in 1991. Today, on a round-the-clock basis, tons of household and industrial waste are trucked in from all over New Jersey and parts of New York. The plant is a disgraceful affront to the citizens of the Ironbound—but one that continues today.

The Ups and Downs of MEM

In my years at MEM, I sometimes became frustrated by the lack of consistency in financial support from local churches and from regional and national church offices. Some executives supported MEM strongly, others were indifferent, and a few were openly hostile. Some denominational leaders were understandably more concerned about the survival of their churches than the future of our ecumenical agency. Just how varied the sympathies could be became clear to me in late 1988, when I clashed with the new Newark presbyter over her decision to evict a Pentecostal congregation from a large old church known as the downtown Lighthouse Temple, a building owned by the Newark Presbytery.

Back in 1974, when members of the predominantly white Lighthouse Presbyterian Church Temple moved to the suburbs and left the downtown Temple building vacant, the presbyter (this is the highest-ranking local job in the Presbyterian Church), Dr. Charles Leber, agreed to allow the Pentecostal

Church of God in Christ congregation to take over the vacant Temple and conduct services there. But soon the congregation was not only worshiping in the building. Under the charismatic leadership of James Parrott, a man who went by the title of "Bishop," it established, with the help of local churches and business establishments, a massive feeding program for the homeless and poor. Four days a week, five hundred to seven hundred needy men, women, and children got hot noontime lunches at the Temple. To better the condition of these poor people, a grant from the Robert Wood Johnson Foundation added a part-time doctor, nurse, and social worker to the Temple staff.

Despite these good works by the Pentecostal congregation, in 1988 the new presbyter, a black woman named Carrie Washington, took a dislike to Bishop Parrot and his congregation. She forced him to turn out twenty-two homeless people then living at the Temple. Claiming that the building was deteriorating and therefore not fit for human habitation, she evicted from the Temple the entire Church of God in Christ congregation in early 1989 and put an end to one of the largest feeding programs for the poor in Newark. Several church leaders in Newark protested to her, but to no avail.

A few weeks later, Bishop Parrott and I talked with Mayor James at city hall. We asked him to donate to the congregation a city-owned building that would be large enough to house a mass feeding program. Much to our surprise, the mayor told us less than a week later that the city would give the congregation an abandoned tire factory that the city owned, along with $200,000 for repairs and renovation. In July 1989, I attended the dedication of this new Lighthouse Center, which was already sheltering twenty-five to thirty homeless men and had ample space for a feeding program on the scale of the one that had been shut down.

Before I left Newark in September of 1990, I drove by the old and partly ruined Temple. The interior, including a magnificent organ, had been repeatedly vandalized. Recalling the hungry and homeless who had patiently stood in line for noontime meals, I felt a pang of sadness. Two years later, a friend sent me a news clipping from the *Newark Star-Ledger* that included a picture of the Temple going up in flames. Probably the Temple was the victim of an arsonist or a fire carelessly lit by a homeless man seeking warmth and shelter. It was a tragic end to this grand old structure, which over successive generations had played an important role in the spiritual life and welfare of the community.

Inter-Church Programs

Although I had my differences with Carrie Washington, I also witnessed stirring examples of unity among churches in Newark. In January

1987, realizing that the twentieth anniversary of the 1967 racial rebellion was fast approaching, I met with Dr. James A. Scott, pastor of the Bethany Baptist Church in Newark and one of the most respected clergymen in the city, to propose that we organize a memorial event. We later invited fifty clergy and lay leaders to a planning meeting that put together plans for a mass gathering which we named the All Church Assembly of Remembrance, Repentance and Recommitment. It was to be held at the magnificent Catholic Sacred Heart Cathedral in mid-September of 1987. We all turned out at the appointed hour, and it was a huge success. More than 125 singers from the choirs of more than a dozen churches in the area performed songs of celebration, after rehearsing weekly for months. The new Catholic Archbishop Theodore E. McCarrick of Newark, Episcopal Bishop John Shelby Spong, Dr. Scott, and Dr. Samuel Proctor, senior minister at Harlem's Abyssinian Baptist Church and a close friend of the late Dr. Martin Luther King, Jr., delivered moving addresses. Worshipers—black, white, and Hispanic—numbered at least 2,300 that night.

Following the event, we kept some of that ecumenical spirit alive when a number of clergy and lay leaders formed the Newark Church Consultation, chaired by Dr. Scott. MEM and I served as the Consultation's secretariat for the next two years. In monthly meetings, we discussed the need for more affordable housing and for reforms of the public schools, the alarming spread of AIDS, and the importance of developing an active youth ministry in every church. But I'm afraid that the Consultation never became a coordinated agency for social change. I was unable, for instance, to persuade the group's leaders or heads of the Newark–North Jersey Committee of Black Churchmen to take a trip to Brooklyn to visit the Nehemiah Homes, a huge housing project of more than ten thousand families that churches had helped to support financially. I wanted us all to meet the church leaders who had founded the Nehemiah Homes—maybe, I thought, this would inspire some of them to start an affordable housing project in Newark.

In 1990, with attendance at our monthly meetings low, Dr. Scott called a meeting of the more faithful among the group to take stock and plan for the future. In this session, many clergy confessed that they often suffered from loneliness and despair about the future of their churches and of the city itself. Some recommended that the Consultation sponsor retreats for pastors and laypeople emphasizing meditation, spiritual renewal, and ways to increase the trust level among the clergy themselves.

I remember being impressed that we were all speaking of these things, and so frankly. Clergy rarely did—the needs of the parishioners were supposed to come first. I discovered in that gathering that many of my colleagues shared some of the same frustrations that I had. It would be well, I thought to myself, if we advocates of social change found time to take seriously the personal needs of our ministerial colleagues—not to mention our own.

MEM's Future

From June 1989 to September 1990, when I left Newark, the board and staff of MEM held a series of lengthy discussions about the organization's goals and strategies. From many meetings with activist clergy, we learned that churches were seeking ways to deal with the growing AIDS crisis, teenage pregnancies, parenting by young couples and single parents, drug and alcohol abuse, crime, and the ever-increasing lack of affordable housing. We agreed that our hoped-for closer relationship with congregations would not lessen our efforts to form coalitions with secular agencies that shared our goals. We approved the following mission statement, which ten years later remains MEM's guiding document. I believe it is a good model for any religious agency seeking to revive churches and to change society fundamentally:

> In order that the participation of churches and denominations may more effectively carry out their missions as agents of God's grace in the greater Newark metropolitan area and in the world, the Metropolitan Ecumenical Ministry exists to
>
> • focus concern and resources of churches and others of good will on problems of racism, poverty, and injustice that exist throughout the metropolitan area;
>
> • support directly and indirectly those moves which will enable those people victimized by racism, poverty, and injustice to participate more fully in the economic, political, social and educational processes, to the end that they will achieve control of and responsibility for their own destinies; and
>
> • mobilize the resources—human, financial, and spiritual of the churches to work toward the realization of those goals throughout the metropolitan area.

Father Jack

My work in MEM is long-since finished, but I will never forget a man who was dear to me and the organization during my later years in Newark. He was Monsignor John Maloney. A man of frequent humor and occasional temper, he was known far and wide as Father Jack. While serving as senior pastor of a large Catholic church, he took an abiding interest in the city's poor.

He was a guiding force behind a rent strike by tenants at the Stella Wright public housing project that in the end forced the city to provide more security guards and maintenance workers there. Instead of paying their rent each month during the rent strike, the tenants deposited their money in cash in a heavy trunk. Father Jack buried the trunk full of greenbacks—at one point they totaled more than two million dollars—in the backyard of his church until the strike was settled. His action and honesty made him a hero among the city's poor for many years.

When Father Jack later became the senior pastor at the large St. Patrick's Cathedral in Newark and served as president of MEM for a few years, I consulted with him often, finding that he knew the community better than anyone. During the summer of 1989 he became seriously ill. He complained to me of constant headaches and weariness. He was hospitalized, and died on October 24, 1989. Two days later, hundreds of friends and parishioners—white, black, and Hispanic—gathered in the sanctuary of his church in Newark for mass and funeral services. It was one of the saddest nights I can remember. I came home grieving the loss of a friend and a wonderful man. Early the next morning, I was hit by a medical emergency of my own—a heart attack.

24

My Brush with Death and
My Spiritual Renewal, 1989–1990

THE HEART ATTACK hit me during a very routine activity, my early-morning run. The exercise regimen that I had adopted in the 1930s in response to childhood illnesses had ever since been how I began my day. In each place that Alice and I lived, I had a standard route of two to three miles that I would run, generally at around daybreak, often with the family dog on a leash. On the morning of October 27, 1989, I put the leash on our canine, Poppy, walked out the front door of our house in Montclair, and began my regular two-mile circuit. I was feeling emotionally and physically drained. I hadn't slept well. I still had Father Jack's funeral of the previous evening on my mind. And grating on me as well was the latest financial crisis in which MEM found itself.

I had run only a few blocks when without warning I felt a painful pressure in the middle of my chest. Clearly something serious was wrong—I knew that such chest pain can signal a heart attack. Fearful, I stopped, something I'd almost never done in decades of running. I walked slowly back to the house. To avoid upsetting Alice, I told her I was feeling unwell and would go to the emergency room of a nearby hospital and see a doctor there. Still feeling a strong pain in the middle of my chest, I drove to the hospital a half-mile away, parked the car in the hospital garage, and walked into the emergency room.

The attending doctor sized up what was happening very quickly. He told me to lie down on a high and what proved to be a most uncomfortable bed. I was given several nitroglycerin pills, but the painful pressure in the center of my chest had grown much worse. A nurse then hooked me up to three intravenous bottles that hung above my bed. Every five minutes a solemn doctor approached me and asked the same question: "On a scale of one to ten, how strong is the pain in your chest?" My first whispered answer was five and a half. An hour later, my answer to the ever-inquiring doctor had dropped to three.

Lying on that bed, I closed my eyes, thankful that I was not in a state of panic. Gradually, though I remained very conscious of the doctors and nurses around me, I began to drift into some other state of mind. Somehow, I felt I was entering into a new reality of a warm embrace by the higher power of God. I was strangely peaceful, convinced that in my moment of need God had enveloped me with his love and had touched my troubled heart. It was a calming sensation that I had never before felt.

I came out of my meditation when I was put on a hard stretcher and taken to the X-ray room. There a doctor cut a hole in my groin, inserted a long plastic tube, and injected watery medicines through the tubes into the vicinity of my heart. I was then taken to a room in the emergency cardiac unit. As I lay on a bed there, I found that the pressure in my chest had almost vanished.

During my ten days in the hospital and two months of recuperation at home, I had plenty of time to consider my mortality and the direction of my life during my remaining days on earth. The immediate cause of my heart attack, I felt from the beginning, was fear that I would not be able to raise $200,000 that MEM needed for the current fiscal year. I was ashamed that I, leader and supposed jack-of-all-trades, was proving to be a failure at the very time we were planning a dinner to celebrate the organization's twentieth birthday. But the heart attack, I knew, had deeper reasons than this. In Newark I had worked myself far too hard over the previous ten years, devoted too much energy to worries and other emotional spinning of wheels. Lying in bed one day, I confessed to myself that I was inclined to measure my success and failure by worldly results alone. Deep in my heart I knew I had failed to heed the counsel of the late Catholic mystic Thomas Merton:

> Do not depend on the hope of results. . . . As you get used to this idea, you start more and more to concentrate not on results but on the value, rightness and truth of work itself. Gradually you struggle less and less for an idea and more and more for specific people. . . . It means that we cannot any longer hope in ourselves, in our wisdom, our virtues, our fidelity. We see clearly that all which is "ours" is nothing and can completely fail. We can no longer rely on what we "have," what has been given in the past, what can be acquired. We are open to God and to his mercy in the inscrutable future. Only then by His grace and His guidance can we be led by Him, by His time, to find Him in losing ourselves.[1]

Would that I had opened myself to this wisdom earlier in my life.

During my recovery, I had much time to reflect. I wrote a brief essay to myself. I concluded:

My heart attack has changed me. For years I have denied my internal pains. If leg weariness overtook me during my morning run, I ran faster to gain my second wind. Now in my slow recovery, every petty twinge in my chest, every feeling of lightness and dizziness, every sign of bodily exhaustion, I interpreted as life-threatening danger signals. Now I am just beginning to relax and to enjoy my leisure. One month after suffering a heart attack, I am deeply grateful that I am still part of God's wonderful and continuing creation here on earth. My heart attack, I believe, was God's way of telling me, "Slow down, Dave. Now in your '70s, don't let stress and worries rule your life. Despite all of your sins and shortcomings, you can rest assured that you are in my hands now—and for the rest of your life on earth and in the life to come."

What I had long lacked, I realized then, was a sense of joy and fulfillment. Without such a sense, I was unable to rejoice in small victories, modest accomplishments, and the everyday experience of being alive on God's glorious earth among other human beings. Somehow my long struggles against the powers of darkness and my obsession with evil in high places had robbed me of ability to celebrate the present moment.

During my recovery, this realization led me to return to the sources of my own Christian faith. I found that the medieval mystic Meister Johannes Eckhart spoke to my current condition. Eckhart lived in Germany from 1269 to 1328 amidst squalor and all manner of persecution, and yet he spoke of the joy coming to him from God's daily presence. In his ninth sermon, entitled "Waking Up to the Nearness of God's Kingdom," he asserted:

> When one has made some spiritual progress, he discovers that there has never been a lighter, more delightful or more joyful life. God is very much concerned always to be present to such a person and teach him or her, so that He can bring the soul to that point where God wants him to follow. Never has a person longed after anything so intensely as God longs to bring a person to the point of knowing Him. God is always ready but we are unready. God is near to us, but we are far from Him. God is within but we are outside. God is at home but we are abroad. The prophet says: "God leads the righteous through the narrow way into the broad path" (Ws. 10:10). God helps us . . . so that He can bring us to the point where we truly know Him.[2]

After the heart attack, our family doctor urged me, for the sake of my health and longevity, to leave Newark. It wasn't advice I wanted, but good advice seldom is. Alice and I soon concluded that it was clearly the right course for us. Eleven months after I walked into that emergency room in October 1989, we moved to Benicia, a small town forty miles northeast of San Francisco overlooking the waters of the Carquinez Strait. We had bought a house there three years earlier, knowing that sooner or later we would need a place for retirement. And it was a family place—two of our five children and three of our grandchildren lived in the area. So in our New Jersey home in Montclair we sorted a lifetime's accumulation of possessions, hired a moving company, and, after a round of farewells, flew west across the continent.

Fortunately, my sadness about departing from Newark was more than offset by several things. In California, I told myself, I might find more time to spend with Alice. I would have more time for travel and a personal spiritual journey. I also knew that I was leaving my Newark work in the hands of four very skilled successors: the able Steve Jones directing MEM, the experienced Steve Finn heading the Newark Coalition for Low-Income Housing, the strong Loretta Smith as pastor of Zion Church, and the inspired Judy Vasile as pastor of St. Stephan's. I will forever remember them and the many other people of Newark who shared parts of their lives with me and left me a more whole and compassionate human being.

Epilogue

AT THE END of an autobiography, the writer often summarizes the wisdom accumulated during the author's long journey of life, in the hope that future generations will be the wiser. I am not fit for such a task because today I feel less like a wise man and more like a scientist who has made some important discoveries but knows that many others remain hidden.

At my present age of eighty-three, I live with the persistent sensation that I am just beginning the search for lasting truth and meaning. If God allows me several more years on earth, I hope to walk many more miles (though now with cane in hand), visit many more places, befriend many more strangers, and experience many more revelations of God's spirit which will open my heart to further truths and glimpses of eternal life on earth and in the life to come.

Much of what I am and what I have done, I owe to my father and mother. They devoted much of their lives to helping others, particularly the poor and downtrodden. Father was kind, singularly devoid of resentment and pride, and quick to forgive. Mother was equally kind, but could be highly judgmental of herself, her friends, her adversaries, and even her own children. During their lives, my parents gave me constant emotional support. From them I learned the importance of love and kindness and of living life not for oneself but for others.

In my long life journey I have tried to identify myself with those who are deprived of the necessities of life on this earth. During the first fourteen years of our marriage, Alice and I worked with farmworkers and industrial workers in the South. In eleven years in the U.S. Foreign Service, followed by eleven more in UNICEF, I tried to better the lives of ordinary people in developing nations of Asia. My eleven years in Newark in the 1980s were essentially a blue-collar ministry in the poorest large city in America.

Throughout my life, I often found myself at odds with the principalities and powers, as real today as when St. Paul referred to them in his letter to the first-century church in Rome. In my life these powers were packing-shed operators, cotton barons, textile magnates, exploiters of children in Asia, powerful corporations and city officials in Newark, and more recently, powerful corporations dominating the economy of California. I discovered that the principalities and powers often invaded and corrupted places supposedly immune to their allure. Some high church leaders, I found, have grown indifferent to the needs of the poor and have ingratiated themselves with the rich. Some trade union leaders have become prosperous business agents now closely associated with corporate executives. Some officials of charitable agencies, though once endowed with a sense of mission, have become mere time-servers and no longer champion the cause of the poor.

Envying the dedication and tactics of the consumer advocate Ralph Nader, I often wished that my life could be simply a story of a good guy overcoming the bad. But the real world—the one I inhabit, at least—was never that simple. I learned that sometimes one must confront, and at other times one must negotiate with the powerful, while hoping to gain some advantage for the poor without losing one's integrity and the trust of the people one is trying to serve. In the end, whether confrontational or not, any person who wants to serve the poor must be able to give the correct answer to the question posed in that old union song, "Which Side Are You On?" The final answer must be based not on vague claims of virtue or good intentions, but on a lifelong record of service.

I owe a debt of gratitude to the following men who have openly sided with the downtrodden and shared with me their motivation and wisdom: Howard Kester, who founded the Fellowship of Southern Churchmen; H. L. Mitchell, brave head of the Southern Tenant Farmers Union; Franz Daniel, the dedicated trade union organizer in South Carolina and other states; Pat Jackson, for twenty years the leading Washington lobbyist for the rural poor; Clarence Jordan, a follower of Jesus Christ and a founder of the interracial Koinonia Farm in south Georgia; Walter Reuther, who from 1935 until his death in 1970 was, in my opinion, the most visionary labor leader in the United States; and Victor Reuther, the senior United Auto Workers official who opened the door for me to work in Asia from 1955 to 1972. Two other men of my acquaintance I regard as saints. One was Jaya Prakash Narayan, the Indian mystic who was a follower of Mahatma Gandhi and a distributor of land to the landless peasants in India. The other was Archbishop Dom Helder Camara of Recife, Brazil, a staunch defender of the poor in the face of church indifference and government oppression. I found each man listed above, even the two saints, to be a peculiar individual with his own strengths and weaknesses—his own virtues and human feet of clay.

From the day when I first contracted sleeping sickness at the age of thirteen, followed by a near-fatal attack of rheumatic fever at sixteen, I have been haunted by the brevity of life itself. My early health crises motivated me to search for the reality of God during the rest of my life. But in subsequent decades, because of my preoccupation with work and my own lack of a disciplined life of prayer, meditation, and Bible reading, I neglected many things of the spirit. These included stilling my restless mind through meditation each morning and waiting patiently each day for the still, small voice of God. Because I knew that my ever-present pragmatism of mind would never satisfy the yearnings of my heart, I have thirsted for the divine presence all of my adult life.

I confess that over the years I have not been a faithful follower of Jesus Christ. Desiring to support Alice and our five children in an adequate fashion, I never considered emulating such a heroic Christian as Father Damian, who forsook wealth and a normal family life to serve lepers on Molokai Island near Hawaii from 1871 until the day of his death in 1889.

Jesus taught that if we allowed worldly greed to become the cornerstone of our lives, we will be full of anxiety, engaged in desperate searches for material security, preoccupied with self-interest and blind to the needs of the poor. But if we devoted ourselves to bettering the condition of other human beings, declared Jesus, we may experience the divine reality of God in our daily comings and goings.

Occasionally in my life, I have experienced flashes of the reality of God. In 1939, with the specter of the Second World War hanging over humanity, I stood among fifteen hundred delegates from seventy-five nations at the World Conference of Christian Youth in Amsterdam, Holland, as we recited the Lord's Prayer together, each in his or her own tongue. I felt then the presence of God in our midst. Less than two years later I was full of anxiety and convinced of my unworthiness to become a Christian minister until a day in 1941 when I read a passage from theologian Martin Dibelius's book *The Sermon on the Mount* claiming that "the personage of Jesus is like a signal that there is another world and that the other world is moving toward the earthly world."[1] Suddenly I found myself on my knees by my dormitory bed, praying and thanking God that amidst despair he had broken into my troubled life and given me new hope.

In November 1945, when I read a telegram from the head of the Farm Security Administration accepting the bid of the Delmo Housing Corporation to purchase nine projects housing 549 farm-labor families, I both wept and rejoiced, thanking God for this unexpected triumph of poor people over the cotton barons. I was reminded of the words of Mary, the mother of Jesus as recorded in the Gospel of Luke: "[The Lord] has put down the mighty from their thrones, and exalted those of low degree; he has filled the hungry with good things, and the rich he has sent empty away" (Luke 1:52–53).

In 1972 I felt God's presence again when Alice, after twelve years of drinking and many days in hospitals and recovery centers, took her first steps toward liberation from her addiction to alcohol. I knew again that God was that mysterious higher power who had touched her life, my life, our family's life, and the lives of the members of Alice's recovering fellowship.

In September 1989, when members of the newly formed Newark Coalition for Low-Income Housing forced the Newark Housing Authority to abandon its plans to destroy nine thousand public housing apartments, I rejoiced again. One more time, God's justice had triumphed over the principalities and powers. And after my heart attack a month later, I experienced the presence of God in the emergency room of a Montclair hospital. In my hour of need I felt enveloped by his divine love. The memory of this liberating experience will remain with me for the rest of my earthly days.

My spiritual search continues. When I left Newark in 1990, I had made a start in my spiritual transformation but still had a long way to go. In California, I felt some resolution of my spiritual quest after I met Matthew Fox, who then headed the Institute of Culture and Creation Spirituality in Oakland. A former Dominican priest, he had been recently dismissed from his order at the reported command of the Vatican. Today Fox is an ordained Episcopal priest. He joyously proclaims that the original blessing of God has already been bestowed on all members of the human race and on all of God's creation. This belief is the foundation of his doctrine of "creation spirituality"—patterned in many ways on the teachings of the fourteenth-century Christian mystic Meister Johannes Eckhart. Fox's doctrines run counter to the firm belief of many conventional Christians in original sin, the alleged conflict between spirit and matter, and the claim that Jesus Christ was crucified as a sacrificial lamb for the sins of fallen humanity.

Fox helped me to recognize my need to "let go" and place my own life in the hands of our compassionate God and to live a redeemed life free of guilt, regrets, and self-condemnation and full of love, sensitivity, and forgiveness. Fox quoted Rachel Carson's observation about the basic difference between wonder-filled children and alienated and spiritually dead adults. Carson's words spoke to my condition as an often spiritually dead adult:

A child's world is fresh and new and beautiful and full of wonder. It is our misfortune that for most of us the clear-eyed vision and the true instinct for what is beautiful and awe-inspiring are dimmed and even lost before we reach adulthood. If I had influence with the good fairy who is supposed to preside over the christening of children, I should ask that her gift to each child in the world be a sense of wonder so indestructible that it would last throughout life.[2]

My regaining of a child's sense of awe and wonder toward all of God's creation, my realization that I and all my fellow human beings are in the hands of a loving God, my admission that I have been privileged far beyond my deserving, my growing ability to count my daily blessings, the ever-present but often buried desire in my own soul to discover "eternal life" here and now amidst the confusion and evils of this world—these are the ingredients, I believe, for living a meaningful and fulfilling life free from the burdens of guilt, worry, and despair.

A possible testament to my spiritual growth was my belated ability to forgive those who I felt had trespassed against me. In my younger years, I hated my adversaries. In my later years, I softened, sometimes allowing them the benefit of doubt. But it was not until 1990, when I left Newark, that I truly forgave, without anger or resentment, those who had obstructed me. Life is too short, I concluded, to be poisoned this way. Meanwhile, I knew that I and my colleagues must continue the struggle for elemental social justice in this world.

In the years since I graduated from Oberlin College in 1939, the world has become far more complicated and at the same time far more challenging. In my college days, an advocate for the poor could join the trade union movement, radical religious or secular organizations, or the Socialist, Communist, or farm-labor parties of the Left. Today in America there is no strong political party of the Left, nor a strong national organization of the Left. Membership in AFL-CIO unions has shrunk because of employer opposition, hostile administrations, and actions of Congress in Washington. Collaboration between a weakened labor movement and powerful corporations and manufacturers has largely replaced confrontation. As the stock market reaches new heights, chief executives directing huge corporations are paid millions of dollars in salary and stock options, while many workers are losing their jobs because of corporate downsizing. With millions of corporate dollars filling the treasuries of the two major parties, most leaders of these two parties appear uninterested in reforming the corrupt political campaign system. In the meantime, at the close of the twentieth century, the ideology of irresponsible selfishness is still infecting the young and old alike.

The income gap between rich and poor in our nation is widening every year. Today millions of workers are unemployed or under-employed in our supposedly prosperous economy. More than 40 million citizens have no health insurance, in part because powerful pharmaceutical firms and insurance companies now dominate the so-called "health industry." More than 40 million Americans, chiefly children, live below the poverty line. Sweatshops abound in factories and fields. The family farm has become an anachronism as corporations and real estate developers gobble up millions of acres of fertile agricultural lands. Prisons are bursting with inmates. Americans, who make up less than 6 percent of the world's population, now consume 60 percent of the world's illicit drugs. Violent crime among youths remains alarmingly high. And in a nation where one out of two marriages ends in divorce, the steady deterioration of the family is threatening the very fabric of our nation's society.

The conditions of life in the Third World countries of Asia, Africa, and Latin America are far worse. For example, UNICEF reports that in developing nations approximately 13 million children under age five die of pneumonia, diarrheal diseases, and vaccine-preventable diseases each year. That's an average of 35,000 a day. If developed countries would spend $25 billion a year to assist the people of developing nations over the next ten years, asserted the late UNICEF executive director James Grant in his 1993 annual report, "it should be possible to bring to an end the age-old evils of child malnutrition, preventable diseases and wide-spread illiteracy."[3]

So far our nation, the richest in the world, and other industrialized nations have not been willing to provide the funds to underwrite this proposed noble endeavor. Yet each year, Europeans pay a total of $50 billion for cigarettes, the Japanese shell out $35 billion for business entertaining, and we Americans spend $31 billion for beer alone. At the same time, in the last twenty-five years the industrialized nations have more than tripled the size of their international arms trade, and today America is by far the world's most powerful arms merchant.[4]

In the end, the dreadful condition of the world's poor, both in America and abroad, will not change because the more privileged have decided to reach down and help the poor. These deplorable conditions, I believe, can end only by the determined action of the poor to empower themselves, to organize in nonviolent action and find allies among the more privileged. It is my hope that in the United States a new generation—not defined by age, but by outlook—will emerge to serve and work with the poor, not in occasional Thanksgiving-basket fashion, but in a lifelong dedication to the radical transformation of the nation and the global economy. Such men and women are also needed in Third World nations where multinational corporations, backed by the World Bank and the International Monetary Fund, are far too powerful. Often these corporations support dictators who rule with brutality for the benefit of the local elites and their foreign collaborators. I pray that members of churches and temples and mosques in America and around the world will play an important role in combating the principalities and powers and transforming the global economy in the twenty-first century.

As a member of the generation of the late President John F. Kennedy—he was born in May 1917, I in June of that same year—I was greatly saddened by his assassination in 1963, and also by the murder of his brother Robert and Dr. Martin Luther King, Jr., in 1968. I have gained comfort and strength, however, from inspiring words spoken by Robert Kennedy at the University of Cape Town in South Africa back in 1967. These same words were repeated by Senator Edward Kennedy in his address at Robert's funeral in New York City's St. Patrick's Cathedral the following year:

> There is discrimination in this world and slavery, slaughter and starvation. . . . There are differing evils and they are common acts of man. They reflect the imperfection of human justice, the inadequacy of human compassion, our lack of sensitivity toward the suffering of our fellows.

> Some believe that there is nothing one man or woman can do against the enormous array of the world's evils. Yet many of the world's greatest moments of thought and action have flowed from the acts of a single man or woman.

> A young man began the Protestant revolution. A young general extended the empire from Macedonia to the borders of the earth. A young woman reclaimed the territory of France. It was a young explorer who discovered the New World. It was thirty-two-year-old Jefferson who explained that all men are created equal.

> These men [and the young woman of France] moved the world, and so can we all. Few have the greatness to bend history itself, but each of us can work to change a portion of events, and in the total of all these acts will be written the history of a generation.

> Each time a man stands for an ideal, or acts to improve the lot of others or strikes out against injustice, he sends forth a ripple of hope. And crossing each other for a million centers of energy and daring, these ripples build a current that can sweep away the mightiest walls of oppression and resistance.

Moral courage is a rarer commodity than great intelligence and bravery in battle. Yet it is the one vital quality of those who seek to change a world that yields most painfully to change.[5]

As I put the final touches on my life story at our home in Benicia, I will continue to try to be one of the courageous people about whom Robert Kennedy spoke. Right now I am campaigning for construction of affordable housing for low-income families in my new hometown. As I celebrate my eighty-third birthday, my heart overflows with thankfulness to God and to my loved ones— to Alice, our five children, our seven grandchildren, and our one great-grandson, as well as their spouses and the innumerable friends we have met along the long and fascinating road of life.

In these words of his hymn "When I Survey the Wondrous Cross," Isaac Watts sums up my heartfelt gratitude to God and to my loved ones as my writing comes to a close:

> Were the whole realm of nature mine,
> That were a present far too small;
> Love so amazing, so divine
> Demands my soul, my life, my all.

Notes

Preface

1. Thornton Wilder, *Three Plays* (New York: Harper, 1957), pp. 99–100.

Chapter 1

1. Stella Fisher Burgess, *A Peking Caravan* (Peking: Maurice Benjamin, 1925), p. 50.

Chapter 5

1. Martin Dibelius, *The Sermon on the Mount* (New York: Scribner, 1940), p. 101.
2. James Tracy, *Direct Action: Union Eight to Chicago Seven* (Chicago: University of Chicago Press, 1996), p. 2.
3. George Houser, *No One Can Stop the Rain* (New York: Pilgrim Press, 1989), pp. 6–9.
4. David Dellinger, *From Yale to Jail* (New York: Pantheon Press, 1993), p. 63.

Chapter 7

1. H. L. Mitchell, *Mean Things Happening in the Land* (Montclair, N.J.: Allheld Osman and Co., 1979), p. 112.
2. David S. Burgess, "Wake Up Theologians," *Christian Century,* December 4, 1946.

Chapter 8

1. Mitchell, *Mean Things Happening,* p. 274. Includes additional material from an unpublished book *Delmo Saga* by the late Rev. Wilder Towle (copy in the David S. Burgess Papers in the Walter P. Reuther Library in Detroit).
2. Towle, *Delmo Saga,* p. 119.

Chapter 9

1. Liston Pope, *Millhands and Preachers: A Study of Gastonia* (New Haven: Yale University Press, 1942), p. 45.
2. David S. Burgess's testimony before the House Committee on Labor and Education (Burgess Papers).

Chapter 10

1. Warren Ashby, *Frank Porter Graham: A Southern Liberal* (Winston Salem, N.C.: John Blair Publisher, 1980), p. 245.
2. Ibid.
3. Ibid., p. 265.
4. Julian M. Pleasants and August M. Burns, *Frank Graham and the 1950 Senate Race in North Carolina* (Chapel Hill: University of North Carolina Press, 1990), p. 245.
5. Ashby, *Frank Graham,* p. 265.
6. Pleasants and Burns, *Frank Graham,* p. 270.
7. Ashby, *Frank Graham,* p. 260.
8. David S. Burgess, "Hucksters of Hate," *Progressive Magazine,* February 1951.
9. Ashby, *Frank Graham,* p. 280.
10. Quoted in Pleasants and Burns, *Frank Graham,* p. 280.

Chapter 11

1. Fellowship of Southern Churchmen document (Burgess Papers).
2. *Time,* September 15, 1956.
3. Mitchell, *Mean Things Happening,* p. 142.
4. Kester's letter is in the Burgess Papers.
5. Robert F. Martin, "Critique of Southern Society and Vision of a New Order: The Fellowship of Southern Society," *Church History* 52 (March 1983): 80.
6. Quoted in Robert F. Martin, *Howard Kester and the Struggle for Social Justice in the South, 1904–1977* (Charlottesville: University Press of Virginia, 1991), pp. 149–50.
7. Martin, "Critique of Southern Society," p. 80.

Chapter 12

1. David S. Burgess, "The Struggle for the South," *Progressive,* January 1953.
2. Jonathan Freemen [pseud.], "Adlai in Dixie," *Progressive,* February 1954.

Chapter 13

1. Sanford Unger, "The FBI on the Defensive," *New York Times Magazine,* May 5, 1988.

Chapter 14

1. Ted Morgan, *A Covert Life: Jay Lovestone—Communist, Anti-Communist, and Spymaster* (New York: Random House, 1999). This book provides a thorough analysis of Lovestone's influence on the international policies of George Meany and his Cold War associates.

Chapter 18

1. Moahammad Aycob and K. Subraujhmanym, *The Liberation War* (New Delhi: Chand and Co. Pvt. Ltd., 1972). I have checked my facts with this most authoritative book about the birth of Bangladesh. One writer is from India, the other a university professor in Pakistan.

Chapter 19

1. Robert Heilbroner, *The Great Ascent* (New York: Norton, 1962). This passage is reprinted with permission from Dr. Heilbroner.
2. Barbara Ward, foreword to *Hunger, Politics and Markets,* by Sutaj Aziz (New York: New York University Press, 1975), p. xvii.

Chapter 22

1. Editorial, *Newark Star-Ledger,* August 11, 1990.

Chapter 24

1. William H. Shannon, ed., *The Hidden Ground of Love: The Letters of Thomas Merton on Religious and Social Concerns* (New York: Farrar Straus, Giroux, 1985), pp. 294–96, and a letter from Merton dated February 21, 1966, and addressed to James Forrest entitled "A Letter to a Young Activist."
2. Quoted in Matthew Fox, *Breakthrough: Meister Eckhart's Creation Spirituality in Translation* (Garden City, N.Y.: Image Books, 1980), p. 141.

Epilogue

1. Dibelius, *Sermon on the Mount,* p. 101.
2. Rachel Carson, *Sense of Wonder* (New York: Harper and Row, 1956), p. 29.
3. UNICEF's Annual Report titled *State of the World's Children* (London: Oxford Press, 1993), pp. 2–3.
4. Ibid., p. 6
5. This quotation from Senator Edward Kennedy's eulogy of his brother is reprinted here with his permission.

Note: The David S. Burgess Papers are in the archives of the Walter P. Reuther Library on the campus of Wayne State University in Detroit. These papers include my letters, my published magazine articles, and numerous reports on UNICEF, labor, church, and political happenings in the United States and abroad.

Index